Advance Praise for

BAD RABBI

"This fascinating book contains the strangest Jews I've ever met in my life. It should appeal to every history buff out there—Jewish, gentile, or otherwise. What's Yiddish for 'Buy this book, or may all your teeth fall out except one to give you a toothache'?"
—A.J. Jacobs, author of *The Year of Living Biblically:
One Man's Humble Quest to Follow the Bible as Literally as Possible*

"Only a historian with the wit and comic sensibility of Eddy Portnoy could succeed in resurrecting these dead and forgotten Jews of New York and Warsaw. Through his painstaking research, we can vicariously experience their desperation and lack of self-control, their strange passions and their various forms of mental illness—predicaments we're just one step away from ourselves."
—Ben Katchor, comic artist and creator of *Julius Knipl: Real Estate Photographer*

"Having devoted his misspent youth to combing the Yiddish press for seedy, shady, and shocking stories, Portnoy, the bad boy of Yiddish studies, brings bad rabbis and other miscreants into the light in this erudite and thoroughly entertaining book."
—Barbara Kirshenblatt-Gimblett, author of
Destination Culture: Tourism, Museums, and Heritage

"*Bad Rabbi* is a masterful set of finely-tuned scholarship and critical zingers that brings detailed archival history of 'downwardly mobile' nineteenth- and twentieth-century Jews alive through vivid, erudite, and spit-take funny storytelling. Portnoy heads straight for the urban immigrant underbelly, opens up the newspapers, and uses portraits of a vanished people and a vanished culture to not just deliver a bygone way of life, but to explode some of our most dominant conceptions of modern Jewish culture."
—Josh Kun, author of *Audiotopia: Music, Race, and America*

"Eddy Portnoy's *Bad Rabbi* is an extraordinary thing: a gateway to the lost world of Jewish street life in pre-World War II New York and Warsaw. The Yiddish newspapers Portnoy mines were free from piety and light on decorum; instead they present a vast, roiling canvas of human behavior in all its extremes, from comedy to horror, with fiercely unbuttoned characters declaiming eloquently as stoopside choruses annotated their rants. Portnoy's book is undomesticated history; it is a time machine to an eradicated past; it is pure pleasure."
—Luc Sante, author of *Low Life: Lures and Snares of Old New York*

"Exuberantly vulgar, blithely unconcerned with gentile opinion, these nuggets of low-class Yiddishism won't let us forget how rough-and-tumble life in Yiddishland really was."
—Michael Wex, author of *Born to Kvetch:
Yiddish Language and Culture in All of Its Moods*

STANFORD STUDIES IN JEWISH HISTORY AND CULTURE
Edited by David Biale and Sarah Abrevaya Stein

BAD RABBI

And Other Strange but True Stories

from the Yiddish Press

EDDY PORTNOY

Stanford University Press

Stanford, California

Stanford University Press
Stanford, California

Printed in the United States of America on acid-free, archival-quality paper

Library of Congress Cataloging-in-Publication Data

Names: Portnoy, Eddy, author.
Title: Bad rabbi : and other strange but true stories from the Yiddish press
  / Eddy Portnoy.
Description: Stanford, California : Stanford University Press, 2018. |
  Series: Stanford studies in Jewish history and culture | Includes
  bibliographical references and index.
Identifiers: LCCN 2017013491 (print) | LCCN 2017015553 (ebook) |
  ISBN 9781503603974 (e-book) | ISBN 9780804797610 (cloth :alk. paper) |
  ISBN 9781503604117 (pbk. :alk. paper)
Subjects: LCSH: Yiddish newspapers—New York (State)—New York—History. |
  Yiddish newspapers—Poland—Warsaw—History. | Jewish newspapers—New York
  (State)—New York—History. | Jewish newspapers—Poland—Warsaw—History.
  | Jews—New York (State)—New York—Social life and customs. |
  Jews—Poland—Warsaw—Social life and customs.
Classification: LCC PN4885.Y53 (ebook) | LCC PN4885.Y53 P67 2017 (print) |
  DDC 071.3089924—dc23
LC record available at https://lccn.loc.gov/2017013491

Typeset by Bruce Lundquist in 10.25/15 Adobe Caslon Pro

For the two-bit nobodies

For most people there is only one small step between vulgarity and refinement, between blows and kisses, between spitting at one's neighbor's face and showering him with kindness.

Isaac Bashevis Singer, *In My Father's Court*

CONTENTS

13   Ever Fallen in Love with Someone
      (You Shouldn't Have Fallen in Love With)?   143

14   My Yiddishe Divorce   147

15   Shomer Fucking Shabbos   175

16   625-Pound Jews and Other Oddities   182

17   Bad Rabbi: Bigamy, Blackmail, and the Radimner Rebbetzin   191

18   You Think You've Got Troubles?
      Stories from Warsaw's Yiddish Crime Blotter   217

      Acknowledgments   237

      Origins and Sources   241

      Bibliographic Sources   245

      Index   255

NOTES ON ORTHOGRAPHY

Most Yiddish words, which are normally written using the Hebrew alphabet, have been transcribed according to the system of the YIVO Institute for Jewish Research, the closest thing in existence to a Yiddish academy. It's not perfect, but it's a decent middle path between a variety of Yiddish dialects. The most problematic aspect of this in practice is that *ay* makes the long *i* sound, like pie. *Kh* is what it sounds like when you clear your throat. Also, an *e* at the end of a word or name is pronounced *eh*. Other than that, it's pretty straightforward. The point here is to allow readers of English to be able to pronounce Yiddish words as they're supposed to sound. Some people will probably be annoyed by the results.

Polish words have also been transliterated phonetically into English. Although this is totally unnecessary because Polish is written with the Roman alphabet, readers of English unfamiliar with the Polish orthographic system will undoubtedly look at a word such as *czajnik* with complete incomprehension, their heads cocked to the side like a dog hearing a high-pitched whistle. Because the bit of Polish that appears (street and town names mostly) comes from Yiddish sources, in which they appear phonetically, I use the YIVO system to transliterate them. As such, I would spell that same word *tshaynik*, which is a degree easier to read and to pronounce for readers of English. Just to see how far I could go, I briefly considered writing the entire book using YIVO orthography. Bot yu no, meybi its not sotsh a greyt aydiya efter ol.

BAD RABBI

A BRIEF AND NOT ENTIRELY UNCOMPLICATED HISTORY OF THE YIDDISH PRESS

Yesterday at approximately 7 a.m., passersby on Bzhozova Street suddenly heard a high-pitched woman's scream: "Catch that bandit!"

The shriek had come from a fat woman with disheveled hair who was running down the street wearing one shoe, holding a rolling pin in one hand and brandishing an iron fire poker in the other. Twenty feet in front of her ran a middle-aged man, gasping for breath. The man also wore only one boot, but held another in one hand and his jacket in the other.

Before confused passersby were able to figure out what was going on, a terrible mishap occurred with the two runners: The man's clothes began to fall off of him and he was forced to stop and cover himself. In the meantime, his pursuer caught up with him and began to beat him over the head with the iron poker.

Chaos ensued. Some of the witnesses tried to get involved and pull them apart. Eventually, a policeman came running and the pair was brought to the precinct, where it was discovered they were a married couple, Moyshe and Yenta Gampel.

From the crime blotter of the Warsaw
Yiddish daily *Moment*, May 5, 1927

The Jews are a strange nation. Some people don't even think of them as a nation. They see them only as people who practice a particular religion. In this day and age, some of them might be right. But a century or so ago, it was a different story. The Jews of Eastern Europe and their diasporas were most definitely a nation. An oppressed, politically and socially disenfranchised nation, they were a distinct ethnic, religious, and social polity living in a number of dominant cultures and among a number of other minorities. Not unlike their brethren elsewhere, Eastern European Jews had their own unique culture, their own foods, their own folktales, their own music, their own literature—all carried by their own language, Yiddish. The only thing they lacked was their own country. Or did they? After all, they lived in Yiddishland.

Where is Yiddishland? It's wherever you need it to be. Yiddish, a 1,000-year-old language based grammatically on Jewish variants of medieval German and written in Hebrew characters, also includes copious amounts of Hebrew, Aramaic, and Slavic languages. It is a fusion language that easily absorbs elements of other languages. Yiddish can have bits of English, French, Spanish, or other languages thrown into the mix, depending on where the speaker lives—and this could be in dozens of places around the globe. Yiddish is terribly flexible and became the way it did in part because of the peripatetic nature of its speakers: Jews who were either on the move or on the run.

You can find anything in Yiddishland. It has food, it has music, it has song, it has dance. It walks and talks in its own unique way. Yiddishland has highbrow literature and trashy novels. It has dirty jokes, expressionist poetry, and brilliant philosophers propounding on a wide variety of linguistic, political, religious, and social matters. A century ago, about three-quarters of the Jews on this planet did their thing in Yiddish. Boxers boxed in Yiddish. Babies shit themselves and cried in Yiddish. Bums begged in Yiddish, and hookers turned tricks in Yiddish. Parents beat their children in Yiddish. Farmers planted crops in Yiddish, and lovers made love in Yiddish. Criminals stole in Yiddish, and scholars researched in Yiddish. This world, now a tiny sliver of what it was before the Holocaust, was vast. Anything and everything was done in Yiddish. And a great deal of this world wound up in the media, because the national sport of Yiddishland was journalism.

There are 8 million stories in the Yiddish naked city, and those in this book are just the tip of the iceberg. That iceberg is the Yiddish press, the largest chronicle of Jewish daily life ever produced. The millions of crumbling, yellowed newspaper pages disintegrating in archives and on library shelves contain some of the most bizarre and improbable situations in Jewish history, products of the concrete jungles that migrating Jews fell into during the late nineteenth and early twentieth centuries. Vaulted out of their small, impoverished Eastern European towns, Yiddish-speaking Jews found themselves in pitiless urban shtetls, where poverty still ruled but where new dangers lurked and life moved at a wicked pace. If migrants didn't also learn to step lively, they were often doomed. And to journalists, Yiddish and otherwise, there continues to be nothing quite so enthralling as quality doom.

Jews responded to new urban environments such as New York and Warsaw as many others did. Some did well for themselves, although most immigrants just muddled through, waiting to hand the reins of upward mobility to the next generation. A great many failed, some of them spectacularly. Although the preference is often for immigrant success stories, it is the screwups, the bunglers, and the blockheads whose stories are often more compelling. Just when they thought their lives were going well, their plans collapsed in a heap, or, as they say in Yiddish, their bread landed butter side down in the dirt. Disaster, misery, and misfortune—there is no better chronicle of these attributes than the Yiddish press, whose readers loved nothing more than a massive failure.

During its early-twentieth-century heyday, the Yiddish press provided its readers with an onslaught of Jewish disaster, a daily chronicle of pitiful problems encountered by newly urbanized Jews. No similar record of Jewish life appeared before, and nothing like it has appeared since. When this press was king of all Jewish media, from the 1880s to the end of the 1930s, newspapers carried far more information than they do today. Without competition from radio, television, and the Internet, the newspaper was the heart of world media. It is difficult to imagine today that not so long ago people got all their news from one outlet: a sheaf of papers they bought on the street from a grizzled old man or a dirty kid with a runny nose. Considering the immediacy and ubiquity of contemporary news delivery, the notion of having to wait for the news, or having to leave your house to get it, just seems weird. People had to wait around—quite literally—to find out what was going on in the world.

What's strange about the Yiddish press is that it didn't really get started in earnest until the Jews hit New York en masse in the 1880s. Before that, one might have expected that Yiddish-speaking Jews would have had loads of newspapers in the Pale of Settlement, the area to which they were restricted by the Russian imperial government. The Pale had more Jews than any other place in the world and, at the turn of the twentieth century, nearly 98% of them claimed Yiddish as their mother tongue. But the Russians didn't want to broaden the worldly knowledge of the subversive fifth column they perceived the Jews to be, so during much of the nineteenth century, they refused nearly every request to publish a Yiddish newspaper or magazine. They restricted the media of other minorities as well, but they were especially severe to the Jews.

Although the Russian government made nominal attempts to modernize this backward community using educational methods in other languages, they didn't meet with great success. Besides, the general attitude of the imperial government toward their Jewish subjects ranged from disinterest to outright antipathy. Perhaps a comment attributed to Konstantin Pobedonestsev, a nineteenth-century adviser to three tsars, summed it up best: "One third of them will convert, one third will starve to death, and one third will emigrate." If this was how the government felt, why would it have bothered to permit something like newspapers, requests for which must have seemed to be just another unpleasant irritant from another minority they didn't like. It has always been in the interest of authoritarian regimes to keep their citizens either misinformed or uninformed, and, as a result, the Russians did their best to keep Yiddish publications to an absolute minimum and the Jews they ruled, clueless.

Culturally, it was an odd situation. Unlike the peasantry, the 4–5 million Jews of the Russian Empire were, thanks to their traditional religious education system, a reasonably literate population—but entirely without any form of mass media. Information about their own communities and the world at large was forced to travel slowly by way of the post office and often inaccurately by word of mouth. Jews doubtlessly saw newspapers in Russian, German, and Polish and could sometimes read them, but their own perspective was shut out of the media equation. In other words, they had no voice. If Jewish readers wanted news about their own community, they had no choice but to accept it through the cultural lens of some other nationality's press. Needless to say, Russian or German perspectives on Jews and their affairs were not exactly what most Jewish readers were looking for.

Those Jews who could read foreign languages were typically better educated and better off financially than most. And because of their exposure to wider European cultures through business contacts and foreign-language books and newspapers, they became more open to different cultural currents and, ultimately, a bit more worldly. Some of these Jews came to understand that their duty to their people was to enlighten them, to uplift them intellectually and to help them engage with the modern world. The question was how to do it.

These Jewish modernizers, known as the *maskilim* (the enlightened ones) strove to bring a mostly religious and superstitious community into the then "modern" nineteenth century. Their greatest hope was that the backward Jewish bumpkins of the Pale and elsewhere would learn European languages, a step forward that would hopefully make them a bit more modern and help them earn citizenship in the countries in which they resided. Although their influence would eventually be significant, most Yiddish-speaking Jews of the period were suspicious of these modernizing types and shunned their advances. In the eyes of many nineteenth-century Eastern European Jews, modernity was a plan to take their culture away from them. Many of them knew that this modernization policy had been successful in Central Europe, where a variety of internal modifications in Jewish cultural and religious practices had already occurred. Beginning in late-eighteenth-century Germany, for example, most of the Jewish population exchanged Yiddish culture for German culture and became something called Germans of the Mosaic (as in Moses) persuasion, the first step to identification as Jews by religion only. What resulted from this process was that German Jews no longer dressed or spoke Jewish and some of their religious services even began to imitate a Protestant service. To Eastern European Jews, there wasn't much Jewish about them at all anymore.

And yet these Jews in transition could hardly be blamed for wanting to be full-on Germans, whose proto-capitalist economy was in solid shape and whose eighteenth- and nineteenth-century culture produced fantastic literature, music, philosophy, and technology. Cultural conditions where Jews lived in Eastern Europe were different: Dominated administratively by the Russians, Jews of the Pale were mostly surrounded by a peasant culture that didn't much appeal to them. Sure, there was a class of educated and wealthy Poles too, but there wasn't much chance of Jews joining that—not unless they converted. As a result, the Jewish masses of Eastern Europe did not have much interest in acculturating to that which they saw around them. But Jewish modernizers kept at it and, after the ascension of Aleksander II to the throne in 1855, things began to creep forward. Known as the Liberator Tsar, Aleksander II freed the peasants and loosened some of the laws restricting the Jews, allowing, for example, wealthy and educated Jews to live outside the Pale.

One of those well-off Jews, Aleksander Tsederboym, an Odessa-based ladies' ready-to-wear dress manufacturer with intellectual pretensions, used his connections to obtain permission to publish a weekly newspaper in Hebrew. Why Hebrew, a liturgical language not spoken by anyone at the time? The tsar's government, despite the new quasi-liberalism, still did not trust the Jews with their own media. Hebrew, the language of prayer and the literary vehicle of a small but growing coterie of intellectuals, was not accessible to the masses as a vernacular, so it would be relatively safe to publish a weekly in a language most Jews did not understand. *Hameylits*, the first Hebrew paper in the Russian Empire, appeared in 1860 and garnered about 150 subscribers—from a population of 4–5 million Jews—a pretty shabby result for the first Jewish paper in the region with such a large potential readership.

Tsederboym, however, was on a mission to educate and elevate his people. When he realized that it could not be done in Hebrew, he came to understand that if Jews were going to read a newspaper, it would have to be in Yiddish, the language that the vast majority of Jews spoke. But there was a hitch.

Men of Tsederboym's intellectual station considered Yiddish a lowly gutter language, a jargon that, some of them said, couldn't generate intelligent thought. Imported from Central European lands where Jews had acculturated to and assimilated into Germanic culture, this idea that Yiddish wasn't a real language, that it was bastardized version of German, was a result of newly Germanized Jews having accepted the dominant culture's negative perceptions of Jewish culture. In other words, as Sander Gilman has pointed out, because German culture conceived of Yiddish as ugly and deformed, Jews who became culturally German also accepted those sensibilities. So began the rift between German and Eastern European Jews.

Yiddish was associated with an immutable Jewishness, something that could not be assimilated into other cultures and a linguistic feature that was thought to prevent Jews from becoming proper citizens in the lands in which they lived. As a result, nineteenth-century Jewish intellectuals held a powerful bias against Yiddish, and many of them thought that Jews would never be able to become civilized if they used that language. After all, true intellectuals wrote and conversed in German, Polish, or Russian, or, if they really needed a classical Jewish language to do it, Hebrew.

So when Tsederboym began to publish a Yiddish supplement to his Hebrew paper near the end of 1862, it was actually somewhat of an embarrassment. In fact, he was so ashamed to publish a Yiddish paper that in the second issue he explained, "We won't wait for jokers to inquire; we're going to admit right here that our coarse Yiddish is definitely not a language, it's really just corrupted German." Ridiculous on the face of it, the statement gives insight into how Jewish intellectuals perceived Yiddish, the language of most of Europe's Jews and the carrier of its culture for nearly a thousand years. There's also the value-added irony of publishing an entire newspaper in a language that Tsederboym claimed wasn't even a language.

Despite Tsederboym's embarrassment, his Yiddish paper with a Hebrew title, *Kol mevaser* (A Heralding Voice), was a hit. It was full of interesting and unusual articles on topics about which Jews had never heard, because they had never been permitted a newspaper in their own language, and readership far outstripped Tsederboym's Hebrew paper, and sold thousands weekly. *Kol mevaser* also became the vehicle in which modern Yiddish literature found its voice, a place where the best writers (writing mostly under pseudonyms because they too were embarrassed to be writing in Yiddish) tested their literary mettle and produced the first modern Yiddish classics: sarcastic satires that appeared each week, serialized stories that were so popular, readers wrote in with bitter complaints if chapters didn't appear regularly. By producing all kinds of new reading material for a mass Jewish audience, Yiddish, a so-called jargon that wasn't supposed to even be a language, was unwittingly becoming modern and was dragging its cloistered and superstitious speakers with it.

In addition to literature, *Kol mevaser* contained all manner of popular historical and scientific articles, subject matter that was entirely new to Yiddish audiences. In issue 3, which appeared in early November 1862, *Kol mevaser* printed an article that described the giant sequoia trees of California. The existence of enormous trees "wider than a house and taller than the highest tower" and estimated to be "eight to ten thousand years old" must have sounded completely unbelievable to the Jews of the Pale. And, indeed, shortly thereafter, the editors published a letter from a reader that asked, "How can a tree be eight to ten thousand years old, when the world God created is only 5,623 years old?"

In a nutshell, this question dutifully evokes the mind-set of the shtetl Jew and helps to explain why the advent of the newspaper was so important to the development of Jewish modernity. In the shrouded world of the shtetl, behind the dual veils of Jewish tradition and Russian oppression, the Jewish masses were mired in a swamp of ignorance. The nineteenth century was exploding with new inventions, new ideologies, new science, new technology, and new knowledge, and the newspaper was the vehicle that mediated news of this new world to the old. Without access to a press in their own language, Jews would be deaf to progress. Quite literally, the Yiddish newspaper transformed Jewish life, hooking readers like fish and reeling them in the direction of the modern world.

Unfortunately, the Russian Empire was a lousy place to greet modernity. Its rulers, despite occasional, brief jerks toward liberalization, did not want an educated or politically engaged populace that might grow to threaten their rule, so even the newspapers they permitted were always subject to severe censorship. And despite the popularity of *Kol mevaser*, subsequent permissions for other Yiddish papers were refused, even though numerous requests were made. In fact, when Tsederboym left grubby Odessa for posh St. Petersburg in 1870, he was not allowed to take the Yiddish paper with him, so he left it with the printer, who, in two and half short years, managed to let the whole enterprise fall apart.

No Yiddish paper would be allowed to appear again in Russia until 1881, when Tsederboym tried his hand with a literary-oriented weekly called *Yidishes folksblat* (Jewish People's Paper), again, the only Yiddish paper permitted in the entire Russian Empire. It lasted until 1889, after which the government banned the publication of any Yiddish paper until 1903 and then allowed only one new paper to lure Yiddish readers away from foreign newspapers, as well as the increasingly popular, illegal underground socialist press. The Yiddish press truly wanted to blossom in Russia, but the tsars and their minions kept cutting the buds.

In the meantime, something else entirely was occurring in the United States. Although Yiddish-speaking immigrants had been trickling in since the Colonial Period, they had never numbered enough, nor were they co-hesive enough, to create the critical mass necessary to require a Yiddish newspaper. But by the 1870s the number of Yiddish-speaking immigrants arriving in New York was on the rise. The odd thing was that it wasn't the Jews who noticed.

Instead, it was Tammany Hall, the corrupt political machine that ran New York City politics. Famous for buying votes and for general corrup-tion, the machine noticed a bump in the number of Yiddish speakers in New York City and wanted to take advantage of it. They cut a deal with an immi-grant Jewish educator by the name of Y. K. Bukhner and paid him to create a Yiddish newspaper that would, first and foremost, supply news to Yiddish readers but, secondarily, convince them to cast their votes for Tammany Hall's candidates. The paper, *Di yidishe tsaytung* (The Jewish Newspaper) wasn't such a grand success, but its 1870 appearance prompted other Jewish immigrants to try their hand at newspaper publication. As a result, a number of different Yiddish papers began to appear in New York during the 1870s, none of them terribly successful either, but still interesting attempts to get into a Yiddish media game that would feed a growing audience.

Back in the Russian Empire of 1881, the Jews were getting fed up. In the wake of decades of oppression and poverty, a major political assassination, a flurry of intense pogroms in the southern regions of the Pale, and a slew of new laws that made their lives even more difficult, Jews began to engage with revolutionary political ideologies in growing numbers. But the one ideology that appealed to most Jews was simply to get out of Dodge: They began to leave—in droves. Some went to Palestine. Many more went to Western Eu-rope or South America. The vast majority of them trundled into the putrid bellies of massive ships and spent two weeks in steerage dry-heaving their way to North America. Between 1881 and 1924, 2 million Jews left the hot mess of Eastern Europe and settled in America, concentrating most heavily in and around New York City, thereby creating the largest Yiddish-speaking diaspora in the world.

In a strange and unfamiliar land, this large, unwashed mass of immigrants needed something to guide them in their new surroundings. That guide was the Yiddish newspaper. That which had required government permission and which had been severely censored in Russia had neither of these impediments in America. As a result, the Yiddish press that existed in fits and starts during the 1870s exploded, and from the mid-1880s through the 1930s hundreds of Yiddish publications—dailies, weeklies, monthlies—appeared on the streets of New York and in other major American cities. The same happened in Warsaw and throughout Eastern Europe, but only after the failed Russian Revolution of 1905. By the 1920s in newly independent Poland, the Yiddish press had become a phenomenon similar to that in New York, and in a strange case of reverse immigration, the Yiddish papers of New York served as models for the Yiddish press in such places as Warsaw, Lodz, and Pinsk.

The Yiddish press catered to virtually every political and social orientation. Everything from anarchist to traditionally religious—and whatever lay between—appeared on newsstands. Among umpteen others, one could find women's magazines, socialist literary magazines, vegetarian monthlies, satirical weeklies, and religious dailies—all available on the corner for just a few pennies. Because the press was the only form of mass media, every organization under the sun published something. Yiddish magazines for Jewish atheists? Jewish farmers? Jewish hatmakers? theater lovers? Yiddish avant-garde poets? artists? It's all there—and more.

Unfettered by government interference and buoyed by the huge influx of news-hungry Yiddish-speaking immigrants, the Yiddish press grew exponentially in America. Without Yiddish universities, the press became not only a central forum for news and information but also a home for literature, arts, and education. Nearly every Yiddish paper, from communist to religiously conservative, published poetry and fiction on a regular basis. Some published columns that described and explained basic political, scientific, and social concepts to an audience of poor immigrant laborers who had no formal education and no way to get one. Most other American dailies did not offer such broad fare to their readers. Fifty or so years after its inception, the original idea to educate the people was still central to the mission of the Yiddish press.

The Yiddish press became a weird locus for literature of every persuasion. Pages were often a wild pastiche, and it was not uncommon to have socialistic poetry on the same page as a chapter from a trashy novel or a column of suggestive jokes next to a translation of Tolstoy. Raucous literary, political, and religious debates played out in the pages of the Yiddish press, only to have their proponents caricatured later on by Yiddish cartoonists. One can read about rabbinic conferences on one page and Jewish circus performers on another. You want to read about innovations in medicine and psychiatry? Go ahead—it's a page away from a story about a Jewish gangster getting his head blown off, or a Jewish girl stabbing her lover to death, and another blink away from the Yiddish crossword puzzle, in which, yes, a six-letter word for "Sabbath stew" is *cholnt*. The Yiddish press was one huge, crazed mash-up of an intensely lived Jewish life that found itself lurching across a wide variety of geographic, political, religious, and social landscapes.

One of the fascinating aspects of the Yiddish press in both the Old and New Worlds was not only the holy/profane intellectual patchwork of the papers' interiors but also the ways in which the news itself was gathered. Before the 1880s there was no such thing as a Yiddish journalist—it was an occupation that had to be invented. Those who reported on all kinds of local matters were typically struggling writers or poets. Nearly every great Yiddish writer was also, at some point in his or her career, a journalist. And as journalists they mined every possible resource inside and outside the Yiddish-speaking community. Another important matter: Before the advent of Jewish-run newspapers, Yiddish speakers had rarely, if ever, served as journalistic sources for news.

Readers of Yiddish acclimated quickly to newspapers. It wasn't as though Jews hadn't seen papers in other languages; there were already models in English, German, Polish, and Russian for them to follow. But how did the Yiddish press differ from those presses? There was certainly a great deal of overlap—that is to be expected. But as the Yiddish press grew, its editors understood that it had to appeal to a unique audience, one that expected and required certain things that were specific to its minority culture.

Some basic issues were mediated and explained in the Yiddish press that one could not find elsewhere. For example, American Yiddish newspapers needed to help immigrants acclimate to their new surroundings, so they did simple things like print articles explaining what this popular American sport "baseball" was and how to play it. The editors didn't think that immigrants would actually go out and play (although some surely did), but they knew that their kids played and that it was culturally important to understand the game. Quite simply, it was part of the process of Americanization. They also described to readers exactly how to vote in an election, something most of them had never done in the old country. Newspapers printed a replica of a ballot and explained how and where to make an *X*. They helpfully added that Yiddish-speaking voters should look for the party symbol as a visual, in case they couldn't read English. The Yiddish press also provided all kinds of helpful tips to immigrant readers, such as how to avoid pickpockets on the Lower East Side, or why it would be beneficial to join a labor union, or how to buy a pair of shoes without getting ripped off. There is a plethora of information to help immigrants live their daily lives. This was a distinct type of information that was extremely important to uneducated immigrants: a guide to life in their new land in their own language—a language they could understand, a linguistic home away from home. Yiddishland really could be any place you needed it to be.

Because their readership was entirely Jewish, the Yiddish papers focused on what was happening in specifically Jewish neighborhoods. This means that, in addition to news about Jewish communities and affairs worldwide, there were many localized stories on specifically Jewish matters—holiday goings-on, Jewish thugs, Jewish prostitutes, Jew-on-Jew crime, matters relating to kosher food—all kinds of things that the journalists of the general press usually didn't bother with because, on the one hand, most of the city's residents weren't terribly interested in specifically Jewish news, and, on the other, they didn't have the access that Jewish journalists had. Or, rather, they didn't have the linguistic facility—they didn't have Yiddish.

Yiddish permitted entry into worlds to which other journalists had none. You need the skinny on a particular Jewish gangster or access to an important rabbi? Do you need to query street peddlers, shopkeepers, or bag ladies about a crime they may have witnessed while panhandling in the Jewish quarter? Yiddish is your ticket of admission to the Jewish street. Without it, you've got nothing.

As Yiddish journalism grew into a profession, specifically Jewish beats developed. The largest internal Jewish minority in Warsaw, for example, was the Hasidim, who made up about one-fourth of all Jews in the city. Newspapers thus assigned journalists to the Hasidic beat to report on the goings-on in and around those communities. More often than not, reporters assigned to write on the Hasidic world either were once Hasidim themselves or were still but had one foot out of the *shtibl* door (a *shtibl* is a small Hasidic synagogue). Knowledge of this world and their connections in it placed them in a perfect position to dredge up details of their internal communal affairs that outsiders could never have had access to. Not only did they already speak the distinct language unique to this community, but they also likely still had relatives and friends on the inside feeding them even more information.

And just as all regular newspapers have court reporters, Yiddish newspapers had rabbinic court reporters. The rabbinic court, particularly in Warsaw, was a rich resource for journalists, not because of the import of certain cases but because of the prevalence of violence between petitioners, especially in divorce cases, where pent-up emotions often boiled over into uncontrollable rage. Editors always knew that a juicy, explosive story was unfolding before the rabbis, and they frequently sent reporters to expose these awful personal moments of marital failure to the Yiddish-speaking world at large. The journalists understood their role as well; the tragic reports from the rabbinic courts were typically written with a heaping side dish of Yiddish snark and mark the spot where Isaac Bashevis Singer meets Jerry Springer.

Along with the creation of a modern Yiddish-speaking intelligentsia whose major forum was the daily press came an occasionally mock-folkloric style of reportage, especially crime stories in which writers treated both victims and perpetrators with sympathy and sarcasm. Journalists sometimes wrote local news as though they were telling the story to their friends or families. Subjects were sometimes called by their first names and even by diminutives. The stories were often written with a humorous tilt and tinged with irony. Even tragic stories were written with a touch of humor. It is another of the striking features of Yiddish journalism: the tendency to hitch humor onto real human tragedy.

Upping the ante, writers sometimes inserted literary jokes into articles and headlines. For example, a 1926 article about a Warsaw merchant's daughter who was taken to the hospital with terrible stomach pains only—to her family's shock and surprise—to give birth upon arrival, was headlined "Khatos ne'urim" (Sins of My Youth). Though it certainly fits the bill, the phrase is also the title of an 1873 Hebrew-language autobiography of Jewish intellectual Moyshe Leyb Lilienblum, which details his youthful intellectual awakening within a traditional world.

The Yiddish press is peppered with inside jokes such as these, references to Jewish literature and lore that serve as ironic markers, dragging high-flown literary works down into the gutter of the Yiddish underworld. A crime blotter blurb describing a violent nighttime gang attack on a group of homeless people in Warsaw who had gathered to collect scraps of food in an outdoor market is titled "Bay nakht afn altn mark" (At Night in the Old Marketplace), which is also the title of a 1907 expressionist play by Y. L. Peretz. Not only were headlines like these funny to those who got the jokes, but they also created a kind of bond between members of the Jewish intellectual class who recognized the references and were in on the wordplay.

Journalistic twists like these created a certain intimacy between writers, their subjects, and their audiences, all subcultures within the broad communities of newspaper readers. And these communities could be quite large. During the 1920s and 1930s Jews made up one-fourth of New York's population and one-third of Warsaw's population. Both cities had a Yiddish readership large enough to accommodate four or five Yiddish daily newspapers, in addition to a plethora of weekly and monthly periodicals. Between New York and Poland there were millions of daily readers of Yiddish. These demographics gave highly concentrated Jewish neighborhoods a distinct ethnic flavor. Nativists complained that walking around the Lower East Side of Manhattan or on Nalevkes in Warsaw was like being in a foreign country. At the time, no one conceived of these neighborhoods as Yiddishland, but that was their cultural reality.

Instead, these Jewish neighborhoods were usually referred to by outsiders as "Jewtown" or "the ghetto," areas that tended to be impoverished and dirty. Garbage and manure-filled streets were densely populated by poor migrants who dressed, spoke, and acted differently. Their emotive language and wild gesticulations were the butt of mockery not only by nativists but also by Jews who had begun to acculturate. Immigrant Jewish neighborhoods in big cities were rife with crime and prostitution. They were considered dangerous. These neighborhoods—also packed with families and the working poor—were full of people just trying to get by and, if possible, to get out.

But in addition to the poverty, crime, and the daily grind, both New York and Warsaw had flourishing Yiddish theater scenes, were major Yiddish intellectual and literary centers, and had raucous Yiddish lecture circuits. Like

ethnic neighborhoods everywhere, they had their own distinct café scenes
and restaurants. These two major centers of Yiddish culture during the late
nineteenth and early twentieth centuries were also the primary cultural centers of their respective countries, a fact that allowed Yiddish culture to feed
into and feed off of the other surrounding cultures. This is significant, because Yiddish never exists in a vacuum. Part of its linguistic and cultural
lifeblood has always been to interface with other languages and cultures, giving and taking what it needs, enriching itself and the others reciprocally.

As Jews flooded into these urban centers, they partook of their various
and sundry entertainments and sometimes created their own unique variants.
Yiddish-speaking freak shows on Coney Island and in Warsaw's Luna Park?
Certainly. Professional wrestling in Warsaw and Lodz? Of course. There were
Yiddish-speaking professional wrestlers—with legions of Yiddish-speaking
fans. Because of their immigrant status—external immigrants in the United
States and internal migrants in interwar Poland—and because of their linguistic difference and their low economic status, Jews in these urban centers
formed part of the underclass and thus participated in its general culture,
which ultimately meant low-culture pursuits. Jews who got rich and were
educated and who wanted to engage higher modes of culture generally did
so in English and Polish. Moving on up also typically meant moving on out,
both geographically and linguistically.

But high literary culture also existed in both cities. Yiddish belles lettres
were a significant cultural force and also a major component of the Yiddish
press. Although Yiddish literature is better known as a discrete cultural product, it would hardly have existed without the press, which functioned as its
main vehicle. Moreover, and as previously noted, most Yiddish authors were
also journalists at one point or another, including such esteemed novelists as
Nobel-prize-winning Isaac Bashevis Singer. Journalism was one of the few
ways a writer could actually make a living. Only in rare cases could one do so
only by publishing books.

As Yiddish journalists, the roles of these literary figures varied. Some
did straight news reportage. Others translated from the foreign press. Those
who had connections in the Hasidic community covered Hasidic-related
news. Writers who grew up in dangerous, poverty-stricken neighborhoods
exploited their own street smarts to get the stories they wanted. Yiddish

journalists thus dredged incredible human interest stories from the Jewish ghettos of Warsaw and New York or even small towns in the middle of nowhere. Warsaw-based journalist Menakhem Kipnis, for example, wrote about everything from folk music to professional wrestling. Also an ethnographer and musicologist, Kipnis was interested in whatever Jews were doing. If Jews were to be found at the circus, he wrote about it. They showed up at wrestling matches? He wrote about it. Isaac Bashevis Singer's older brother, Israel Joshua Singer, who was much more famous in his time, wrote a huge number of brilliant human interest stories about all kinds of bizarre goings-on among the Jews of Poland during the 1920s and 1930s. When accused of writing sensationalistic tripe, he sneered right back and said, "Good journalism is also good literature."

And Singer doubtlessly was right, for the most part. The papers are full of riveting tales, some beautifully crafted; others, not so much. Shackled by deadlines and an urgency to get news out as quickly as possible, journalists did not always have the time to shape their stories into high literary form. Instead, we wind up with intense little narratives that are pared down to a bare-bones minimum. Even then, with a little bit of context, these stories can be unpacked and unfurled as the explosive little culture bombs that they seem to be.

Many of the reporters of the Yiddish press remain nameless. Thousands of blurbs from the Yiddish crime blotter had either no byline at all or only an initial or two that supposedly identified the author. The names of the many writers who mediated the raw energy of street Jews to large-scale newspaper readerships are unknown. It may be that, because they frequently dealt with criminals and informers, they did not want their names made public. And then, they may not have wanted their names on seemingly insignificant stories about Jewish urban blight and were saving their real bylines for their serious literary endeavors.

In the often contentious world of Yiddish letters, the worst insult that could be heaped on a writer was to call him a producer of *shund*, or sensationalistic trash. With the huge increase in the number of newspapers came an attendant increase in the number of writers: good, mediocre, and absolutely awful. Recalling the early days of the Yiddish press in the Polish capital, one Warsaw-based journalist, Aren Fridenshteyn, wrote, "If Jews were once 'the people of the Book,' they have now transformed themselves into a 'people of the pen.' No nation has so many writers, poets, journalists, and plain old spillers of ink of all kinds like we Jews do" (Bal Haturim 1938: 44). The huge number of Yiddish periodicals produced during the late nineteenth and early twentieth centuries bears this out proportionally. Books, mind you, we haven't even discussed.

Emerging from a culture for which the written word enjoyed a venerated status, writing and writers played an enormously important role in the modernization and secularization of Jews. "The writer had become a kind of rabbi, a new rabbi. Not one that takes queries and payments, not one who gives blessings and advice, but one who teaches. He says something new, something beautiful, something electrifying," noted self-serving critic Aleksander Mukdoyni about the role of the writer in modern Jewish society in the early twentieth century (1955: 35). For an increasingly secular Jewry, writers and journalists were part of a new intellectual class that was supplanting rabbis as a communal authority.

Not that rabbis didn't continue to garner respect—they did. In fact, for the *amkho*, the poor, explosively angry, and occasionally half-witted Jewish underclass, rabbis retained a high-value societal position. But in the new urban environment the secular writer seemed better placed to provide guidance to the common man than the Old World rabbi. Yiddish journalists and writers became authority figures, doling out advice to troubled newcomers who were having difficulty acclimating to the city, and thereby helped turned newspapers into a major social force in Jewish life.

The Yiddish newspaper was also a place where Jews could be Jews. There was nothing exotic about them here. They could be brilliant or stupid, religious or secular fanatics, or they could be average and uninteresting. A chronicle of Planet Jew, the Yiddish press opens a window onto everything one could and could not imagine Yiddish-speaking Jews doing. Jewish opium addicts? Jewish tattoo artists? Jewish drag queens? They're all there. Everything from the highest levels of literature, philosophy, politics, and science to the lowest levels of beggary, poverty, pimpery, prostitution, and inept stupefaction. Every echelon of Jewish life appears; all of it smuggled its way into the Yiddish press in tiny, convulsive news blurbs—and all to the absolute delight of its readers.

When it came to the novelties of reporting on Jewish life in big cities, even the Yiddish journalists themselves understood they were onto something interesting. A 1932 article in the Warsaw daily *Unzer ekspres* (Our Express), took notice of the plethora of headlines in its own pages that were exposing the previously unknown goings-on in the city's nightlife: "A Secret Gambling Den Has Been Uncovered with a Roulette Wheel and Baccarat"; "Arrests Made After Lesbian Night Club Discovered"; "A Secret Narcotics Den Was Uncovered: Opium and Cocaine Found"; and so on. The list of urban Jewish subterranean enterprise goes on and on. And although none of it is the stuff of what most people think of as Jewish history, there it is—in black, white, and Yiddish.

Similar sounding tales can be found in other urban newspapers throughout the world. But a few factors conspire to make the Yiddish press a little bit weirder than others. Well aware of the language's high-value Hebraisms and homey Slavicisms, Yiddish readers and speakers, many of them partly or fully multilingual, became masters of ironic juxtapositioning. Throw in the added irony of the self-perceived chosen people shunting about the planet in tatters, abused and oppressed at every turn, living in hovels among criminals and prostitutes, combine that with the low political and social status of Jews, mix in an exceptionally high literacy rate and a tradition of argumentation, and you wind up with a people who cannot help but mock themselves and everyone else. What produced humor in Yiddish—a language that some erroneously claim is inherently funny—was its speakers and writers, who had no choice but to express themselves under social and political conditions that were nothing less than absurd. One of the by-products of the twisted Jewish road to modernity was an awareness, in Yiddish, that there really was something funny going on.

Another significant factor concerning the uniqueness of the Yiddish press is the Jews themselves. Put in the strange position of living as an unloved and sometimes virulently despised minority throughout Europe, Jews had a semipermanent position as the continent's Other. Even Jews who assimilated and converted to Christianity were often still suspect and were derided for their immutable Jewishness. They weren't to be accepted as naturalized Europeans but were perceived as loathsome infiltrators. If Jews who converted to Christianity, either because of true belief or for societal benefits, were perceived as poseurs, those who stuck with what they had and maintained their own culture—Yiddish speakers, in other words—were considered complete aliens on European soil. They spoke their own strange language, ate a weird diet, dressed differently, and, with their often Mediterranean looks, were sometimes also physically different from their neighbors. Europeans never really liked foreigners (mind you, they don't much like each other either) and, as you may already know, the story does not have a happy ending.

But while they were there, the Jews of Eastern Europe created a fantastic culture, their own explosive variant of urban creativity. What Yiddish produced in Europe—Yiddish literature, theater, music, satire, from the smallest joke to the fattest philosophical treatise—is a stunning example of what a minority culture can do, even while under the boot. Europeans should be proud to know that it flourished on their soil, and they should punch themselves in the face every day to remind themselves that they destroyed it.

Again, the story is different for the millions of Jewish immigrants from the mess that was Europe who brought their culture with them to the United States, where, for a few generations during the late nineteenth and early twentieth centuries, Yiddish culture flourished on a mass scale as well. With a social dynamic that was far different from that of Europe, Yiddish culture declined slowly, chipped away by the forces of acculturation and assimilation rather than incinerated. Jews loved America so much that they conceded 1,000 years of culture for it.

⌢

This book is an attempt to retrieve some of the flotsam and jetsam of Jewish history, focusing specifically on what happened to Eastern European Jews as they tried to make their way into new urban and industrial environments. Most of these stories are sourced in the Yiddish press, although in some cases they have been augmented with material from the English-language press. But Yiddish serves as the core, and its culture provides the context in which the protagonists lived their lives and did their deeds.

The contents appear in a vaguely chronological sequence, beginning with a nineteenth-century immigrant abortionist in New York City and followed by a murderer, an alcoholic poet (I know, not much of a novelty perhaps), violent gangs of Jewish mothers, and a Lower East Side clairvoyant. From there we go transnational for some Jew-on-Jew Yom Kippur violence in both New York and Warsaw. This is followed by a series of Warsaw-based narratives ranging from journalistic snark wars in the Yiddish press to Hasidic brawls, professional criminals, beauty queens, divorce court, and hardcore promoters of Sabbath observance. From there we briefly return to the United States for a look at Jewish professional wrestlers. Turning back to Warsaw, a rabbinic bigamist on hard times is considered, followed by a flurry of examples from Warsaw's raucous Yiddish crime blotter. Some chapters are short; others are longer and more detailed. All depend on how much information was available. The episodes are discrete and are as disconnected as the lives that appear in them. What unites them is deviance, disaster, and Yiddish.

Part of the reason this collection of stories came about was a desire to learn about how Jews lived before World War II. What was life like for migrant Jews in cities like New York and Warsaw? What did the city do to them? How did it affect their culture? Irving Howe's *World of Our Fathers* provides an excellent, if flawed overview of the world of Jewish immigrants in New York City. No book can cover everything, and although Howe's book provides a broad outline of the main features of Jewish life in New York—labor, politics, press, literature, and theater—many of life's other features are left out. One of those is the nitty-gritty of daily life, the quotidian grind, the stories of the criminals and lowlifes, the human detritus that gets washed away and forgotten, the undocumented losers, failures, and freaks who are so common in immigrant neighborhoods of big cities.

Warsaw, an even more unwieldy Jewish city than New York, has no English-language chronicler like Howe. There are a number of fine memoirs, some excellent anthologies, and one great historical work, but none of them address pre–World War II Jewish urban life in a broad narrative style as *World of Our Fathers* does. The Yiddish press—covering the big stories, the small stories, and everything in-between—is perhaps the best available chronicle of pre-Holocaust Jewish life in Poland. The press, however, was not created to function as a historical narrative; its job was to report the news to its daily readers. But distinct narratives can be extracted from its pages, bits and pieces cobbled together that bring detail to the stories of the unknown and unsung Jews, some of whom lived on a knife's edge but didn't know it or didn't care.

We will never have anything close to a complete picture of the Yiddish world that was. But dredging up even a little enriches our sense of it because it reveals how much we do not know. These little bits, these leftover crumbs of Jewish life, are so rich and so compelling that it continues to be worth the effort to pore over thousands of crumbling newspaper pages looking for the big stories, the small stories, and those that reveal the unexpected in a Jewish world that has disappeared.

The stories in this book do not tell us a great deal about these cities' famous writers, musicians, businessmen, communal leaders, or politicians. A fair amount of that work has been done and can be found in the domain of traditional historiography. Instead, these forgotten stories offer a look at the seamy underbelly of Jewish urban life, a peek into the depths of Jewish poverty and insanity, into the frequently troubled world of migrants in big cities, where any misstep is potential news. The lives of average people hit the headlines only when someone gets pushed out of a window or when somebody throws acid into another's face—in other words, when disaster strikes. With such "Jew bites dog" dramas, it goes without saying that these stories of Jewish lowlife do not represent the great masses of Jews; they found their way into the newspaper precisely because something went terribly wrong. As a result, they are not exactly representative of the majority, but, in the hinterlands of their narratives, they evoke an idea of what is supposed to be Yiddish normal.

Looking at the press to find out what life was like in a certain society must therefore be done with a watchful eye and with great care. In fact, if the study of human society were based only on newspaper reports, it would quickly be determined that we are a society composed mainly of criminals and deviants. The reality, as most people are aware, is that human society is, for the most part, pretty damn dull. And that is one of the reasons people read the papers.

So what is the historical value of these stories to us? Because it is clear that they are not broadly representative of Jewry at large, what do they show us? In every society some level of the populace is considered—by those who do the record keeping—lowly, uncultured, uneducated, poor, dangerous, frightening, ugly, and worthy of attention only from a safe distance. And yet, even from a protracted distance, these Jews have something to say about themselves. They are easily stereotyped, yet they break the mold into which they are supposed to fit. They are secular, religious, and a little bit of both. The prewar Yiddish press, a complex mix of shtetl folklore and urban poverty, reveals multitudes of mediocre Jews, many of whom lived on the verge of modernity yet were often backward and stupid. They worked odd jobs. They were desperate and they were frequently violent. But whatever they did, whether they were brilliant or slack-jawed stupid, they were all part of the Jewish story, rising, falling, and failing with Yiddish on their tongues.

And, for the most part, historians have ignored them. Whereas social history has become an important element in the field of Jewish studies, Jewish historiography has tended to be a relatively conservative field and, for a long time, most of its worker bees have not much liked stepping too far away from normative history. As a result, rabbis, communal leaders, businesspeople, politicians, traditional artists, scholars, writers, and their related institutions fill the rosters of Jewish history books—not that there's anything wrong with that. To be honest, it's vital. But even the growing number of Jewish social history texts tend to place their emphasis on acculturation and upward mobility. Granted, it is much easier to focus on traditional personalities and economic and social strivers because they typically leave paper trails. Bums, drunks, murderers, small-time crooks, and the legions of two-bit nobodies usually do their best to disappear without a trace. Coupled with the destruction of this Jewry in Europe, documentation is often limited. This is the reason that the Yiddish press becomes such an important resource for discovering information about downwardly mobile and marginal Jews. If it hadn't been for the resourcefulness of Yiddish journalists, we probably would not have any records of these things at all.

What we do decide to record is telling: History's mandate should cover a broad swath, but nostalgia dictates that we remember only certain things. Unpleasant matters might get lip service but are rarely dwelled on. Family lore conveniently forgets that Zeyde the antiques dealer was actually Zeyde the beggar, or that Bubbe the saintly seamstress was also Bubbe the hooker, who turned tricks during the slack season to make ends meet. These elisions are the lies we tell ourselves to elevate our pedigrees and to make ourselves look palatable in the mirror of history. But along the way, if we decide to ignore the sometimes ugly realities of our pasts, we lose some of the pieces of the story that make us human and we do a disservice to the historical record.

It has been said that the telling of history rarely comes close to the way life was actually lived. History, as it is told, lacks the tastes, the smells, the aching tedium, the frustration, the fleeting excitement, and the spontaneity of everyday life. This is part of the reason that literature sometimes works as a stand-in for often dry historical texts. But is it a good one? Journalism may not be able to convey these things either, but what it does provide is a slightly less contrived, more immediate, and an arguably more authentic representation than either historical or literary works.

If ordinary people have any familiarity with pre–World War II Eastern European Jews, it usually comes from such hypermediated pop culture fantasy phenomena as *Fiddler on the Roof*, the paintings of Marc Chagall, or perhaps the photographs of Roman Vishniac. Then there's the Holocaust and its many mediations that also contribute to the image of this world. It is not a particularly nuanced conception: hunched-over rabbinic scholars, swaying yeshiva boys, women selling goods in the marketplace, wholesome families, scholars, musicians, writers, maybe a pogrom here or there. It is a historical image that can be rich and compelling, but one that has also become saccharine and glib. It is also only a small part of the picture. True stories of downwardly mobile Jews plucked out of Yiddish dailies not only help expand our conception of this world but also explode many of our preconceived ideas about it.

It should not normally require mention that the presence of the sometimes unsavory Jews in this book does not mean that all of them are like this, but their history as a despised minority warrants it. What it does mean, though, is that Jews are not exceptional. They have their freaks, their criminals, their morons, their vicious bastards, and their complete bores. They are not all Einsteins, even if some of them think they might be. Uneducated, ugly, and boorish but sometimes clever, creative, and resourceful, the *amkho*, the uniquely Jewish rabble, deserve a place in the historical record. Every culture has characters like these—the only difference is that the main players are Jews and that the events generally occurred in a Jewish context, a fact that lends some unique cultural characteristics to the stories.

Another aspect makes these stories unique: The Jewish culture that existed when these stories took place is largely gone. Yiddish mass culture has disappeared. Either destroyed in the Holocaust or worn down by acculturation and assimilation, its vessel was the Yiddish language. Though English is a weak substitute (the poet Chaim Nachman Bialik claimed that reading in translation is like kissing through a handkerchief), one can still tell the tales, the stories of an urban Jewry experiencing the birth pangs of modernity and expressing their angst in a language that was rich in folklore and folk-ways, a language that crashed head on with the modern city and that made it its own. They are the stories of the common folk, the rabble, the people who don't make history but who are crushed by it. For most of human history they have been nameless and faceless. Only thanks to the advent of the press and mass culture do we know anything about them at all. Fragments of fragmented lives that wound up at the bottom of birdcages or as wrapping for dead fish, their stories briefly caught the eye of distracted readers, shocking them, entertaining them, and, perhaps most important, functioning as a moralistic directive, telling them how *not* to behave.

Destroyed in a bacchanalia of hatred in Europe and slowly killed by kindness in America, Yiddish culture is a tiny sliver of what it once was. Its main vehicle, the newspaper, once had circulation in the millions. A raucous chronicle of Jews and their ancient culture in a cage match with modernity, the Yiddish press allows us to see the interior of a fascinating culture that exists today only as an echo of an echo.

For 2,000 or so years the common denominator of Jewish culture has been the retelling of their ancient stories. For these same millennia the tales of the listeners themselves never made the cut, but they still deserve to be heard. Here are but a few. Millions more are waiting to be told. Welcome to the Yiddish naked city.

CHAPTER 1

JEWISH ABORTION TECHNICIAN

New Yorkers sometimes complain that their city stinks. They have no idea. During the nineteenth century, when New York was a horse-powered town, the stench of manure and urine was gag-inducing, especially in the dog days of summer. It was on one of those steamy days near the end of August 1871 that a bulging trunk was delivered to the baggage room at the Hudson River train depot. It sat undisturbed until a baggage agent noticed an odor emanating from it that was so pungent that even the city's generally putrid stink failed to mask it. Concerned about the fetid contents, the agent called his supervisor, who, after getting a whiff, decided they'd better open it up.

The contents of the trunk horrified the workers who jimmied it open. Crammed into the 2-foot-wide, 8-inch-high box was a comely, naked young blond woman. Even while decomposing, the girl was a stunner, if we are to believe the words of a news pamphlet that described the body. "A tangled mass of the most beautiful golden hair fell in waves over her shoulders, which must have been white as Parian marble, and eyes of blue, that even death's horrors cannot pale," it read. "The limbs were white and shapely and the feet tiny and delicate. The arms and hands were faultless in their symmetry, and every feature showed refinement and grace."

This chapter was originally published in *Tablet Magazine* (August 20, 2009) and has been expanded for this book.

Figure 1.1. Opening the mysterious trunk. Source: *The Great "Trunk Mystery" Murder of New York City*, 1871. Courtesy of Harvard Law School Library, Historical and Special Collections.

The morgue report was less forgiving. The coroner estimated that the girl, thought to be around 20 years old, had been dead for three days. The body showed no signs of having sustained blows, but her "lower parts" were severely swollen. More to the point, the coroner discovered a placenta stuck in her uterus, a possible sign that she was the victim of metroperitonitis, that is, internal hemorrhaging from an abortion gone wrong. He was also puzzled over how the 5'2" young woman had been pretzeled into the trunk. Rigor mortis would have forced the perpetrators to break her limbs to make the corpse fit, leading the coroner to conclude that the woman must have been stuffed into the trunk while she was still alive.

While the hows of her death were being solved by the coroner, the police went about trying to identify the corpse. They interviewed the baggage master and his assistants. When news of the story broke, a number of people who had missing friends of similar description showed up at various precincts around town to see whether their missing blond girl was the one who had surfaced in the trunk. But none of them matched. The only clue was that the woman who dropped off the trunk was thought to be nervous about something.

After interviewing Robert Vandevort, the Hudson Depot baggage master, police turned to a street orphan who was known to help out around the station and who had earlier directed an unknown woman with a trunk to the baggage department. The boy, Alexander Parks, told police that he remembered that the horse-drawn car that brought the woman and her trunk to the station had the name Pickett stenciled on the side of it. Inspector George Walling, the police captain in charge of the case, ordered that the boy be taken on a tour of the entire city, to every location where trucks stood for hire, in order to locate the driver. Not wanting to leave anything to chance, Walling put nearly every cop on the force on the case.

It turned out that a truck driver by the name of William Pickett had shown up at Bellevue Hospital after reading the morning's news about the girl in the trunk and was greatly upset, thinking he was the driver who brought her to the station. Pickett was brought to the 18th Precinct station house by one of Bellevue's wardens, where he was met by Inspector Walling and a slew of other cops eagerly waiting to hear his story.

Pickett explained that the previous Saturday he was at his usual spot, 29th Street and Third Avenue, when a woman approached him and asked if he could pick up her trunk at 687 Second Avenue. She wouldn't be there, but if he rang the bell and said he'd come for the trunk, they'd know what he meant, she said. She paid him $5 in advance and told him to meet her at the Hudson River Railroad Depot. Pickett went to the address, knocked on the door, and was led into the basement, where he saw a number of women and a tall man. The police asked Pickett to describe the man, which he did in such detail that one of the cops present, a Sergeant Rooney, immediately sussed out that it was Dr. Jacob Rosenzweig, an abortionist on his beat.

Rooney took off his uniform and put on his street clothes. He then accompanied Pickett to 687 Second Avenue and knocked on the door. The sign outside listed a "Dr. Ascher." A number of cops, also in street clothes, stationed themselves in various places on the block. A woman and a girl, Rosenzweig's wife and daughter, respectively, opened the door and told the callers that the doctor was out and that they weren't sure when he'd be returning. Rooney and Pickett stepped outside and began to walk down the street, away from the house. Rooney caught sight of Rosenzweig walking into a liquor store at the other end of the block. As Rosenzweig left the

ARREST OF DR. JACOB ROSENZWEIG.

Figure 1.2. The arrest of Dr. Rosenzweig. Source: *The Great "Trunk Mystery" Murder of New York City*, 1871. Courtesy of Harvard Law School Library, Historical and Special Collections.

shop, Rooney approached, but the doctor caught sight of him and tried to take off. Rooney tackled him and, after a brief struggle, a swarm of cops cornered the man. Rosenzweig was brought immediately to the 18th Precinct. Police also corralled a servant girl from the house as well as a "Jew peddler boy," as the *New York Times* referred to him, and brought them to the station house for questioning.

When Sergeant Rooney pushed Rosenzweig into the station house, Inspector Walling immediately grabbed the suspect, set him in front of Pickett, the truck driver, and asked what he could tell him about the trunk delivered to the Hudson rail yards. "What trunk?" Rosenzweig claimed to know nothing about it. Walling wasn't buying it and had the doctor locked in a cell. The servant girl, the Jewish peddler boy, and Pickett were told they could leave.

In the meantime the dead girl's body was put on ice, and a parade of curious gawkers ambled by in an attempt to identify her. A number of people claiming missing friends took a look, but none matched the girl in the trunk. A seamstress from Paterson, New Jersey, by the name of Harriet Williams, whose daughter had gone missing a week before, was too upset to see if the festering corpse was her beloved little girl. Instead she dispatched the family's doctor and dentist, who identified the girl by an unusual vaccination scar and a missing eye tooth. The girl's aunt showed up shortly thereafter to make a definitive identification. The victim's name was Alice Augusta Bowlsby.

Everyone in Paterson considered Alice Bowlsby a virtuous young woman and wondered what kind of malevolent lothario could possibly have put her in this situation. The answer became apparent when Walter Conklin, the son of a well-off alderman and silk mill owner in Paterson, was denounced by his own mother as Alice's seducer. Humiliated, Conklin shot himself in the head; when his body was discovered, police found a note in his pocket with the address of one of Rosenzweig's offices, one on East 24th Street. Connecting the doctor to the body in the trunk was becoming easier.

Despite Conklin's role in initiating the affair, Rosenzweig was pegged as the villain and was publicly excoriated. After all, it was he who allegedly packed the girl in a trunk and tried to mail her to Chicago. In papers ranging from the *New York Times* to the *Milwaukee Sentinel*, journalists referred to him as a "miscreant," "devil," "fiend," "monster," "murderer," "slaughterer," and, perhaps most devastatingly, a "pirate of human happiness."

THE LATE ALICE AUGUSTA BOWLSBY, THE VICTIM OF THE "TRUNK TRAGEDY."

Figure 1.3. Portrait of the victim, Alice Bowlsby. Source: *Frank Leslie's Illustrated Newspaper*, September 16, 1871.

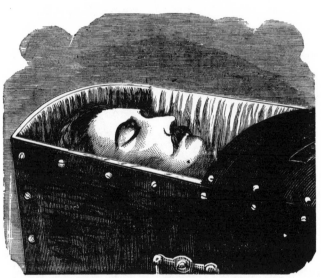

WALTER CONKLIN, Alice Bowlsby's lover. as he appeared in his coffin.
Walter Conklin, Alice Bowlsby's Geliebter, wie er in seinem Sarge aussah.

Figure 1.4. Walter Conklin, the lover of Alice Bowlsby, in his casket. Source: *The Great "Trunk Mystery" Murder of New York City*, 1871. Courtesy of Harvard Law School Library, Historical and Special Collections.

Many journalists had been following the abortion issue and it was a hot topic at the time. Just a week before the malodorous trunk showed up at the rail yards, the *New York Times* had published "The Evil of the Age," a two-part exposé on the abortion industry in New York City. Their crusading reporter, Augustus St. Clair, visited a number of providers, including, coincidentally, Rosenzweig, whom he described as "a fat, coarse, and sensual-looking fellow, without any traces of refinement in person or manners and [who] does not bear the faintest appearance of the educated physician. None but the wretched creatures, who, driven to desperation by their condition and the fear of discovery by friends, would place any confidence in his skill."

·DR." JACOB ROSENZWEIG, ALIAS "ASCHER," ETC.

Figure 1.5. Jacob Rosenzweig, a.k.a., Dr. Ascher, the abortionist. Source: *The Great "Trunk Mystery" Murder of New York City,* 1871. Courtesy of Harvard Law School Library, Historical and Special Collections.

It didn't help that during his interview for the paper, Dr. Rosenzweig, who became increasingly agitated by St. Clair's aggressive questioning, suddenly lunged at the journalist, who pulled out a revolver to ensure that he could escape unharmed. St. Clair's negative portrayal of Rosenzweig would surely augur badly for the doctor.

Short and plump, Rosenzweig had curly light brown hair and searing blue eyes; he looked like a treacherous, diabolical Jonah Hill. He claimed to have attended medical school in Warsaw (an unlikely possibility for a Jew at that time) and to have received a diploma from an unnamed medical college in Philadelphia, though it was subsequently reported in the *New York Times* that Philadelphia was the center of the country's bogus diploma industry.

In covering Rosenzweig's arrest, St. Clair reported that Rosenzweig "claims to be a Russian, but his voice has the twang of a German Jew," and he proceeded to quote him in foreign-accented English: "These other fellows are all humpugsh; they bromish to do somting vot they don't do. I poshitively do all operashunsh widout any danger, and as sheap as anybody."

Despite his journalistic bona fides and his fine foreshadowing of vaudevillian stage Jew dialect, St. Clair did not appear to know much about Jewish immigrants. In reality, Rosenzweig hailed from Plotsk, a shtetl 60 miles from Warsaw in Russian-ruled Poland. He was married with four children and lived in an apartment building at 22nd Street and Second Avenue that housed a variety of ethnic types, but mainly Irish immigrants. In fact, the Rosenzweigs were the only Jews in the building. Although the city was not yet home to a large number of Jews, postbellum New York City saw more and more Eastern European Jews settling on the Lower East Side. Only a year earlier, the city's first Yiddish paper had been launched, an indication of a growing community.

Rosenzweig arrived in the United States in 1865, though it is unknown what kind of work he did when he got there or how he became an abortion provider. Whatever it was, he wasn't doing too badly: Five years after his arrival, the 1870 census lists him as a doctor with a net worth of $1,500, which may not sound like a lot, but that he had any net worth at all after five years in the country was not too shabby. It also made him, according to the census reports, one of the richest people in the building.

As for his *nom de travail*, "Dr. Ascher," Rosenzweig had purchased his main office on Amity Place (now 3rd Street) from a man of that name, whose sign Rosenzweig kept intact, leading him, at that office anyway, to answer to the name Ascher. In building a case against Rosenzweig, the Manhattan district attorney suggested that the intermittent alias was proof that Rosenzweig was the Jekyll and Hyde of the abortion trade. And yet it was also common for immigrants to purchase existing businesses and leave the old name to ensure the return of previous customers. This was probably Rosenzweig's intention in leaving Ascher's name.

What is not entirely clear is how Rosenzweig got into the abortion racket in the first place. The medical profession in the 1870s was fairly sketchy, and anyone who put up a shingle reading "Doctor" and paid a $10 "physician revenue tax" was legally recognized as such by the state. This allowed all manner of quacks to present themselves as medical experts and to advertise all manner of elixirs, which claimed to cure everything from cancer to scrofula. According to some press reports, there were hundreds of abortion providers in New York City and, it was argued, the city could not function without them. The daily press, including the *New York Times*, was littered with their advertisements, which brought in an estimated $150,000 per year per newspaper, an indication of just how lucrative the trade was.

Similar to advertisements placed by other providers, one of Rosenzweig's in the *New York Herald* promised, "Ladies in trouble guaranteed immediate relief, sure and safe; no fees required until perfectly satisfied; elegant rooms and nursing provided." None of the adverts mention the word *abortion*, but readers understood what was being talked about.

Despite the veiled language and secrecy, abortion was perfectly legal in the early 1870s. Accidentally killing a patient, stuffing her body in a trunk, and shipping it out of state, however, was not. Put on trial for medical malpractice and manslaughter, Rosenzweig's first day in court was not a good one. His attorney, William Howe, a man described in the press as "indefatigable," didn't turn up. He later claimed to have been ill. He was replaced by a lesser known temp by the name of Abe Hummel. Rosenzweig was reported to have been shocked at the change, and when Hummel asked for a postponement because the defendant's real attorney was sick, the judge refused, telling the substitute to carry on. The first activity after the grand jury was empaneled was for them to view the body, which, a good ten days after it had been discovered in the trunk, had turned into "a loathsome, putrid mass of flesh." It probably didn't smell too good either.

The trial was quick, and the jury took less than two hours to convict Rosenzweig of second-degree manslaughter. He was sentenced to seven years of hard labor in Sing Sing Prison. At the sentencing, the judge griped that Rosenzweig should have been tried for murder in the first degree and sentenced to death. Lucky.

Two days after the trial ended, on October 30, 1871, Rosenzweig arrived at Sing Sing. Meanwhile, his lawyers had quickly lodged an appeal; the court had been swayed by public opinion, they claimed, and, in addition, had disallowed evidence in Rosenzweig's favor. After serving a year and a half, a period during which the press gleefully reported that Rosenzweig had made a jailhouse conversion to Christianity and led the prison choir, the erstwhile abortionist won a new trial. Unfortunately, however, in the interim his sensational case had

Rosenzweig. Counselor Howe.
Sergeant Rooney.

Coroner Schirmer.   Alexander Potts, the witness. Watch
                                                   Capt. Cameron

NEW YORK CITY.—CORONER'S INQUEST, AT BELLEVUE HOSPITAL, SEPTEMBER 1st, IN THE CASE OF ALICE AUGUSTA BOWLSBY, VICTIM OF THE TRAGEDY
ALEXANDER POTTS ("PADDY").—SEE PAGE 7.

Figure 1.6. Courtroom scene from the Rozensweig trial, Source: *Frank Leslie's Illustrated Newspaper*, September 16, 1871.

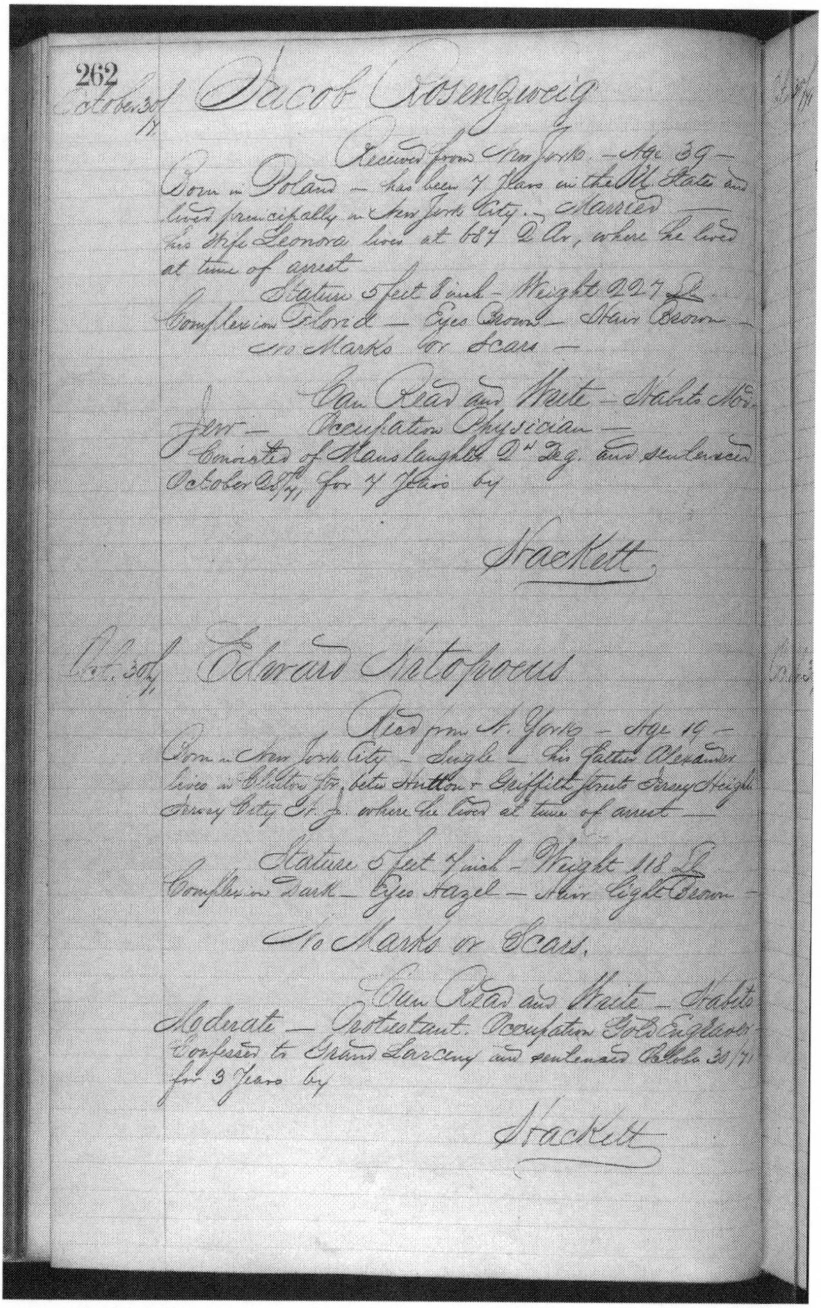

Figure 1.7. Jacob Rosenzweig's admission notes, New York Sing Sing Prison. Source: Inmate admission registers, 1842–1852, 1865–1971 (bulk 1865–1971). New York (State), Department of Correctional Services, Series B0143. New York State Archives, Albany, New York.

helped spur the state legislature to pass a law criminalizing abortion, which now meant that he would be tried for murder.

His previously AWOL attorney, William Howe, cried foul, and rightly so, because Rosenzweig's malfeasance occurred before the new law was passed. In the end, a second trial never took place; double jeopardy applied, and Rosenzweig was set free and left the country without a trace while journalists like St. Clair were left to hound other well-known practitioners, such as the Grindles and the van Buskirks, two married teams of abortion providers, and the legendary Madame Restell, whom the press nicknamed "the wickedest woman in New York."

Although advertising for abortion was proscribed by the Comstock Act of 1873, those dedicated to solving the problem of unwanted pregnancies continued to place ads in papers for items such as "Female Monthly Regulating Pills," "Dr. Melveau's Portuguese Female Pills," and "Old Dr. Gordon's Pearls of Health." Nonetheless, crusading Victorian-era journalists and politicians were still itching to rid the city of what they considered the scourge of abortion, which, as Horace Greeley, editor of the *New York Tribune*, argued, was the most "infamous and unfortunately common crime—so common that it affords a lucrative support to a regular guild of professional murderers, so safe that its perpetrators advertise their calling in the newspapers." In fact, his *Tribune* was one of the few papers that refused to print ads for abortion.

It was the Rosenzweig case that opened the floodgates for the anti-abortion crusaders. With the advent of the Comstock Act, authorities began hounding all providers. Madame Restell, the best known abortionist in the city, was arrested in 1878 and committed suicide on the first day of her trial. As a result, abortion providers were forced underground, and although abortion was a dangerous practice in the 1870s because of the lack of advanced medical technologies, it became even more so in the wake of total proscription.

Dr. Jacob Rosenzweig, Madame Restell, the Grindles, and other abortion providers might have professionalized their trade had their activities been supervised and scrutinized by the state. But crusaders like Augustus St. Clair and Horace Greeley drove the profession into the back alleys, which resulted in even more accidental deaths. Legalization of the practice was left up to the states, most of which proscribed the procedure until it was legalized nationwide in 1973 under *Roe v. Wade*.

No one knows what became of Rosenzweig after he was alleged to have left the country. One interesting aside is that the press, which reported widely on his case, did not focus on the fact that he was a Jewish immigrant. Other than Augustus St. Clair's brief dalliance with Yiddish dialect, journalists mostly ignored his ethnic origins. It is of note that the next time a Jewish immigrant got caught up in a murder trial, only a few years later, the Jewishness of the perpetrator would become an issue of great significance.

CHAPTER 2

THE HEBREW GIRL MURDERER
OF EAST NEW YORK

Her head was thrown back, the arms were raised above the body, as though in the last moments of her life the girl was desperately defending herself, and the lower part of the face and neck were disfigured with gashes. A deep gash four inches long was in her right cheek; her neck was cut from the lobe of the left ear to the center of the throat, and there was another gaping wound in the right side of the neck. The blood had so dyed the skin that it was not possible to tell whether she was white or an octoroon.

. . .

The body lay in a furrow between the rows of corn stubble, and all the ground about it for several feet that was not covered by snow was red with blood, the deepest stain being closest to the body. The corpse was frozen, and the wound in the face and the wrinkles of the garments were filled with snow.

The Murdered Jewess, 1876

It was a frigid December morning in 1875 when a farmhand discovered a frozen corpse that had been lying at the edge of a cornfield for a number of days in the East New York section of Brooklyn. The police were called, but they were stumped by the find: No one had been reported missing. Once the body was brought back to the precinct and word spread, locals thronged to the police station to see who it was; over the course of a Tuesday afternoon, 2,000 people shuffled past the disfigured corpse, but no one recognized the dead girl. This could mean only one thing: She came from across the river—from Manhattan.

Detectives in Brooklyn began to question the streetcar conductors and the horse car and ferry drivers, any of whom might have seen the victim on her way to her unfortunate fate. One conductor on the Broadway–East New York route was sure he remembered such a girl; she stood out because she was not wearing a hat and because of her "exceptionally small and exquisitely shaped feet." The conductor had also taken note of her companion, "a swarthy Polish Jew of forbidding mien."

In 1875 a few hundred thousand Jews were living in America, making up only 0.5% of the total population. In the decade following the Civil War, they had worked quietly to establish a reputation as solid, upstanding citizens. An 1867 editorial in the Philadelphia *Sunday Dispatch* decrying the refusal of certain insurance companies to insure Jews described them as

> fully the peers of any other religious sect in the country. We seldom or never hear of the failure of a Jewish merchant; Jews are very rarely accused or convicted of crimes, and the community is not charged with the support of Hebrew vagabonds and paupers in our almshouses and prisons. All of these facts speak very highly for the Jews, and show them to be orderly and well-behaved citizens.
>
> *Sunday Dispatch*, April 21, 1867

A relatively innocuous bunch, Jews were just one more ethnic curiosity in a greater melting pot. Even though they did suffer discrimination (even a wealthy Jew could not stay in quality hotels), compared to how they were

Figure 2.1. Site of the murder of Sara Alexander, East New York. Source: *Di Yidishe tsaytung*, c. March 1876. Courtesy of the Library of the Jewish Theological Seminary.

treated in Europe, America was remarkably free and welcoming. At the time, Americans had no obvious reason for a widespread dislike of the Jews, but they were about to get one. And his name was Pesach Rubenstein.

Pesach Rubenstein would have been considered a typical Jewish immigrant fleeing oppression and poverty in Russian-ruled Poland. Arriving in 1873 in his late 20s, a few years after his parents and siblings immigrated, he worked as a peddler and itinerant jewelry salesman, saving enough money to bring his wife over from the old country, not an uncommon practice at the time. His entire family lived together on Bayard Street, and Rubenstein, who was fervently religious, went to synagogue every day at the shul across the road.

The Rubenstein clan was a hardworking bunch of peddlers, and they made enough money to hire a relative named Sara Alexander to work as a housemaid. Rubenstein became particularly close to the girl, who nursed him back to health when he was stricken by consumption. The two were seen out together frequently, but no one thought too much of it; Alexander and Rubenstein knew each other from the old country and were related as well: Her father was his great uncle.

On Sunday, December 12, 1875, the Rubenstein family went to a wedding. Beforehand, Sara had helped some of the women get dressed. The family then went off to the affair and she left the Bayard Street apartment to go home but never arrived. The following day, her brother John showed up at the Rubenstein household asking if anyone had seen her; he was beginning to worry. The family told him that she had been there the day before but that she had left late in the afternoon after they'd left for the wedding.

One of the Rubenstein girls accompanied John Alexander to the police station to report the missing girl. The police helpfully suggested that they take a look in some of the nearby whorehouses, whose pimps often seduced poor young neighborhood girls and forced them to turn tricks. They did have a look, but Sara was not to be found. By Monday evening when she still had not come home, her brother paid for an announcement to run in the next day's *New York Sun*:

> A girl missing—since the afternoon of the 12th—age 17 years—stout—middle height—face dark—dressed in a light colored dress with a black overskirt—striped shawl—small gold earrings with red stones—Any information will be received by J. P. Alexander, No. 30 Essex Street.

Coincidentally, the announcement ran on the very same page as a small article describing the sensational discovery of a young woman's body, dressed quite similarly, in a cornfield in East New York. Indeed, it was Pesach Rubenstein's father who made the connection between the two. He went to the police station clutching a copy of the *New York Sun* and told them he recognized the girl as Sara Alexander, an employee in his household.

The police informed John Alexander, and while he ran to the morgue to identify her, two detectives were dispatched from Brooklyn to the Rubenstein home on Bayard Street to begin their investigation. The detectives were particularly interested in Pesach Rubenstein. His close relationship with the victim was well known, but he had also acted strangely when he learned Sara was missing. He told his family that he had dreamed that she had been abducted by "loafers" and murdered in a field 10 miles from the city. They thought it odd that Pesach had suddenly developed the skills of a psychic medium, deeming it unusual, even for him.

When the detectives arrived at the Rubensteins', Pesach had not yet returned. When he did, he found detectives pumping his stepmother for information. They questioned him too, and although he remained calm under questioning, mainly discussing the nature of his relationship with the victim, the police did peg him as an odd but harmless religious fanatic. But his demeanor changed when he was asked to identify the body at the morgue. The blood drained from his face, and he resisted to such an extent that the cops had to physically force him out of the house. On the way to the East River ferry, one of Rubenstein's friends, a local busybody by the name of Moses Harris, loudly harangued the police, saying that Rubenstein was "a religious man and would not cheat a man out of a cent," much less murder a girl in cold blood. But the police, whose interest had been piqued by his strange behavior, were not convinced.

With Rubenstein in tow, Brooklyn detectives arrived at the morgue just as the coroner finished examining the battered corpse. According to a report in *Pomeroy's Democrat*, the wounds inflicted on Alexander were done by a person "possessed of demonic fury," and when

the blood was washed away, there were great gashes running down each side of the face, meeting deep in the centre of the throat, and they showed that the knife had been twisted and gouged about in the flesh to make the work sure. There were incised wounds on both hands, across the fingers, such as were dealt by the assassin, as she knelt on the cold ground imploring for life.

Rubenstein went white as the cops dragged him into the morgue. The girl's body, covered with a cloth, lay cold and motionless on a stone slab. As one officer pushed Rubenstein closer to the body, another snatched the cloth away, exposing the open gashes on her neck. His lips quivering, Rubenstein threw his arms in the air, let out a hideous shriek, and jumped backward, falling against a window. Even though his odd demeanor had already piqued their interest, Rubenstein's crazed reaction at the morgue convinced the cops that they had their man.

And although the police already knew about Rubenstein's strange "dream," they still could not quite figure out a motive for the slashing, that is, not until the coroner's report brought a crucial new piece of evidence to light: The victim was five months pregnant. As the police inspected Rubenstein's clothing, they found drops of what looked like blood on his jacket and even on his fringed undershirt. Moreover, he had mud and vegetation on his boots that resembled the mud found on Sara's knees. The police immediately arrested Pesach Rubenstein for murder. He protested, claiming

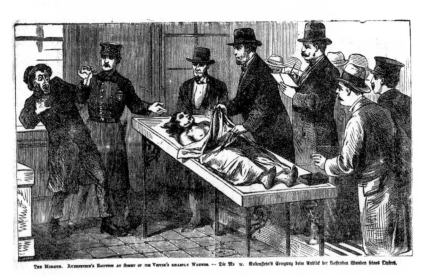

Tae Morgue. Rubenstein's Emotion at Sight of the Victim's ghastly Wounds. -- Die Mo ue. Rubenstein's Erregung beim Anblick der klaffenden Wunden seines Opfers.

Figure 2.2. Pesach Rubenstein is shown Sarah Alexander's body in the Brooklyn morgue. Source: *The Murdered Jewess*, 1876. Courtesy of Cornell University Law Library, Trial Pamphlets Collection.

absolute innocence—the evidence, after all, was entirely circumstantial—but for Gilded Age New York City cops, this was enough to make an arrest and set up one of the trials of the century.

The trial for the murder of Sara Alexander began on February 1, 1876. More than 300 prospective jurors crammed a Brooklyn courtroom hoping for a place on the jury, and the gallery was packed with spectators for the duration of the twelve-day trial. One of the news reports politely commented that the audience jamming the gallery, a motley group hoping for a good show, were in dire "need of soap and water."

The trial started with Rubenstein pleading not guilty, and his family stood firmly behind him. Compounding matters was the small number of rabble-rousers who insisted that the whole thing was a setup, proclaiming to the press that Rubenstein had been framed only because he was a Jew. There were, in fact, no Jews on the jury; the one who had shown up in the crowd had been excused—apparently, the defense team didn't want any extra help from local tribesmen.

The Rubenstein family's initial position was that Pesach could not possibly have murdered Sara, because he had been in shul on Bayard Street while the crime was being committed in East New York. But that idea was shelved after it became apparent that the Rubensteins couldn't line up their witnesses, so they defaulted to plan B. That Sunday afternoon, the family had attended a wedding, followed by a game of cards at home. According to this story, Rubenstein had gone to bed at 7 p.m. The only problem with this image of a family idyll was that it contradicted subsequent testimony that Rubenstein came home at 9 p.m. that night, went up to his room, and proceeded to run around "howling, screaming, crying, muttering, and moaning like a maniac, thrusting himself upon the bed and jumping out again, and keeping up this infernal noise almost the whole night."

The defense provided over a dozen witnesses who could "prove" that Rubenstein didn't do it. Eyewitness testimony, mostly given by family members and friends, placed Rubenstein in various places—in synagogue, on Hester Street, or in shops on Maiden Lane—during the time the murder was alleged to have taken place. A few of Rubenstein's brothers tried to pin the crime on a local shoemaker named Nathan Levy, who had been seen "frequently" with Sara Alexander, but Levy had a solid alibi. Rubenstein's attorneys also tried to discredit witnesses for the prosecution who said they had seen Rubenstein and Alexander on the way to East New York. They even got one alleged eye-witness's brother to tell the court that his testimony was worthless because he was "loose a screw." The defense focused on the circumstantial nature of the evidence—that Rubenstein could have picked up mud and blood on his boots shopping for fish at Fulton Market and that anyone who had stabbed some-one in the throat would be drenched in blood, not just speckled.

Rubenstein's supporters stopped at nothing. One anonymous do-gooder attempted a smear campaign against the victim, sending two letters to the Brooklyn chief of police indicating that Sara Alexander was in the employ of not one, but two houses of ill repute. Members of Rubenstein's family appar-ently cased their own neighborhood for locals who would swear that Pesach was either at their house at the time of the murder or across the street at the Emil Jacob synagogue. One of these was Jacob Apt, a ritual slaughterer with a reputation as somewhat of a village idiot. Apt testified that he was on his way to work and sat with Rubenstein on the Broadway streetcar that contin-ued on to East New York. The problem was that, upon cross-examination, it was discovered that Apt never took the Broadway car to work.

Medical evidence was then introduced in an attempt to prove that Ru-benstein was suffering from a tubercular cocktail of infectious diseases that

Figure 2.3. Sara Alexander and Pesach Rubenstein. Source: *The Murdered Jewess,* 1876. Courtesy of Cornell University Law Library, Trial Pamphlets Collection.

rendered him physically incapable of committing the deadly crime. His doctor was called to testify about the exact nature of his consumption and the way in which he bled constantly from his lungs, but this compelling evidence was undone by Rubenstein himself when it was noted that the spittoon provided to him by the court remained remarkably empty throughout the trial. In fact, for most of the twelve-day ordeal, Rubenstein barely moved at all, sitting stock-still, described variously by the press as "repulsive," "pale, haggard, idiotic, corpse-like, and filthy" and as having a "sallow, death-like face" that was the image of "utter despair." The only time Rubenstein moved a muscle was when he collapsed one day in the courtroom. One of his sisters ran over and poured ice water on his face, bringing him to. She tried to feed him an apple, but he claimed he was too weak to bite into it. She later informed the press that her brother was weak because he ate no meat in prison, though, she added, he happened to be very fond of herring.

Despite their creativity, all of Rubenstein's ruses and alibis fell flat. His fate was sealed by passengers and conductors, all of whom fingered him as having been on a tram to East New York together with the victim on the night of her death. Making matters worse, the murder weapon was a rare brand of "segar knife" sold only by a particular Division Street manufacturer whose distinctive trademark was to use three rivets instead of the more commonly used two. On the witness stand, the manufacturer's 12-year-old daughter clearly recalled selling the knife to Rubenstein, who wanted it so badly he didn't care that it wasn't completely finished.

That very knife, which was caked with Sara Alexander's dried blood and bits of flesh, was found among the corn stalks near her body. That Rubenstein's clothing was flecked with "a blood-like substance" and that his boots were speckled with mud and vegetation matching the East New York cornfield did not help his case. The soles of his boots also matched the blood-soaked boot prints in the cornfield. In a period that lacked DNA testing or even fingerprinting, the Brooklyn police managed to build a case on circumstantial evidence that would convince the jurors to convict him. In fact, the jury took only about an hour to do it.

With the words, "And now, Pesach Rubenstein, listen to the sentence, which is that you be taken to the jail from whence you came, and that on Friday, the 24th day of March next, between the hours of 9 o'clock in the

Rubenstein, by pulling down his long curl, takes the most solemn oath known
by his race, and protests his innocence.

Rubenstein entwickelt seine lange Haarlocke. leistet einen Eid, der von seiner Race für den
heiligsten erachtet wird und betheuert seine Unschuld.

Figure 2.4. Rubenstein displays his *peyes* as a guard against sin. Source: *The Murdered
Jewess*, 1876. Courtesy of Cornell University Law Library, Trial Pamphlets Collection.

morning and 2 o'clock in the afternoon, you be hanged by the neck until you are dead. And may God have mercy on your soul," Rubenstein became the first Jew to be sentenced to hang in America. In a last dramatic attempt to demonstrate his innocence, Rubenstein stood trembling before the court and unwound his foot-long ritual side curls to prove that it was impossible for him to have murdered the girl, for his *peyes* kept him from committing sin. With the curly locks spilling over his shoulders, he said, "That is my witness that I never had my hand on any woman, never touched a woman, and that time will find out that I am innocent and the jury have made a mistake." The display fell on deaf ears. He was led out of the courtroom amid the howling sobs of his relatives and remanded to cell 2 in the Raymond Street Jail.

The Rubenstein trial was a huge media sensation, and newspapers across the country, from the *New York Times* to the *Idaho Avalanche*, printed stories about the "Jew Murderer." Appearing in virtually every newspaper in the country, the Rubenstein saga marks the first major interface between American media and the Jews. Because, perhaps, Rubenstein was deeply religious, this aspect was heavily considered. Also under the microscope was the notion of Jewish cultural differentiation. A flurry of articles appeared, such as one in the *New York World* that explained how and why most Jews weren't anything like Polish Jews, who were an odd bunch of freaks. Not only did the newspaper industry take note, but also the trial was so popular that its entire transcript was published shortly after its completion in book form. In addition, four murder pamphlets, small illustrated booklets containing dramatized narratives of the events, appeared in the wake of the trial. It had become a nineteenth-century American tradition that major murder cases saw the publication of murder pamphlets, typically one per case, a few more for more popular ones. But four was exceptional—an indication of genuine popularity.

The small English-language Jewish press of the day, on the other hand, was enormously embarrassed and barely even noted the case other than to state that is was bad for the Jews. Interestingly, the Yiddish press, which itself was a new phenomenon in New York, apparently had no issue whatsoever with publicizing the case and did so using many of the illustrations that had appeared in the popular murder pamphlets. Their take was that Rubenstein, who they also misidentified as a rabbi, was totally nuts.

Figure 2.5. Front and back pages of *Di Yidishe tsaytung*, c. March 1876. Courtesy of the Library of the Jewish Theological Seminary.

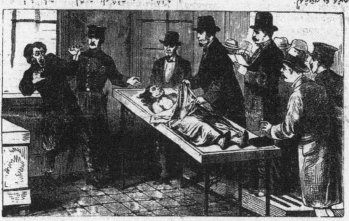

חדושים!

דער מיסיסיפּיער זעלצער אזוי יעצט דיא פאהנע דער די
שען אראנזשאמענט אין אמעריקא עטדראגען האט נון אונז
פאנגען אים אלאמעל שואכע דיעזע נעדערזינקען צו לאספטען
זיט קורצע צײט אזוי דיעזער פּוסח על שתּי הסעיפּים·
איסטער דעם דאם ער דיא פּריינדיגע נאהמעלע פאנגעלע דעם
מרדם אבנעדריקט, פינדען מיר אין ארטיקעל אבער ערדיך
טען איינער שולע פיר ארמע ידישע קינדער אין באל-
טער קסיריט; עס הײסט אין דעם זעלבען ארטיקעל דאס
אינע קריסטליכע פרויא אײן פֿריא לאקאהל צו דיעזעם
צועק מעהר געאיעצען האט, וואט דאאזעלבסט זײט צוויא מא
נאטה אײן נעטטפלעיער יעדע אם שבת 50 ידישע קינדער
אונטערריכטעט אוים איהר גיט, זייא זים נאהמע-
קיינע צײט האט אומזאגסט צו אונטערריכטען, זאל זיך אײן
ראבבינער אדער חזן אונד אײן אומגעהינגער לעהרערן לערנען
דער הײלינען זאכע אנגענומען זײל דיא טיארכער רײכע- יעדען
נעבין קיינע מיטטעל האבען פיר ארמע ידישע קינדער
אײנע שולע צו מאכטען

ני-יאָרק-טען!

פּאַריז פֿאָרגעס מאטאַט איזט ל אנשפאן געשטאַרבען
ער מיתה דער שוויגער פֿאַסטער פֿון דעם באראן ש ראטהשילד
אנגליין ער נאך זאך רײך וואהרע האט ער זײנע קינדער דיא בעסטע
ערציאונג געבען לאספטען זעם אלטטעסטע טאַכטער דיא שאהן
אך דיא נעבעדער-עססטען אין פארים וואהר בײ איהם גענאראן
פֿון ראטהשילד אם דאנטאַג-טאאננט האט איהם ראטה שילד
אײן פּאַנסטסעא צוגעזיקטען אין דער האַנד געעכנען אונד-
האט איהם געגעעט ער זאל מיט אונ אין זיינעם הויזן נעהמען
נאך דעם דאקטערניטס פעסט אַלם אנשיל דער פֿאסטער
דער גלעקליכע פֿלעה דאם פאקעפטגעפענט פאנד ער פריי דריך
יט ער על-זא זיינ זאג אויף פינף מיליאן פֿראַן פרוזין זײן מוחל
עם שטאַאנד אין דען פֿרײ פאַלגעודעם, איום דאנקבא-קײט
דאם איהר אייך ליעבע טאַכטער מײנעם זאהן צום-וײב
געשען האט געהמען דיעזע קלײנע געשענק פאַדן מיר אן
איהר זאלט דיעזעם אלם מיטגעבע פיר אײהרע יינגערע
טאַכטער בעהאלטען פאַראַן דיא ראטהשילד

Even after the trial ended, Rubenstein's increasingly bizarre death row antics provided plenty of fodder for the papers to keep the story alive. This would probably have been the first time American periodical readers were treated to stories about someone on death row who lit candles on Friday nights, "shook" as he prayed, and wore "tassels" on his "apron," as well as strange little boxes with long leather straps on his head and around his arm. His fellow inmates, who called him Ruby for short, thought he was crazy.

In the meantime, Rubenstein allegedly offered a cell mate $2,000 to help him escape, though it was apparently turned down. Just a few weeks into his stay at the notoriously filthy and vermin-filled Raymond Street Jail, he began to refuse to bathe. His next-door neighbor, a happy-go-lucky murderer named Andreas Fuchs, who was in for beheading a man and stuffing his heart and liver down a coal chute, offered to take Rubenstein out for a lager if he'd clean himself up.

Rubenstein spent nearly all his waking hours in a hysterical bob and weave of prayer, shuckling for up to four hours straight. When he wasn't praying, he spent his time curled up on the dank floor of his cell. He refused most food, maintaining a starvation diet. The administrators of the Raymond Street Jail officially refrained from intervening, saying that they did not want to offend his religious sensibilities, but the reality was, they thought he was out of his mind and so left him to his own devices, even when he stopped eating completely.

There were still those among Rubenstein's family and their supporters who were convinced that he was innocent; their belief was based on the conviction that such a deeply religious Jew could never have been involved in such a gruesome murder. His family tried numerous times to petition for a reprieve, and the court did agree to review the case, even granting a stay of execution in mid-March. This was the one bright spot in Rubenstein's stay in prison; to celebrate the possibility of a new trial, the press reported that he cooked some eggs and herring and made himself a giant fruit salad.

Inexplicably, however, his hopes did not remain high, and he quickly returned to his ascetic routine. After a few weeks of crazed praying and fasting in a filthy, dank, airless jail cell, Rubenstein was perilously close to death. In an apparent last-ditch attempt to save his own life and/or make an open-casket funeral more palatable, he put in a request for a doctor and a haircut. The prison doctor prescribed tincture of iron and cough medicine, both of which

Rubenstein's singular manner of praying.
Rubenſtein's ſonderbare Manier beim Gebet.

Figure 2.6. Rubenstein's "singular manner of praying." Source: *Rubenstein, or the Murdered Jewess*, 1876. Courtesy of Harvard Law School Library, Historical and Special Collections.

Rubenstein at his very peculiar Religious Devotions.

Rubenſtein bei ſeinen eigenthümlichen religiöſen Andachten.

Figure 2.7. Rubenstein praying. Source: *The Murdered Jewess*, 1876. Courtesy of Cornell University Law Library, Trial Pamphlets Collection.

RUBENSTEIN CURSING DETECTIVE ZUNDT.

"You have brought me to the Gallows. My blood shall haunt you around the world!"

Rubenstein verflucht Detektiv Zundt.

„Du hast mich an den Galgen gebracht   Mein Blut soll dich durch die Welt hetzen!"

Figure 2.8. Rubenstein curses the detective who arrested him. Source: *The Murdered Jewess*, 1876. Courtesy of Cornell University Law Library, Trial Pamphlets Collection.

Rubenstein refused. When the barber arrived, Rubenstein asked only that he trim the giant, matted dreadlock that had grown on top of his filthy head.

On May 8, Rubenstein allegedly made a deathbed confession to Fuchs, his murderer next-door neighbor, but by the next morning, Rubenstein was too weak to eat even a piece of dry bread. Lying on his wooden pallet, he began to groan and his breathing became labored. Eventually a deputy arrived and told two guards to prop him up. As they did, Rubenstein began twitching violently and foam began to pour out of his mouth. He expired a few minutes later, after which the prison doctor showed up to officially pronounce him dead.

The authorities argued over who was to blame for the prisoner's premature death. Jail officials claimed that they didn't want to offend Rubenstein's religious sensibilities by preventing him from following his crazed starvation diet and shuckling. The coroner said that if the prisoner had lived in clean quarters and had been fed decent food, he would have survived to attend his own hanging. Whatever the cause, with his passing, Rubenstein denied the legal system the chance to hang him from his neck until he was dead.

The Pesach Rubenstein murder trial can only be described as not so good for the Jews. In the aftermath, effigies of Rubenstein were found hanging in the trees of Brooklyn, and according to complaints lodged with a new Yiddish weekly called *Yidishe gazetn*, people accusingly screamed "Rubenstein, Rubenstein!" at any random Jew who happened to pass by. Even more embarrassing, one of the day's popular songs came to be called, "My Name is Pesach Rubenstein." High-tone Jews were aghast at blaring headlines such as "Hebrew Girl Murderer," but the Jewish community largely adopted an ostrich mentality toward the trial, hoping that if they ignored it, it would go away. One of the major Jewish newspapers of the period, the *Jewish Messenger*, contained no mention of the trial, despite the fact that the case had made headlines in every major American newspaper of the day. The official organ of Reform Judaism, *The American Israelite*, did chime in briefly, mainly to note that Rubenstein's Orthodoxy was in no way an impediment to his becoming a murderer. As noted, the Yiddish press was the only Jewish concern that seemed to have no problem discussing the case, but only Jews could read Yiddish, so there was no reason to discuss the matter in hushed tones. Their take was that Rubenstein was an overly religious nut, and so his passing was

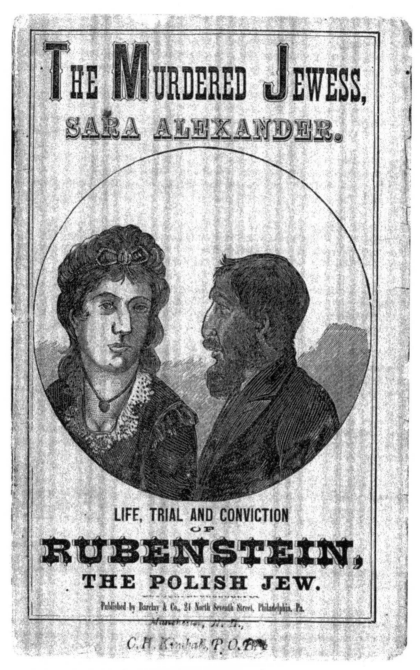

Figure 2.9. The Murdered Jewess cover. Courtesy of Cornell University Law Library, Trial Pamphlets Collection.

Figure 2.10. Rubenstein, or the Murdered Jewess cover. Courtesy of Harvard Law School Library, Historical and Special Collections.

no great loss. Indeed, the reaction of most Jews was one of collective shame: One lunatic had disgraced the entire community.

From a historical perspective, there are two points to note. First, it is hard to overemphasize how long the story stayed in the national consciousness. Simply put, Americans loved reading about the case. Pesach Rubenstein, religious fanatic and killer of a pregnant woman, was considered a national weirdo. Four sensationally illustrated murder pamphlets were printed, and one entrepreneurial publisher even printed the entire courtroom transcript as a book—something that was done only for the most high-profile of trials. No Jew in America had ever made the papers in the way Pesach Rubenstein had. In fact, it is more than likely that the stark engravings of Rubenstein putting on tefillin in prison and unfurling his *peyes* (side curls) in court were the first images most Americans had ever seen of such things. The case affected the Jewish community deeply. *Forverts* editor Abraham Cahan noted in his autobiography that when he arrived in the United States in 1881, Jews were still talking about the Rubenstein trial. In addition, a 1910 article in the *Forverts* noted that the affair was one of the major events of the previous century.

This leads us to my second point. This episode was not terribly good for the general perception of Jews in America, which is likely why most of the Jewish community chose to ignore it. But what's worse is that later historians also chose to ignore this first major interface between Jews, the justice system, and the press in America. Maybe you can't blame them. After all, who would want to write about a shameful popular murder trial that might embarrass the entire Jewish community?

In the end, murder never really caught on as a form of conflict resolution among the Jews. Instead, they seem to prefer feigned outrage, flailing arms, and raised voices to a "segar knife" in the throat.

CHAPTER 3

THE JEWISH MAHATMA

During the final decade of the nineteenth century, a man known variously as the Mahatma and the "apostle of the Kabbalah and the Emissary of the 37 masters" could be found traipsing around the western United States and prophesying about catastrophes in Paris and future civil wars in the United States. With a leonine shock of gray-streaked black hair, he would stand before journalists and spectators and comment nonchalantly in Yiddish-accented English, "I'm going to shake the foundations of your world." Whether or not his predictions shook those foundations is unclear, but he was popular enough to draw large audiences to his occult performances throughout the 1890s.

Before all that, he was a Hebrew poet and scholar known by the perhaps less exotic name of Naftali Herz Imber. Born into a Hasidic family in 1856 in Zlotshev, Poland, the same Galician shtetl that birthed the mercurial Yiddish poet Moyshe-Leyb Halpern and the mercenary tabloid photographer known as Weegee (whose mother was also an Imber), young Naftali was alleged to have been deaf, mute, and paralyzed until the age of 7, when he underwent what could only be called a miraculous recovery and subsequently became known in the region as a brilliant talmudic and kabbalistic prodigy. He also dabbled in poetry—a matter that might strike any Hasidic parent as boding

This chapter was originally published as "The Futurist" in *Tablet Magazine* (October 15, 2009) and has been expanded for this book.

poorly for his future as a serious religious scholar. But his talents were such that in his teens he wrote a poem on the occasion of Bukovina's joining the Austrian Empire that earned him an award from Emperor Franz Joseph. Imber was becoming irrepressible.

A peripatetic young man, Imber broke out of claustrophobic Zlotshev while still in his teens and traveled throughout the Austro-Hungarian Empire before leaving for Palestine in 1882, where he published *Morning Star*, his first book of poems. To earn his keep, he served as the secretary to the English adventurer Sir Laurence Oliphant, a Christian millennialist who, in an attempt to hasten the apocalypse, developed a plan in 1879 to lease the northern portion of Palestine for resettlement of the world's Jews. Thankfully, perhaps, the plan did not come to fruition.

While living with the busy adventurer in the German Templar colony near Haifa, Imber allegedly had an affair with Oliphant's wife. But, more important, Imber was influenced by Oliphant's mystical beliefs, which became the basis for his long-term interest in extrasensory matters. Imber left Palestine in 1887, returning briefly to Europe before leaving for India and, finally, the United States, where he arrived in 1892 to start a career as a professional mystic.

Imber's American sojourn was marked mainly by itinerancy, an increasing obsession with the occult, and a tendency toward hard drinking. During a short stay in Boston in 1894, Imber married a local Brahmin named Kate Davidson, whom British Jewish writer Israel Zangwill referred to as an "American Christian crank." Although the marriage would not last long, the couple went west, seeking audiences with other mystics, rivals whom Imber routinely denounced as "bluffers."

Appearing before audiences dressed in flowing white robes, Imber offered sometimes remarkable prophecies. In an 1896 prediction reported in the *San Francisco Call*, he warned Americans to stay away from Paris, where a major disaster would soon occur. It was not clear what was to befall the City of Lights, but, according to Imber's prognostications, something terrible was about to transpire. And he was not wrong: Within six months, an enormous fire broke out in Paris's Bazar de la Charité, the result of a film exhibition during which a projector set a pile of highly flammable film alight, killing hundreds and destroying many city blocks. It was this prediction that secured his reputation as a quality psychic.

Figure 3.1. Imber in Palestine, c. 1883. Courtesy of the YIVO Institute for Jewish Research.

Le Petit Journal

SUPPLÉMENT ILLUSTRÉ

Le Petit Journal

Le Supplément illustré

Huit pages : CINQ centimes

ABONNEMENTS

Huitième année

DIMANCHE 16 MAI 1897

Numéro 339

INCENDIE DU BAZAR DE LA CHARITÉ
LE SINISTRE

Figure 3.2. The Bazar de la Charité fire, as shown on the cover of *Le Petit Journal,* May 16, 1897. Source: Bibliothèque National de France.

In 1897, at an event in Los Angeles, Imber predicted that in fifty years' time, a Jewish state would come into existence violently in Palestine and that, in the future, power from the sun's rays would provide energy to heat homes and power transportation. A serious drinker, Imber also prophesied that California wines would one day rate among the best in the world.

Was Imber a genius or a prophet? That these predictions came true seems absolutely remarkable.

But like most prognosticators, Imber was wrong about a few things as well. In October 1897 the *Los Angeles Times* reported on one of his visions: In 2010, Imber claimed, a new civil war would break out in the United States. Imber's prediction was that the ultraliberal state of Kansas, whose female governor will have declared that "the West for Westerners," will secede from the Union. Kansas will be joined by Illinois and Missouri, prompting the eastern states to launch a war against all the western states, which will have supported the secessionists. The west will rout the east, and the two sides will remain separate. The eastern states, which will then wage war with Canada and annex most of it, will be governed by what Imber called "the Manhattan Empire," and the western states, which will take on Mexico and annex most of it, will be governed by Chicago. Meantime, he said, California will split in two, with Los Angeles as the capital in the south and San Francisco as the capital in the north. This was, as is evident, not as much of a winner as some of his other predictions.

Around the time Imber made his second civil war prophecy, he and his young wife attempted to settle in San Francisco, but, perhaps unable to compete with the memory of the city's most famous Jew, Emperor Norton, and afflicted with the Jewish disease known as *shpilkes*, he disappeared and abandoned his wife. According to reports in the *Los Angeles Times*, Imber resurfaced shortly thereafter in a police lineup after having been arrested for disorderly conduct in a Los Angeles flophouse. During an altercation with another resident, who had tried to hold him down and cut off his long hair, Imber went wild and, stalking the hallways of the place all night, screamed about cutting out his assailant's heart. Imber stood with a black eye before the judge, the *Times* reported, and explained, "Conzidering ze zituation zat I was hit by a drunken man and called a little sheeney only to show ze anti-semitic feeling, is it any wonder zat I got angry, Your Honor?" Unmoved, the judge found him guilty and levied a $20 fine.

Imber subsequently made his way back to New York City, leaving his work as a seer behind and cementing his reputation as a poet, writer, and obstinate alcoholic. "Fascinating, sub-lovable, dirty, handsome, impudent," noted a 1904 *New York Times* profile of him. Yiddish writers such as Aaron Davidson commented in their memoirs on Imber's infamous pub crawls. Ever the obstreperous one, Imber's sojourn in New York failed to calm him. In 1902 the *New York Times* reported that the police again had to intervene in the Mahatma's affairs after he disrupted a meeting of the Ohole Shem Hebrew research society, a group of scholars led by Rabbi Solomon Schechter, the esteemed dean of the Jewish Theological Seminary. Imber allegedly lost control himself over an orthographic issue and began ranting and threatening violence, so the intellectuals of Ohole Shem called the cops.

Imber's mercurial personality notwithstanding, his genius and eccentricities found benefactors, one of whom was philanthropist Judge Mayer Sulzberger, who provided the Mahatma with a monthly stipend of $30. However, it quickly became apparent that the alcoholic Imber was not to be trusted with money, so Sulzberger put Abraham Freidus, the chief librarian of the New York Public Library's Jewish Division, on the case. Freidus, a brilliant bibliographer, was himself somewhat of an unusual character. Besides being of short stature, he suffered from a glandular disorder that caused bulging eyeballs and morbid obesity, a fact that resulted in him receiving the untoward nickname "The Hippopotamus." Obsessed with Jewish celebrities, Freidus was wont to spend his time among those of the Lower East Side and made it a habit to attend funerals of the rich and famous. It is even alleged that he skipped his own mother's funeral to go to that of a well-known writer.

But outside his mania for fancy funerals, Freidus could be trusted. So to keep Imber's drinking under control, the librarian doled out $1 per day, delivered in whichever book Imber requested at the library, a location where, evidently, he spent an enormous amount of time: Imber's 1905 U.S. passport application lists his home address as the New York Public Library.

But hard drinking and hard schnorring took their toll. As he lay dying and penniless, Imber willed his rheumatism to his enemies and, to the writers of the Yiddish press, his broken pen. After his death in 1909 at the age of 54, one of the eulogies in the Yiddish press commented that he was the only true Jewish bohemian. A few days later, a letter appeared noting this fact was

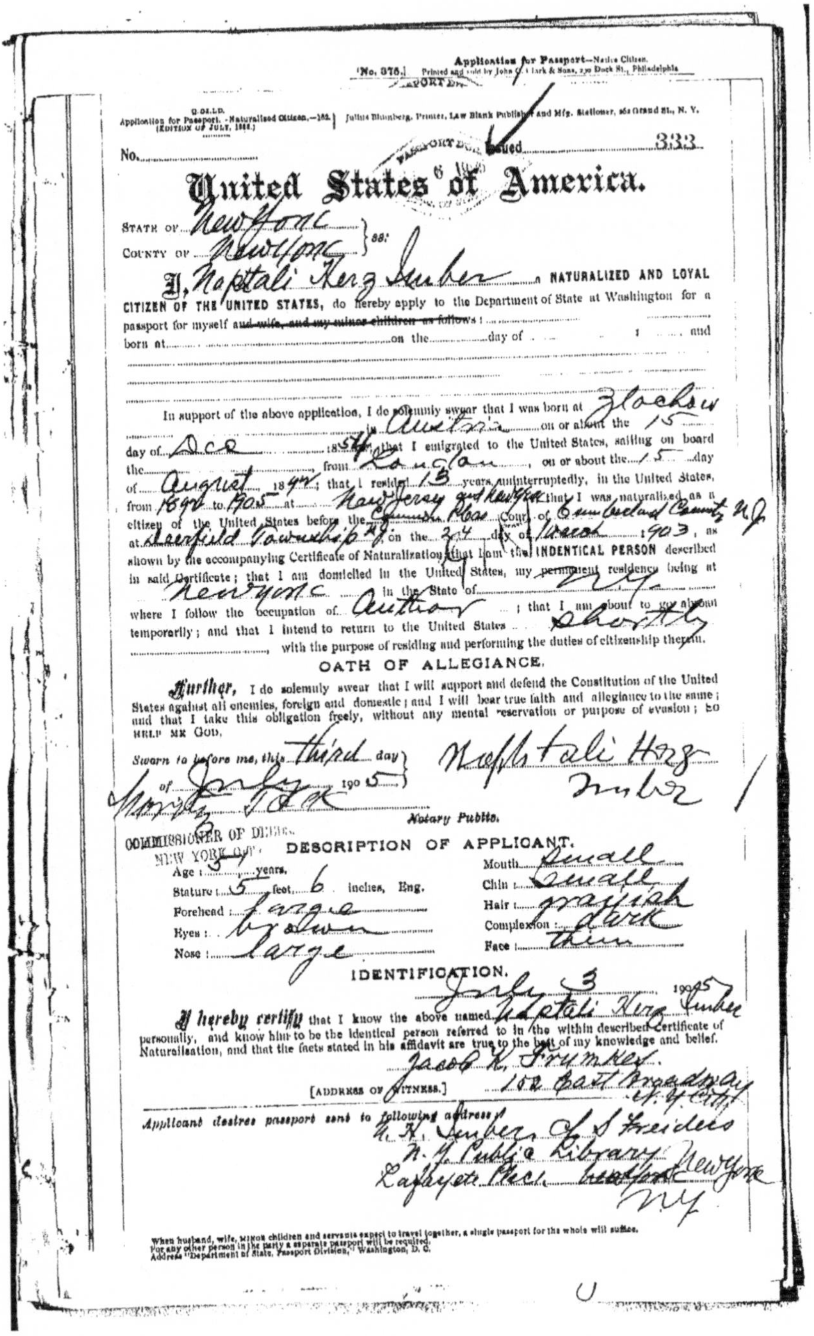

Figure 3.3. Imber's 1905 passport application. Source: U.S. National Archives.

Figure 3.4. Imber, age 49, New York, 1904. Courtesy of the YIVO Institute for Jewish Research.

incorrect, that Imber was not a Bohemian at all and, in fact, from Galicia. Yiddish readers, apparently, were not always the brightest of bulbs.

Although his past as a clairvoyant and a cantankerous, knife-wielding drunk is not particularly well known, Naftali Herz Imber was never an unknown quantity. He was best known among Jews for his poetry, famous enough, in fact, that an estimated 10,000 people attended his funeral. Although he also edited a short-lived journal called *Uriel* that focused on Kabbalah, his cultural bona fides were due to his status as a poet. In fact, before he passed, he managed to buy a burial plot by trading a poem for it. But Imber's best known work, initially titled "Tikvateinu" (Our Hope) was written while he was on the road in Romania in 1877. He tweaked it a bit after arriving in Palestine a few years later, eventually changing the title to "Hatikvah" (The Hope). Put to music, the poem was chosen as the anthem of the Zionist movement and ultimately became the national anthem of the State of Israel.

Imber was known to have attended a number of Zionist congresses. At one of them he showed up completely bombed and had to be escorted out by security. He managed to hang around outside until the end of the meeting, when "Hatikvah" was sung. "They can kick me out," he said, "but they still have to sing my song."

CHAPTER 4

THE GREAT TONSIL RIOT OF 1906

"The Lower East Side is a volcano of superstitious ignorance," howled an article in the *New York Tribune* at the tail end of a steamy June in 1906. Referring to masses of immigrant Jews prone to the kind of mass hysteria that occurs every so often in the quarters of the poor and ignorant, the *Trib* wasn't exactly in the wrong.

It was a hot June 27, 1906, when the Jewish volcano on the Lower East Side erupted, spitting forth 50,000 furious immigrant mothers. Descending on the neighborhood's public schools en masse, an enraged army of Yiddisha mamas demanded to see their children after a rumor spread that doctors from the New York City Board of Health were in the schools slashing their children's throats.

Greeted by locked doors, the screaming throngs encircled the school buildings and set to pounding on doors and smashing windows. The kids inside were baffled and doubtlessly frightened. On Essex Street some white-hot Jewish mothers clambered up ladders they'd brought with them in an attempt to break into P.S. 137 through the second-floor windows.

During the rampage, gangs of immigrants cursed out principals, fought police, and attacked anyone in the street bearing the slightest resemblance to

This chapter was originally published as "Sore" in *Tablet Magazine* (August 19, 2010) and has been expanded for this book.

a doctor—and, according to the *Tribune*, this meant anyone wearing spectacles. Some of them raided vegetable pushcarts for ammunition, whereas others posed more serious threats, such as one young man who cornered an actual member of the Board of Health and pulled a revolver on him.

Just what was going on here? Word had spread like wildfire among the Jews of the Lower East Side that uptown doctors had come to downtown public schools and were, as described in the Yiddish daily *Di varhayt*, "cutting the throats of Jewish children." After a two-hour assault, the ragtag army achieved victory: Their children were released early and alive, thereby proving that no such slaughter had taken place. Twelve schools on the Lower East Side had to be shut down early on account of the chaos.

Thrilled at having gotten a miraculous half-day's vacation, the children didn't even know what the ruckus was about. "I dunno sir, I t'ink the school exploded," one boy told a reporter from the *Evening Post*.

How is it that a simple rumor managed to upset so many thousands of mothers to the point where they besieged neighborhood schools in fits of violence to demand their children? As with many hysteria-inducing rumors, this one contained a kernel of truth. A week earlier, scores of Jewish students at P.S. 100, an elementary school on Cannon Street on the Lower East Side, had been absent from school, prompting one school principal to

Figure 4.1. Headline excerpt from the *New York Sun*, June 28, 1906. Source: Library of Congress, Chronicling America digital collection of historic American newspapers, chroniclingamerica.loc.gov/ (accessed April 17, 2017).

propose the brilliant idea that, because the neighborhood's immigrant children probably do not receive adequate medical care, they should probably undergo tonsillectomies. This idea was suggested to their parents, some of whom complained that the trip uptown for such a procedure wasn't possible for people who worked twelve-hour days, six days a week. What's more, the 50-cent doctor's fee was too high. So, taking the initiative, P.S. 100's thoughtful principal kindly arranged for doctors from Mt. Sinai Hospital to come to the school and perform the operations locally.

Directed by the city Board of Health, doctors performed eighty-three tonsillectomies at P.S. 100. Allegedly, most of the children were back in class the following day. According to the *New York Tribune*, none of the operations were performed without parental consent, and, they added, there were no complaints. A tonsillectomy, apparently, was no big deal.

But *Di varhayt* claimed otherwise. They reported that not only did many of the young patients not even bother to get their parents' permission, but also they had been sent home with permission slips that their Yiddish-speaking parents did not understand and so they just signed the papers. Some of the children apparently even signed the slips themselves.

"First of all," *Di varhayt* editorialized, "the poor and unhappy immigrant mothers who suffer the stifling heat and confinement of the tenements can't even read. And secondly, they aren't able to understand the technical English on the permission slips that was being read to them." All they knew was that when the children returned home from school after their procedures, they did so drooling mouthfuls of blood, barely able to speak. Shocked, their parents asked what happened. "Doctors cut our throats," the children replied.

Rumors of a wholesale slaughter began to leap like wildfire throughout the tenements and sweatshops. As the gossip wended its way through the neighborhood, the story ballooned from "doctors cut our throats" to "two children died" to a wild "83 children died." Local street corner orators got into the act, screaming about the massacres in the schools, comparing them to the wave of pogroms that were then taking place in the northeast sector of Russian-ruled Poland, reports of which were all over the Yiddish papers. According to the *New York Sun*, 16-year-old Esther Blaustein was pulled off the back of a wagon and arrested for inflaming the crowd with a fiery Yiddish speech in which she claimed to have seen teachers killing children in the school. Another street corner pontificator claimed to have seen teachers chopping children's heads off.

But, as the *New York Tribune* noted, "One merit of the Yiddish mob is that it indulges more in vociferation than violence. It shrieks epithets without stint, hurls a few vegetables and breaks a few windows, but never destroys life and property in the style of Southern lynchers, striking mechanics, railway men, and mine workers." Thank heaven for small favors.

On the other hand, the *New York World* reported the story of a telephone repairman who was observed by a phalanx of angry Jewesses on the corner of 8th Street and Avenue C with a pliers hanging from his tool belt. Someone in the crowd claimed he was a doctor and that his pliers were used to yank out the tongues of their little boys and girls. Within seconds, he was mobbed and beaten senseless. It took police from two different precincts to rescue him.

Coming on the heels of a particularly brutal pogrom in Bialystok that had just been reported in the Yiddish press—accompanied by gruesome photos of the dead and wounded—the Lower East Side surgeries morphed, in the eyes of gullible parents, into evidence of an American pogrom. Accustomed to fear of such violence in Europe, many of the recent arrivals believed that such things could happen even in America. Newspaper reports noticed this stark difference between hysterical immigrant parents and their American children.

But if the *Tribune* implied that the Jews were superstitious dupes prone to wild overreaction, the Yiddish *Di varhayt* shot back that the fault lay with the Board of Health and the school's principal for stupidly sending home permission slips that had not been translated into Yiddish. *Di varhayt* also launched into a tirade about how Irish principals have no respect for Jewish immigrant parents and essentially do whatever they want with the children.

Nearly all the Yiddish papers decried the overwrought reaction of the mothers, but they understood why it happened. The "Stupid Women" headline that appeared in the conservative *Morgn zhurnal* was the one Yiddish exception. In an attempt to fully blame the Lower East Side's Jews for the riot, both the *Tribune* and the *New York Times* alleged that a nefarious group of neighborhood Jewish doctors had spread the rumor because they were furious that uptown doctors were performing tonsillectomies on local children for free, when they could be getting 50 cents a pop. True or not, the Yiddish press opted not to remark on that theory.

Figure 4.2. Headline excerpt from the *New York World,* June 27, 1906. Source: Library of Congress, Chronicling America digital collection of historic American newspapers, chroniclingamerica.loc.gov/ (accessed April 17, 2017).

The *Tribune* also took the opportunity to bemoan the episode as one of a series of events that plagued the overcrowded and frequently obnoxious Jewish quarter. Four years earlier, they noted, Jewish women rioted against local butchers, and three years earlier they had rioted against doctors who were treating their children for trachoma. These same immigrant women joined together most consistently for "landlord riots," which exploded every time rents were raised, and for bank riots, which occurred every time a Jewish bank went belly-up, leaving its poor immigrant depositors with bupkes.

The implication was that the Jews were a people who would explode into an orgy of anarchy on a hair trigger; a whole neighborhood of overly emotional, potentially violent immigrant women could easily detonate when things did not go their way. Although accurate in part, this assessment did not take into account the fact that Yiddish-speaking immigrants had neither the linguistic faculty nor the basic knowledge as to how to handle administrative issues through traditional conduits. Heading into the streets with your neighbors and a rolling pin was simply a more expeditious way of dealing with issues you had difficulty expressing in a new language.

And it wasn't just the Jews. Two days after Jewish mothers rioted, the Italians got into the act, besieging the schools in Little Italy, demanding their children. On the morning of June 28, 1906, according to the *Tribune*, little Maria Boldini arrived at school and told her teacher, "Look out Mees Jackson. Lassa night da mans tolda my pa evera kid getta da troat cut. Read in da pape dis a morn. My pa, my ma—he's ver mad. He's drink by Tony Baccigalupi's place an' he's take da knife, maybe so."

But after having been attacked two days earlier by rampaging Jewesses, the teachers wised up and brought the children to the windows to show the mob of Italian women that they had, in fact, not been harmed. Seeing that nothing had happened, the mothers calmed down and went away.

The great tonsil riot fizzled quickly. Having occurred at the tail end of the school year, it was forgotten almost immediately as students graduated and parents kvelled. The police, however, were still unsettled and, according to the *New York Times*, posted squads of cops outside the heavily Jewish schools on Essex and Grand Streets, where, on the last day of classes, graduates performed scenes from *The Merchant of Venice* to their Yiddish-speaking parents, none of whom rioted or even panicked. Well, with a pound of flesh involved, maybe they panicked just a little.

The events in question—another feverish episode in a neighborhood that exploded in fury every once in a while—were summed up quite nicely in the *Evening Post*, in which a local woman offered a simple explanation for the behavior of the neighborhood's women: "We Jews are an excitable race."

CHAPTER 5

RIVINGTON STREET'S WHEEL
OF (MIS)FORTUNE

One of the items that historians have done a neat job of obscuring as irrelevant to the modern Jewish experience is the role of performance psychics in Jewish life. Legitimized as prophets in the ancient period, they were shunted aside in subsequent eras as shysty products of their times or, if they needed to be legitimized in some way, categorized as special mystics. But up until the modern period, science and mysticism still mixed in weird and uncomfortable ways; for example, mathematician and physicist Isaac Newton was a big fan of alchemy and divination, among other matters of the occult. (Apparently, rationality has never been beholden to the laws of motion and gravity.) During the nineteenth century, when science and reason began to edge out the occult, the terms *fraud* and *charlatan* were weaponized to discredit those who worked as palm readers, phrenologists, and telepaths. But that did not make them disappear or make their customers, who ranged from the deeply impoverished to the nobility, any less interested in their abilities. Wealth and education were never any barometer for potential belief in the paranormal.

Indeed, Jews have worked in the occult for as long as there have been Jews. Instances of necromancy and other occult activities are peppered throughout the Bible and the Talmud, as well as later rabbinic texts. In-

This chapter was originally published as "In the Palm of His Hand" in *Tablet Magazine* (June 18, 2009) and has been expanded for this book.

deed, prophesying is hardwired in the tradition. Numerous biblical and talmudic approbations exist with regard to these matters, among them a warning in Deuteronomy 18:9–12 that states, "When thou art come into the land which the Lord thy God giveth thee, thou shalt not learn to do according to the abominations of those nations. There shall not be found among you any one who maketh his son or his daughter to pass through the fire, or who useth divination, or an observer of times, or an enchanter, or a witch, or a charmer, or a consulter with familiar spirits, or a wizard, or a necromancer. For all who do these things are an abomination unto the Lord, and because of these abominations the Lord thy God doth drive them out from before thee."

Enchanters, witches, charmers, wizards, and necromancers were supposed to be personae non grata for the Israelites, whose consolidation of many into one god is often conceived of as a form of progress. Ancient Jewish texts have a special animus for necromancy—attempts to contact the dead. So offensive is this otherworldly profession that the biblical penalty for it is death.

But Jews have made a stock-in-trade of either ignoring certain laws outright or creating flexible interpretations that permit enough wiggle room to get over, under, or around them. In the case of the occult, it seems to be a case similar to that of traditional admonitions not to go to the theater—a dictate that Jews have roundly ignored.

As a result, Jewish history is chock full of performance psychics, from palm readers to telepaths, necromancers to nasologists. If a particular psychic occupation exists, you can be fairly sure that some Jew did it at one point or another.

And even with the advent of the Enlightenment and the political and social emancipation it brought in its wake, Jews were expected to have abrogated this silliness. But shtetl superstitions simply migrated in various forms to cities, where, in an attempt to slap a veneer of sophistication on their ancient crafts, occultists often presented themselves as scientists or professors. They could be found in Jewish neighborhoods in Warsaw, Krakow, and New York City plying their trades.

One such specimen, a man named Abraham Hochman, came to prominence in mid-1890s New York, following the 1895 publication of his *Fortune Teller*, a popular booklet he claimed to have reprinted several times, as were

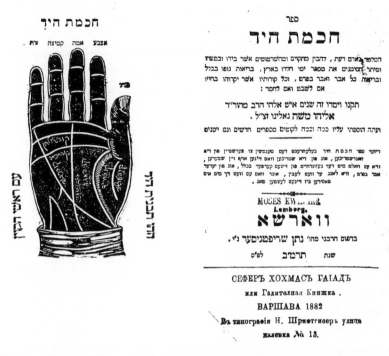

Figure 5.1. Cover and illustration from *Khokhmes hayad* (Wisdom of the Hand), an 1882 Yiddish reprint of a 1799 reprint of a Hebrew palm reading manual that dates to the sixteenth century. This is just one of many examples of such Jewish occult manuals. The frequent reprinting of such manuals over many centuries is but one indication of their popularity. Courtesy of the YIVO Institute for Jewish Research.

his subsequent Yiddish publications on astrology and fortune telling. Operating out of a building he owned at 169 Rivington Street, Hochman was a Lower East Side fixture who told fortunes, read palms and foreheads, and tracked down lost spouses and kin for people in the neighborhood. He kept innocent men out of prison, found lost property, and, occasionally, knew which horse would come in at the track. When business flagged, he contacted journalist friends and pulled psychic stunts to attract customers, who reported on them assiduously in the Yiddish press.

Even the *New York Times* was not immune to the lures of Hochman. Tongue in cheek as it may have been, the *Times* reported on the 1904 story of how Hochman's psychic abilities helped to locate Jacob Greenberg's (of the Essex Street Greenbergs) missing horse, cart, and an errant load of grapes.

Figure 5.2. Cover of Hochman's fortune-telling guide, *Di geheyme kraft oder di shlisl tsu der nevue* (The Secret Power, or, the Key to Prophecy), 1909. Courtesy of the YIVO Institute for Jewish Research.

Occasionally, when Hochman did something really dramatic, news of his exploits would appear in the general press. The *New York Sun*, among other outlets, reported on an episode in May 1904 when a bushy-haired Hochman waltzed into the Essex Market Police Court and inexplicably paid the bail for one Abie Langener, who had been arrested with seven other youths on a burglary charge. The magistrate asked why Hochman was paying bail for someone he didn't know.

"I can read the future!" he declared to the court. "I have read this man's mind and know he is innocent. I can also read your mind. You will discharge him when the case comes up before you tomorrow. If he were guilty, I would know it and I would not bail him out. I will be here tomorrow to show you that my predictions come true."

Figure 5.3. Advertisement in Yiddish for Hochman's psychic services, c. 1905. "Prof. Hochman is the greatest artist of mind reading. No one in the world even compares to him. He tells everyone the absolute truth and future." Courtesy of the YIVO Institute for Jewish Research.

Hochman did, in fact, show up the following day. And, sure enough, when Langener and another suspect were brought before the court, the magistrate released them due to lack of evidence.

"What did I tell you?" said Hochman.

The psychic was mobbed outside the courthouse by hundreds of the accused's friends, who, according to press reports, practically tore off his clothes. It is not clear why this would be necessary and, in any case, the courthouse bailiffs came outside to rescue Hochman from his demonstrative well-wishers.

But Hochman was usually surrounded by a mob, though typically of what was referred to as "wildly gesticulating women." The stoop of his Rivington Street studio was frequently crammed with flailing ladies, often accompanied by children, all desperately trying to find missing husbands and fathers. These men ranged from immigrants who had conveniently "forgotten" about their families in the old country, to men who could not tolerate the cramped quarters of their 300-square-foot tenements and their half-dozen screaming kids, to jerks who ran out of money and disappeared. The epidemic of runaway husbands was so severe among the Jews that the *Forverts*, the largest-circulation Yiddish daily in the world, began running the "Gallery of Missing Men," a page full of mug shots and descriptions of these nefarious characters to help locate them and bring them to justice. The situation was so bad that in 1905 a quasi-governmental agency, the National Desertion Bureau, was founded to help Jewish women and children whose husbands and fathers were on the lam.

Locating missing husbands was a Hochman specialty. He gained quite a bit of fame for this ability when, in 1903, the press reported on the predicament of Minnie Cohen, whose husband went missing for a month. Minnie decided to avail herself of Hochman's services. With a dollar in hand, she made her way through the labyrinthine snarl of panhandlers and pushcarts to Hochman's office. He informed Minnie that her husband would be up to no good at the corner of Pitt and Grand Streets at exactly 10 o'clock that night. So sure was he of his prophecy that he promised to give her $50 if he was wrong. With unshakable faith in the Hebrew Seer of Rivington Street, and with hope in the possibility of getting a wad of cash if her runaway husband didn't show, Minnie pulled a cop out of the Essex Street station and told

Figure 5.4. The *Jewish Daily Forward*'s "Gallery of Missing Men," February 20, 1923. Founded in 1909, this feature served as a rogues' gallery of runaway Jewish husbands and fathers. Courtesy of the YIVO Institute for Jewish Research.

him about Hochman's prediction. Officer O'Grady went with her, perhaps out of sheer curiosity. When they got to the corner of Pitt and Grand, Minnie's truant husband was there, scratching his back on a lamppost. Officer O'Grady arrested Minnie's husband and brought him into the station, where he was held on a $100 bond and instructed to begin paying his wife Minnie $2 a week in alimony. "Venus is ascendant—husbands beware!" Hochman announced to the women gathered on his stoop.

With this kind of publicity, Hochman concluded that he could expand his psychic constituency further than the local Hebrews. He went straight for the top. One day in the spring of 1905, Hochman trundled into the Grand

Street clubhouse of Tammany Hall thug Florrie Sullivan, grabbed the local strongman's hand, and told him that he dreamed that the horse King Pepper was going to come in first, with a payoff of 8 to 1. Sullivan, who forswore belief in the occult, nevertheless took a bet on Hochman's advice. King Pepper won, making Sullivan a small fortune. Hochman's gambit worked; he wound up as the Sullivan gang's official mind reader and phrenologist.

Hochman was so successful with local politicians that his youngest son Frankie's 1906 bris brought out a full police battalion and included performances by Yiddish theater actors. The massive event was besieged by thousands of well-wishers who devoured 320 pounds of chicken and six crates of fruit. An entire block of Rivington Street was closed down for two days on account of this sumptuous affair.

As may be evident, Hochman loved a good Jewish party, and, as a sidebar to his psychic industries, he had colorfully illustrated *ketubot* (Jewish wedding contracts) printed and sold at a wedding hall he owned. He even published his own Passover Haggadah, which included a number of advertisements for his psychic services as well as other products and services. Hochman's Haggadah is the only one in the world that, right after the ten plagues, has an advertisement for a doctor who specializes in constipation.

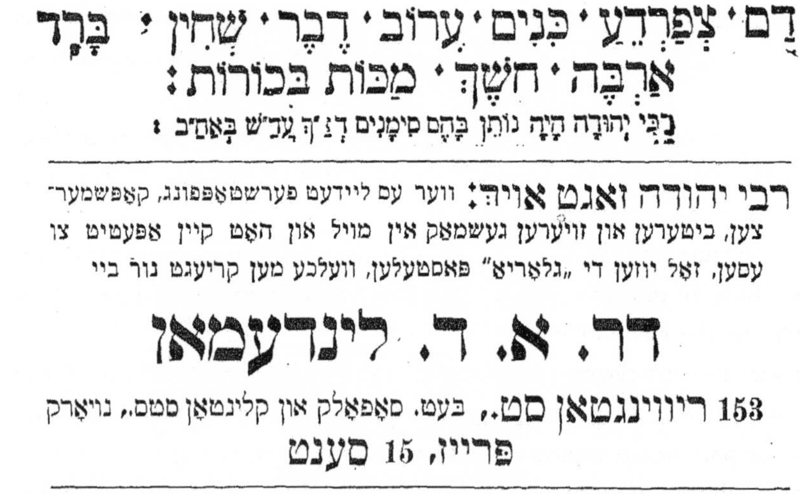
דם · צפרדע · כנים · ערוב · דבר · שחין · ברד
ארבה · חשך · מכות בכורות:
רבי יהודה היה נותן בהם סימנים דצ"ך עד"ש באח"ב:

רבי יהודה זאגט אויה: ווער עם ליידעט פערשטאפפונג, קאפשמער־
צען, ביטערען און זויערען געשמאק אין מויל און האט קיין אפעטיט צו
עסען, זאל יוזען די „גלאריא" פאסטעלען, וועלכע מען קריעגט נור ביי

דר. א. ד. לינדעמאן

153 ריווינגטאן סט., בעט. סאפאלק און קלינטאן סטס., נויארק
פרייז, 15 סענט

Figure 5.5. Excerpt from Avraham Hochman's Haggadah shel peysekh in reyn yidish, New York, n.d., www.hebrewbooks.com.

But not everyone was so enamored of Hochman's psychic exploits. In 1903 Sadie Reed visited the professor's Harlem office to test his mettle. After entering and introducing herself, she demanded proof of his psychic powers. Hochman claimed he could guess her husband's name if she wrote it on a piece of paper and placed it inside a bible he gave her. She complied, but while she stared into the crystal ball he told her to focus on, she allegedly caught him sneaking a peek at the piece of paper she'd put in the bible. Still not dissuaded, she told the seer that her husband was a heavy drinker and needed help. He put a stone in a glass of water and told her the stone had properties that would help him. Miss Reed paid and left. She returned shortly thereafter with news that the magic stone had worked on her husband but that now she needed help because of a pain in her side. Hochman concocted a potion for her; she paid him and left.

Although Mrs. Reed may have seemed to be an initially skeptical but ultimately happy customer, it turned out that she was an undercover detective for the County Medical Society, there to investigate Professor Hochman's activities. As a result, Hochman wound up in court having to defend himself, which he did with aplomb after changing Sadie Reed's skeptical mind.

Despite his detractors, Hochman frequently used his powers, or at least his connections, for good. As a member in good standing of the East Side Businessmen's Protective Agency, he arranged, together with another Tammany strongman, Big Tim Sullivan, to provide holiday fare for local indigents. And provide they did: During Passover 1907, Hochman and his crew showed up on Grand Street with 52,000 pounds of matzos, two carloads of potatoes, 24,000 eggs, and 600 gallons of wine to provide more than a thousand poor families with holiday fare.

The same year, Hochman invented the internet—but only for the Lower East Side. In 1907 the *New York Tribune* reported that a well-known East Sider by the name of Hochman had dubbed himself "the wireless news expert" and had rigged a 40-foot pole to the roof of his Rivington Street house. Hochman explained to reporters how a series of colored flags run up the pole would inform journalists of the nature of important stories. For Hochman, "important stories" actually meant "news of births and weddings" and was apparently a scheme to create a buzz for a nearby wedding hall he owned.

Unlike most clairvoyants, Hochman was happy to share his secrets, publishing his prophetic techniques in books and articles. As he explained in his book *The Key to Prophecy*, he based his method on what he referred to as the "astro-biblical chart," which anyone could use to answer questions such as "Will I fall in love?"; "Should I take dance lessons?"; "Does my husband know I've been bad?"; "Should I get a job as a tailor?"; "Is my landlord in love with me?" Determining the answer required readers to hold some herbs or nuts in the right hand, count backward by 7's with the left hand, add whatever remained to the number of the question, and find the corresponding number on the astrobiblical chart, which provided the name of a Hebrew symbol and a natural element. Then, inquirers were to take the Hebrew symbol and the element and consult Hochman's system of charts for another number, which led to the answer chart, whereupon a person would punch in the original number subtracted after the initial step of nut holding and backward counting. A bit convoluted, perhaps, but how could it miss?

One of Hochman's major innovations had little to do with phrenology or mind reading. In fact, it was his knack for self-promotion and performance—his Haggadahs, *ketubot*, and suddenly mysterious appearances in various locales—that increased his fame. But Hochman's success as a clairvoyant was limited and, around the end of World War I, his advertisements in the Yiddish press began to disappear. In the end it appears he gave up the occult for something far less ephemeral: real estate.

CHAPTER 6

YOM KIPPUR BATTLE ROYALE

When Jews decide to chow down on Yom Kippur, it is usually done clandestinely: sneaking tasty morsels in a dark pantry or disappearing into a diner in some nearby non-Jewish neighborhood. But furtive noshing was not always the heretical path of choice on the Day of Atonement. A little more than a century ago, a range of leftists held massive public festivals of eating, dancing, and performance for the full twenty-five hours of Yom Kippur, not only as a way to fight for their right to party but to unshackle themselves from the oppressive religious dictates they grew up with. After all, what do you do when prayers and traditional customs no longer hold any meaning yet you still want to be part of a Jewish community? Eating with intention on a religiously sanctioned fast day allows you, in one fell swoop, to thumb your nose at the religious establishment and create a secular Jewish identity.

Yom Kippur dances, organized initially by anarchists in the mid-1880s, started in London and migrated to New York and Montreal. Smaller nosh fests and public demonstrations were also celebrated by Jewish antinomians in other locales. Unorthodox Jews in interwar Poland could pull hundreds of locals into small venues on Yom Kippur in shtetls such as Kalish and Chelm; in larger cities, for example, Warsaw and Lodz, they could sell out 5,000-seat

This chapter was originally published as "The Festive Meal" in *Tablet Magazine* (September 24, 2009) and has been expanded for this book.

circuses. Heresy could also be big business; tickets for early 1890s Yom Kippur events in New York City cost 15 cents for anarchists; capitalists who deigned to attend had to pay double.

Advertised in the Yiddish press, Yom Kippur balls, lectures, and nosh fests were decidedly communal events created by and for an alternative community. You had to be a Jew to avail yourself of a free blintz given out by a Jewish organization in Warsaw on Yom Kippur. Otherwise, it just wasn't heresy. Yet it was not just provocation that motivated people to engage in what critics would consider a supremely obnoxious activity. Some people partook to spite a god they did not believe in. Others participated to antagonize their parents, and still others to harass the religious establishment. In fact, harassment may have been the biggest draw.

In addition, holding an antireligious Yom Kippur event was often a way to get free publicity. New York's Herrick Brothers Restaurant caused a riot on Yom Kippur in 1898 when it became apparent that the venue was staying open for the holiday, because, the Herricks said, they were socialists and did not believe in such stuff. In fact, they had even placed advertisements in the *Forverts*, a socialist paper, indicating that they would

Figure 6.1. Advertisement for a Yom Kippur concert and ball at Clarendon Hall, New York City. Source: *Di varhayt*, 1889. Courtesy of the YIVO Institute for Jewish Research.

RIOT ON THE EAST SIDE

Mob of Hebrews Again Attacks Diners in Division Street.

THE POLICE ARE KEPT BUSY

Crowd Could Not Stand the Sight of
Their Co-Religionists Eating on
the Day of Atonement.

Figure 6.2. Headlines of events at Herrick Brothers Restaurant. Source: *New York Times,* September 27, 1898.

be keeping the restaurant open on the holidays and that it would be open to both Jew and Gentile.

So as the autumn sun went down on the Lower East Side and a good portion of its denizens made their way to local synagogues, hundreds took a quick detour, falling with fist and nail upon the diners at the packed Division Street restaurant. As the *New York Times* wryly noted, "If their customers didn't have enough respect for the holiday, it would be pounded into them."

The restaurant became a flashpoint for religious Jews who were looking for a fight. Hundreds of them gathered outside, waiting for diners to come out. One such postprandial customer was Louis Silverstein, who was set upon and attacked by a mob of boys and men. He was rescued by the police, who managed to arrest some of his assailants. The gangs of religious attackers even tried to pounce on a group of four uniformed Jewish soldiers who had just left Herrick Brothers. But one of them, Morris Sherman, shot his revolver in the air, scattering the crowd. Unfortunately for the would-be attackers, the police beat them as they tried to escape and a number sustained injuries. Louis Rotner, according to the *Times,* had his nose broken by a billy club, and another man, who refused to give his name, had his two front teeth knocked out.

It was, no doubt, a Yom Kippur to remember.

For a generation of immigrants, many of whom had grown up in religious homes, these Yom Kippur shenanigans were a full-on revolt against Jewish tradition. And although synagogues were generally active and frequently packed on holidays in immigrant Jewish neighborhoods, the number of Jews who were actively engaged in subverting tradition was large enough to be considered a mass movement. In fact, the number was so large that in 1907 the sensationalist socialist Yiddish daily *Di varhayt* penned an editorial asking its readers to be tolerant of those observing Yom Kippur. The editors explained that it was people's right to be religious in a free society, but it was not really clear whether their pleas actually worked. Nearly every year there were pitched battles between radical and religious Jews. And it was also never entirely clear in which direction the balance was tipped. That same year, it was reported that the New York City Police stationed extra cops on the Lower East Side to protect the atheists from religions hooligans.

Regardless of which side was in control, there was always action. In 1915, for example, the *New York Sun* reported that a Lower East Side cooperative restaurant a few doors down from a synagogue on East Broadway not only insisted on keeping its doors open on Yom Kippur but also hung out a "Free Lunch" sign and, to top it off, handed out free cigars. At some point during this provocation, some religious Jews from the synagogue down the block lost their patience and heaved a big rock through the restaurant's large plate-glass window. The radicals inside left their food and promptly marched outside, starting a battle royale between themselves and the religious folk, a bloody fight that was eventually suppressed by the police.

Yom Kippur fisticuffs, it should be known, were not unique to New York City. Warsaw, with its large Jewish population, was also a flashpoint for Jew-on-Jew Day of Atonement fury. Similar to its New World manifestations, engagement in public fressing was typically the result of political orientation, something made clear by a post–Yom Kippur report from *Haynt*, one of Warsaw's daily Yiddish papers in 1927.

> In the nonreligious sector everything went according to tradition. The Independent Socialists organized a *Kol nidre* evening in which various "cantors" and "cantorettes" performed in a Jewish fashion. And there was rejoicing in the house.
>
> This year, the Free Thinkers also fulfilled their "holy mission" and held a meeting during *Kol nidre* at the Worker's House on 23 Karmelitska Street in which religion, Yom Kippur, and atheism were discussed.
>
> And if the meeting itself went without incident, they went out into the Jewish streets the morning of Yom Kippur and hawked old issues of the magazine *The Freethinker* while people were on their way to shul. On account of

Figure 6.3. The Freethinker magazine, anti-high holiday issue (Lodz, Poland, 1926). Courtesy of the YIVO Institute for Jewish Research.

this, a number of fights occurred between religious Jews and the "holy rollers" who sold the magazines.

A few incidents also occurred during the day, when a group of Free Thinkers poured onto Karmelitska, Dzika, and Nalevki Streets, some with lit cigarettes and others with apples in their mouths.

On account of this provocation, a serious battle occurred between the "demonstrators" and the religious passers-by. Water was dumped from a window on Karmelitska Street onto the heads of the Free Thinkers.

Also, a free lunch was organized at the Worker's Home at 23 Karmelitska Street for those who were not able to eat at home because of their parents or wives.

The number of takers for this free lunch was so large that the line for tickets stretched all the way to the front gate of the building, where a large crowd gathered. Some protested against those eating; others defended them. Occasionally the arguments became so heated that the police had to intervene.

Similar scenes also occurred at the Bundist "Worker's Corner," on 9 Pshiazd Street, where the struggle for lunch was so great that the screams and yells could be heard all the way in the street. In addition, some of those eating showed off their big appetites [by dining] in front of the windows, bringing forth much anguish among the religious Jews who were passing by.

The "struggle for lunch" was indeed intense. Yom Kippur battles broke out between religious and antireligious Jews worldwide as a result of these annual provocations. Some years, though, events passed peacefully. In September 1925, for example, *Moment* reported that an antireligious mass meeting held in a theater during the evening of Yom Kippur in Warsaw, during which speakers fulminated furiously against religion in general and against Yom Kippur specifically, ended without any violence whatsoever.

And yet on the same night at about the same time, angry protesters gathered outside the Workers' Kitchen on Pshiazd Street, yelling at those eating inside. As the protests escalated, rocks were thrown, and as soon as the tinkling of smashed glass was heard, the socialists burst out of their kitchen armed with sticks to drive the crowd away. The Warsaw police, always loathe to interfere in Jew-on-Jew violence, managed to arrest youths from both camps on just another typical Yom Kippur in Yiddishland.

CHAPTER 7

ATTACK OF THE YIDDISH JOURNALISTS

Newspaper readers do not often consider what kind of behind-the-scenes insanity goes into the articles they peruse. I am not referring here to either the intrepid news gathering or the hysterical keyboard pounding of writers on deadline. The insanity in question has to do with what happens to a journalist's work once he or she hands it in, namely, the tension-filled relationship between writers and editors.

Is it true, as some writers contend, that editors wantonly destroy perfect copy? Or do they artfully reshape a writer's prose into a more cogent and readable text? The editor-journalist relationship is as fraught as that between mohel and baby during the circumcision ceremony. The mohel has no choice but to snip; the baby has no choice but to cry, but he drinks a little wine and learns to live with the damage.

Renowned for its minor and major disputes, the Yiddish press was a place where editors ruled inky fiefdoms, cracking the whip over writers who served as bitter and often disloyal subjects. Editors controlled the fates and livelihoods of writers and journalists, many of whom thought the press functioned as a kind of commercial department of Yiddish literature, something over which they felt they should have more control.

This chapter was originally published as "Print War" in *Tablet Magazine* (September 16, 2010) and has been expanded for this book.

Most of the battles in the Yiddish journalistic world never left the perimeter of the editors' desks. But on occasion these spats leapt out of the editorial offices and onto the pages of the papers, making for some of the juiciest Yiddish snark this side of Pinsk.

For example, when famed columnist Hillel Tseytlen (a.k.a. Zeitlin) jumped ship in late 1910 from Warsaw's daily *Haynt* to a new competitor, *Moment*, his former editor, Shmuel Yatskan, was furious but temporarily held his tongue.

Tseytlen was one of *Haynt*'s most popular columnists. Born into a family of Lubavitcher Hasidim, he strayed from his yeshiva studies after discovering Spinoza, Nietzsche, and a slew of other Western thinkers. Like any shtetl kid in the process of denuding himself of tradition, he moved to the city—Warsaw, in this case—and involved himself in Jewish political matters and journalism. But Tseytlen never completely gave up his traditional ways, and an interest in Kabbalah eventually brought him back, not only to full religious observance but also to an assiduous promotion of Jewish tradition in his newspaper columns. This was a novelty in the new world of Jewish journalism, most of whose writers had grown up religious, had become secular, and stayed that way. Tseytlen was one of the few who went back—and yet he worked and functioned in a completely secular brand of media long before Orthodox Jews decided it was kosher to print their own version of the news.

Tseytlen's former editor, Yatskan, was also a Litvak plying journalism in Warsaw. An ordained rabbi from the highly regarded Ponevezh Yeshiva, Yatskan was a major figure in the Yiddish press, having founded some of Warsaw's early Jewish dailies, including *Haynt*, which eventually became the best-selling Yiddish paper in Poland.

With an understanding that a popular newspaper should have a broad mandate, Yatskan printed a lot of sensationalistic trash along with high-quality literature and excellent cultural and political criticism. His papers always appealed to the widest possible audience.

That's where Tseytlen fit in. Able to synthesize abstract philosophical ideas about Jewish culture, religion, and modern society into readable opinion pieces, Tseytlen was one of the paper's major assets. In particular, his columns appealed to religious and traditionally oriented readers, a significant

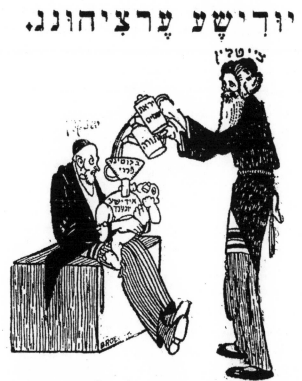

Figure 7.1. A 1910 cartoon portraying how Tseytlen and Yatskan worked together. Tseytlen (standing) pours Torah and piety into a funnel marked "The Bloody Woman" (a torrid potboiler published by *Haynt*), which then goes into a baby marked, "Jewish youth." The caption reads, "Reb Hillel Tseytlen pours in some Torah and piety so the suckers won't complain." The cartoon represents the idea that Tseytlen functioned as a kind of religious beard for the paper. Courtesy of the YIVO Institute for Jewish Research.

portion of the readership. So when he decided to abandon *Haynt*, it was a devastating blow for Yatskan, who was losing his most popular writer.

Yatskan and Tseytlen sniped at each other for a while, printing what in Yiddish is called *soydes fun kheyder*, or "secrets from the schoolyard." The strange thing was that all of this sniping took place in the pages of a newspaper, the purpose of which was to print news, not the details of a bitter personal fight between two journalists. But in a world without Twitter, the newspaper is where everything happened and where Tseytlen and Yatskan duked it out. Words like "hypocrite," "trash," "liar," and "provocateur" were bandied about briefly, and then things seemed to settle down. The appearance of tranquility was deceptive, however, and by September 1913 Yatskan could no longer control his anger at Tseytlen's departure and rekindled the fight by printing a blurb in *Haynt* by an unnamed "correspondent" from Pinsk.

> Seeing how Hillel Tseytlen is still around and unashamedly screams before the public in regard to his holiness and complains about the "lies" that are being spread about him, that he, tragically, is a "holy man" who is being hounded for his religiosity, and also has the audacity to compare the accusation against the victim of the Kiev blood libel with himself, it is my duty to remind him of the fact that when he was here, in Pinsk giving a lecture, I, along with numerous others who can verify it, saw with my own eyes, as the others saw with theirs, how in the train station buffet he ate a pork chop, with a roll, followed by a cutlet.

Although this rambling sentence (21 lines of one newspaper column) was a grammatical mess, it was also a finely crafted accusation, attacking Tseytlen for his hypocrisy, arrogance, and, the ultimate transgression, the consumption of *treyf*. And in public, no less.

A Yiddish version of fake news, the accusation was the last straw. Tseytlen and the *Moment* staff responded in the paper by saying that Yatskan and *Haynt* were rank liars attacking a former colleague who had left for good reason. In printed testimonials supporting their besmirched colleague, dozens of journalists sided with Tseytlen.

Haynt, as well as another daily, *Der fraynd*, pounded away at Tseytlen, attacking him for all manner of sin, ranging from writing on Shabbos to violating Yom Kippur. The writers of *Moment* shot back, asserting that Yatskan wrote a fake Torah, printed pornography, and promoted conversion to Christianity, claims Yatskan said were "a product of unscrupulous swindlers and a gang of Sodomites who created a horror story comparable to some of the worst crimes ever committed." No one ever accused Yatskan of subtlety.

To Tseytlen's readers the attacks were devastating. How could their beloved writer, a *frumer yid* (a religious Jew), stand accused of such heinous transgressions? Thousands signed petitions and wrote letters of support, dozens of which *Moment* published. *Haynt* claimed that it was all a ploy: The letters and the names were all fakes.

Figure 7.2. Cover of the September 1913 issue of the Yom Kippur humor magazine *Kapores. Haynt* editor Yatskan waves a chicken with Tseytlen's head in preparation to sacrifice it for the holiday. The caption reads, "Did you ever see such a chicken? I tried to *shlog kapores* with it, and look at the trick it played on me!" Courtesy of the YIVO Institute for Jewish Research.

Yiddish cartoonists had a field day: Tseytlen's bushy beard and shock of long hair made for great caricatures. With the battle coming to a head just before Yom Kippur, Yosef Tunkel, the brightest satirical light of twentieth-century Yiddish, found the perfect analogy for this tempest: the *kapores* slaughter ritual, a custom in which Jews, on the eve of Yom Kippur, wave a chicken over their heads three times and then kill it to expiate their sins (the Jew's, not the chicken's).

Tunkel drew Tseytlen's bushy head onto the chicken that Yatskan performs the *kapores* with, while chicken Tseytlen defecates. The image perfectly captured their unhappy relationship. By the time this cartoon appeared on the cover of Tunkel's special Yom Kippur humor magazine, the organized Jewish community had begun to freak out because the mudslinging had gotten so out of hand that the Polish press had begun to report on it in a series of "look at these crazy Jews" articles. Ever sensitive about their position in society, something had to be done.

In response to the journalistic melee, a number of community leaders decided to create an arbitration panel to put an end to the ugly public dispute. In the end, however, there was no need; by early October 1913, the Mendel Beilis blood libel trial was underway in Kiev. This huge story, about a Jew who was framed for killing a Christian child to make matzos, dominated the headlines through the fall, and the Tseytlen-Yatskan skirmish fizzled into Yiddish oblivion.

A fine example of the esteem in which editors and journalists—Yiddish or otherwise—hold one another, the episode reflects the nature of their relationships and what happens when egos cannot take insults. For those actually involved, these episodes could be painful. For readers, it was all gravy with which to smother their *kapores* chickens.

CHAPTER 8

SUICIDE JEWS

"People really love suicide," wrote journalist Efroyem Kaganovski in 1929 in the Warsaw daily *Unzer ekspres*, "because a suicide always has some kind of sensational story, some kind of letter from which people can extract some kind of essential truth."

The "essential truth" that Kaganovski was referring to here is elusive and slippery. What is true is that suicide stories in the press not only often end with a bang but are also riveted with drama and emotional excess, a painful trifecta that is essential to attracting readers. Although suicide occurs among all peoples, the Jewish variant that was reported on in the Yiddish press had its own unique attributes.

Although suicide is categorized as a type of murder in the Jewish tradition, its illicit nature has not stopped many a Jew from shuffling off his or her mortal coil. Statistics indicate that, although Jews may be less apt than other groups to commit suicide, they are not removed from it altogether. At certain times and in certain places suicide has increased among Jews, particularly when economic, political, and social conditions have gone south. There are other variables as well. One nineteenth-century German statistic indicates that as rates of assimilation grew among Jews, so did

---

This chapter was originally published as "Death Toll" in *Tablet Magazine* (June 17, 2010) and has been expanded for this book.

rates of suicide. After all, there is nothing like a conflicted identity to make one feel like ending it all.

Because of suicide's disreputable status in Jewish law and because, as is so often the case, it was frequently a mystery why a close friend or relative threw him- or herself off the top of a building or drank a vial of poison, suicides were frequently a source of embarrassment to survivors. The departed became the topic of dark family secrets. But once the Yiddish press came along, it was tough to keep anything in Jewish life private.

In Warsaw in the 1920s and 1930s, for example, reporters wrote with gusto about the huge number of suicides. There are stretches in which one finds at least one and sometimes several suicide reports per day. Not only were Jews killing themselves on a regular basis, but also Yiddish newspaper readers seemed to love nothing more than a juicy story with an unhappy ending.

Figure 8.1. A suicide cartoon from the April 1, 1927, issue of *Der blofer* (Warsaw). The caption reads, "In the Near Future: [Man 1] What's going on? Where's everyone running to? [Man 2] They say there's a man over there who has never tried suicide!" Courtesy of the YIVO Institute for Jewish Research.

"The number of suicides has increased in a frightening manner on the Jewish street. Not a day goes by without at least a couple of Jewish suicides," began an August 1931 article in *Moment*. The story tells of three suicides that occurred the previous day: 19-year-old Benyomin Levin killed himself by asphyxiation; 26-year-old Yitzhok (no last name given) poisoned himself with iodine; and 38-year-old Dvoyre Berger jumped out a fourth-story window. The last two deaths were understood to have been undertaken as a result of severe poverty, a typical reason for many Warsaw Jewish suicides, especially during the Depression.

Reporters who worked the suicide beat were usually anonymous, although authors of note, including Dr. Gershon Levin and Shaul-Yitzhok Stupnitski, wrote articles every few years decrying the plague of suicides that had descended on the community and asking what could be done to stop them. Levin, for one, argued that the large number of Jewish suicides was the result of alienation from traditional life, the laws of which acted as a cork, plugging potentially explosive personalities.

But no population in the Jewish community, religious or otherwise, was immune to suicides; every group from the secular to the Hasidic, and everyone in between, experienced them. The religious orientation of the victims generally was not reported, although some of the suicides had specifically religious components to their executions. According to *Haynt*, in February 1931 in the Polish shtetl of Lusiev, Shevakh Halperin ended it all by jumping into a well while wearing his tallis and tefillin; in August of the same year, Anshel Gotfried wound up as a floater in Lemberg's biggest *mikve* after drinking a vial of poison.

A number of souls who had failed in their attempts tried again and again to kill themselves. "For the third time, the nervous tallis dealer Avrom Aba Lehrer tried to commit suicide," reported Warsaw's *Haynt* in September 1927. "A few months ago, on a beautiful summer's night by the light of a full moon, he attempted to hang himself from a beam under a wooden bridge on the Vistula near the Citadel. But the rope was too weak and it broke. Lehrer fell between the pillars of the bridge and lay there all night with the noose still around his neck." Botched or unusual suicide attempts spun off into the creation of "suicide comedy" in the pages of the city's Yiddish humor magazines. Dark times called for dark humor.

"It's a strange thing," wrote Reb Yoyne in *Unzer ekspres* in January 1926, "I think to myself, all our suicides are incessant scribblers—they all write letters." Having come across a report of a particularly poetic suicide note written by a person who claimed his suicide will be unlike all those other "banal, unoriginal, and unartistic" suicides, that his will be the "loftiest expression of uncertainty," our critic comments, "Perhaps it's gone so far that, even within the suicide industry, there are those who are seen as frauds, and those few original masters in this line of work have been shunted aside and sit in the shadows, unable to exhibit their originality because of these fakers."

"Who knows?" he added. "Maybe there will come a time when the real suicides, those truly capable and talented suicides, will open courses in the practice of their art, where one will learn how to commit suicide, not in a banal, common way, but the way it should be—'the loftiest expression of uncertainty.'"

So many suicide reports appeared in the papers that one humorist, writing in *Haynt*'s humor section in 1928, wrote a parody of the genre in order to expose the sensationalism inherent in the frequent reporting of these little tragedies.

SUICIDE OF A GIRL ON THE DAY OF HER WEDDING

A terrible tragedy took place yesterday on Pavia Street, where 17-year-old Rivka M. threw herself out of a fourth-floor window on the day of her wedding. Critically wounded and with few signs of life, the victim was brought to the Jewish Hospital. It is rumored that the girl committed the terrible act because she discovered that her fiancé had a Christian lover.

*   *   *

Correction

We have been informed that the story above is not entirely correct. First, the tragedy took place on Gnoye Street, not on Pavia. The victim's name is not Rivka M., but Gedalia T. He didn't jump from the fourth floor, but instead went to Kozhenik [a nearby town]. He wasn't critically wounded, but was washing his socks. He was not taken to the Jewish Hospital, but was taking out a loan. He doesn't have a Christian lover, but an uncle who is a tailor.

While it does seem somewhat odd to mock suicides, the snarky manner with which the daily press often wrote about the topic is inescapable. For example, the suicide attempts of Pinye Rogochinsky, a young Warsaw socialist, were roundly mocked in the press. Rogochinsky was described as "a 'true socialist,' who walked around dreaming about a fantastic future and who also had no real interest in actual work." Rogochinsky, they added, lived with his three brothers and had been known previously in the press as the "Shabbos Suicide," for his failed attempts to kill himself on the Sabbath. One day, reported *Moment* in March 1927, after having caught a cold, he stayed home in the rented room that the brothers shared on Stavski Street. At about 11 that morning, neighbors heard screams. They tried to open the apartment door but to no avail; it was locked. They could hear Rogochinsky thrashing about as his wails grew louder. When they finally broke the door down, the neighbors found him gutted with a knife, which was still in his hand, and lying in an expanding pool of blood. Rogochinsky looked up at his neighbors and screamed at them, "Down with the bourgeoisie!"

Among those who attempted to confront the Jewish suicide crisis in a serious fashion was one Reuben Gildenstern. Having grown up in early-twentieth-century Palestine, he traveled to Europe after receiving a large inheritance. While abroad, Gildenstern, who spent two years on the Russian estate of Leo Tolstoy as a literary groupie, fell in love with another Tolstoy hanger-on. His affections went unrequited, and he wound up attempting suicide a total of eight times. In a 1926 interview in *Moment*, he said he had no regrets about "remaining among the living" but had decided to dedicate his life to helping those with similar temptations to resist them. Gildenstern created a club in Vienna where survivors of attempted suicide could enjoy one another's company. He also attempted to launch a Budapest-based German-language magazine called *Der Selbstmörder*, or "The Suicide." His plan was to hire only what he called "one-time suicide candidates" not only as his writers and editors but also as typesetters and printers. He thought that these people were the only ones who could understand what it meant to feel the need to kill oneself. He was adamant on this point, which is perhaps why the magazine never came to fruition.

But the ever-resourceful reporters of Warsaw's Yiddish press could always be counted on to bring in a good suicide story. And during the 1920s and 1930s, at least a handful appeared each day in the crime blotter. Suicide was considered a type of murder, after all, and thus required investigation. Whether it was the story of the woman who was sliced in half after capriciously diving under the wheels of a tramway car while on an afternoon stroll with her father-in-law or the high-school student who hanged himself in detention or the spurned lover who drank poison and leaped out a fourth-story window into the courtyard of his ex-girlfriend's building, these minor daily tragedies kept the readers of Warsaw's Yiddish press horribly entertained.

Here are but a few samples of Yiddish press accounts of such tragedies.

THE ANATOMICAL INSTITUTE RETURNS THE BODY OF A JEWISH SUICIDE BECAUSE THE BONES ARE WORTHLESS

Moment, April 1927

As readers remember from December of last year, a young Jewish girl committed suicide by jumping from the fourth floor (on Targova St.) because she was not able to recover from tuberculosis.

That victim, Rokhl Weinstein, left a will saying that her body should be donated to the Anatomical Institute so "it can be helpful in finding a cure for this dreadful disease" of which she was a victim. That exact expression was taken directly from her will, which she had scrawled in ink on her body. Not wanting to deny her wish, the dead girl's family did not try to oppose her decision and the body was sent to the Anatomical Institute, where it has been for the last four months.

On Saturday, the Burial Society received a notice from the Anatomical Institute, saying that the body of Rokhl Weinstein is of no value for scientific inquiry, because the most important bones were damaged by the tuberculosis. Therefore, they do not need the body and request that they take it.

Yesterday, the Burial Society picked up the body and the burial takes place today.

And so ends the tragic life story of 17-year-old Rokhl Weinstein. Even her bones are worthless. Even the humanitarian efforts she attempted in her last moments could not be fulfilled.

*   *   *

JEWISH BOY COMMITS SUICIDE IN THE COURTYARD OF HIS EX-FIANCÉE ON 19 MILA ST.

Moment, May 1927

Around 9 a.m., a number of residents of 19 Mila Street watched as a young man leapt out a third-story window.

The victim landed on the thick electrical wires that spanned the courtyard on the second-floor level and he remained there, dangling.

Many people came running to see what happened after hearing screams. In the midst of the chaos, no one could figure out what to do.

In the meantime, after hanging on the wires for a number of minutes, the victim fell onto the brick street, receiving horrible bruises over his entire body.

Emergency services were called, and the doctor who arrived determined that the victim drank a large dose of iodine before jumping.

The victim was brought to the Jewish Hospital on Tshista Street in critical condition. It appears that the victim was 18-year-old Yekhiel Braf, who had only a mother in the town of Kotsk. He came alone to Warsaw a few years ago and lived with his cousin, Khaym-Dovid Braf, on 20 Mila Street.

The young man had studied to become a tailor and earned a decent wage. Recently, he began going to dance halls with his friends, where he showed off his skill as an excellent dancer.

Not long ago, Yekhiel made the acquaintance of Ms. Brontshe P. (19 Mila St.), also known as Brontshe the Cossack. She was also an excellent dancer, and Yekhiel quickly fell in love with her.

Because Brontshe liked going out with elegant gentlemen and partying, the boy spent his entire savings on dates and theater tickets.

During Passover, Yekhiel went to visit his mother in Kotsk. He went to tell her that he had found his *basherte* and that he was preparing to get married.

During this time, however, Brontshe met another young man who was better off financially than Yekhiel. When Yekhiel got back to Warsaw, Brontshe made it clear that she didn't want anything to do with him.

Yekhiel took it real hard. He stopped working and would walk around for days at a time as if there were a black cloud over him.

Yesterday at about 6 a.m. he went over to Bzovski's Pharmacy on Mila Street and bought a bottle of iodine. He went home with the bottle of poison with the intention of taking it in bed. But after getting in bed, his plans suddenly changed: He decided to go kill himself in the same house where his unfaithful "bride" lived.

At about 8:30 a.m. he left home for 19 Mila Street. He wandered around the front gate for a while because he thought Brontshe might pass by and he would get to see her one last time.

Finally, he went up the stairs, drank the bottle of iodine, and jumped out the window.

When Brontshe found out about it, she also wanted to poison herself. But residents saw what was happening and they stopped her. The condition of the victim is critical, but not hopeless.

*   *   *

LOOK, I'M TAKING MY OWN LIFE!

Moment, March 1933

Yesterday afternoon, a young man arrived at 21 Gzhibovska Street in the offices of the Burial Society and walked up to the third floor.

Standing by an open window, the young man yelled, "Look, I'm taking my own life right here, so the Society will be able to bury me even faster!"

With these words, the young man drank down a small bottle of iodine and jumped out the window.

It later became known that the young man was 24-year-old Leyzer Zielni (Gzhibovska 78).

He was brought to the Jewish Hospital in critical condition.

The reason for his suicide was unemployment.

CHAPTER 9

BATTLE AT THE BRIS

As industrialization swept Europe in the late nineteenth century, cities grew exponentially, bulging with newcomers seeking better jobs and better lives. Already a quasi-urban society in Russian-ruled Poland, Jews also began to move en masse to big cities, such as Warsaw and Lodz, both centers of commerce. Warsaw, the seat of Polish politics and culture, became a magnet for migrants of all kinds. By the turn of the twentieth century, the future Polish capital's population was at least one-third Jewish. Also drawn by the lures of city life, numerous rabbis and Hasidic rebbes and their followers moved there. In fact, by the start of World War I, Warsaw had at least fifty Hasidic rebbes and thousands of their followers as permanent residents.

In general, the courts of Hasidic rebbes were initially based in specific towns. Instead of being known by their real names, rebbes were often referred to by the name of the town from which they hailed. Thanks to shifting borders and mixed local populations, towns in Eastern Europe often had Polish, Russian, Ukrainian, and Yiddish names. Hasidic rebbes, for obvious reasons, were usually referred to by the Yiddish name of the town. For example, the Bialer Rebbe, Yitzhok Yankev Rabinovitsh, was from Biala (Biała Podlaska in Polish); the Bobover Rebbe, Shloyme Halbershtam, hailed from

This chapter was originally published as "Grudge Match" in *Tablet Magazine* (July 16, 2009) and has been expanded for this book.

Bobov (Bobowa in Polish); and the Gerer Rebbe, Yitzhok Meyer Alter, was
from Ger (Gora Kalwaria in Polish). As such, these rebbes were popularly
referred to as "The Bobover" or "The Bialer." In everyday Yiddish, or in the
newspapers, when "The Gerer" was mentioned, everyone knew that it was
a reference to the rebbe from Ger. Incidentally, Hasidic courts are essentially dynasties, with succession typically (but not always) going to a son of
the rebbe.

Hasidic rebbes could move anywhere, but they always retained the names
of their original towns. So, for example, when the Gerer Rebbe moved to
Warsaw, he remained the Gerer Rebbe, as did all subsequent Gerer rebbes. As
it happens, the Gerer court still exists and is now headquartered in Jerusalem.

Just as a Hasidic rebbe's home in a shtetl functioned as his office and
general headquarters, so did his new home in the city. As sect leader, the
rebbe's presence was enormously important to his Hasidism, and his disciples would come from near and far to ask advice and request divine
intervention in matters holy and profane. Numerous Hasidim were so attached to their rebbes that they moved to Warsaw just to be near them. This
often placed them close to other Hasidic sects whose rebbes had also come
to live in the capital. This proximity made inter-sect disputes a far more
in-your-face affair than they had been when the rebbes and their followers
were in their separate shtetls. And disagreements between Hasidic sects
were legion.

Such disputes occurred for a variety of reasons. Within the sects themselves the disagreements usually had to do with jealousy over particular
disciples who were closer to the rebbe than others, and often the disputes had
to do with rabbinic succession. Between different sects anything was possible. Disagreements could arise over when to start praying, which *nigunim*
(melodies) to use, or what kind of kugel to eat on Shabbos and when to eat
it. Some sects suffered from such long-term disputes—for example, the feud
between the Sandzer and the Sadagurer or that between the Belzer and the
Munkatcher Hasidim—that nobody could remember what it was that initially set off the antagonism. Essentially Hasidic variants of the Hatfields
and the McCoys, these disputes were often furious and sometimes violent.
Such a feud occurred with two groups of Hasidim whose leaders had moved
to Warsaw just after World War I, the Porisover Rebbe (Rabbi Yeshoshue

Osher Hurvitz-Shternfeld) and the Kolibyeler Rebbe (Rabbi Uri Yehoshue Osher Elkhanan Ashkenazi). This disagreement had an unknown cause that resulted in bad blood between them and all of their followers for many years.

In early 1925 the Porisover Rebbe, a widower, remarried. A year later, his first child, a son, was born. In an attempt to bury the hatchet with the Kolibyeler Rebbe, the Porisover invited him to the newborn's bris. Moreover, he designated the Kolibyeler Rebbe to serve as the boy's *sandek*, the godfather who cradles the child while the mohel performs the circumcision. This was a beautiful gesture, and the Kolibyeler Rebbe gracefully accepted. The Porisover Rebbe, however, neglected to inform his own followers of his changed attitude toward the Kolibyeler. After having doubtlessly heard censorious homilies from their rebbe against the evil Kolibyeler over a period of years, the Porisover Hasidim were flabbergasted by his largesse and did not quite know how to react when they saw the Hasidic chieftain of their most despised enemies accorded such esteemed treatment.

The party for the bris was huge. Rabbis and their acolytes packed the Porisover Rebbe's large apartment; everyone who was anyone in Hasidic Warsaw was in attendance. Wine poured like water, and the Porisover Hasidim got drunk and obstreperous. To protest their rebbe's decision to reconcile with his former archenemy, they openly defied their leader's call to join in the opening prayers of the bris ceremony.

Taking note of his followers' silence, the Porisover Rebbe invited the Kolibyeler Rebbe to recite a blessing, which further infuriated the Porisover Hasidim. "Raboysay, mir veln bentshn [Gentlemen, let us make a blessing]," the Kolibyeler intoned. The Porisover Hasidim couldn't take it any more and met the call to prayer with forced, hysterical laughter. Their rudeness was shocking, but given the number of celebrants and the noise, the ruckus died down and the ceremony soon continued.

One of the Porisover Hasidim finally chimed in with a prayer and was joined by his peers. But another guest, the son of the Zvoliner Rebbe, refused to let their obnoxious outburst pass without incident and blurted out, "It's more appropriate to laugh at your singing than at the Kolibyeler's."

Their patience already thin, the drunken Porisover Hasidim were quick to react. One particularly inebriated fellow, Avremele Gritser, stuck his face into the Zvoliner Rebbe's son's and told him to shut up. He called him a brat and cursed him as a "villain of Israel." (Like their clothing, Hasidic cursing is relatively modest.)

Seeing his son berated by a drunken Hasid infuriated the Zvoliner Rebbe, who grabbed Gritser by the *kitl* (silk robe) and warned him that if he didn't stop insulting his son, he'd get punched—twice for good measure. Gritser looked at the Zvoliner Rebbe and shot back, "Oh yeah? And you'll get four punches."

With that, the Zvoliner Rebbe's son dropped Gritser with two blazing punches.

Already on edge, the Porisover mob jumped on the Zvoliner Rebbe and his son and began to beat them mercilessly. Performing what is known in Yiddish as "taking out a mortgage," a beating that entails holding someone down while others pummel him, the Zvoliner father and son took a serious pounding.

Hearing the inhuman screams of the two Zvoliners, neighbors came running. They rushed into the rebbe's apartment and found the Zvoliner Rebbe and his son lying immobile on the floor groaning, their clothes ripped to shreds.

The two pummeled men were then dragged out of the building by a gaggle of Porisover Hasidim and thrown into the street. Only with the help of two passers-by were they put into a *droshke* (horse-drawn carriage) and taken home. Inside, the party continued as though nothing had even happened: The bris was completed, and merrymaking and dancing followed.

But shortly thereafter, the daughter of the Zvoliner Rebbe burst into the apartment with a policeman. The officer asked that the owner of the house, the Porisover Rebbe, step outside. His followers, however, circled the wagons and would not allow the policeman to approach the rebbe. The Zvoliner's daughter, described by one Yiddish reporter as "a girl with a sharp tongue," began to howl that her father was beaten and stomped on and that she demanded satisfaction. After a tense standoff, the Hasidim relented and the policeman returned to the station house with the names of the rebbe and the other brawlers.

The Zvoliner's daughter told the group of Yiddish journalists that had assembled to report that they had not heard the last of her. She would press charges. In the end, it was not clear whether she did or not. Many intra-

Jewish disputes, particularly those based in the religious world, were resolved through quiet intercession. Most people thought that having these small internal convulsions in the Hasidic world reported in the press was hugely embarrassing, and they did not want to create further possibilities for the airing of Yiddish dirty laundry in the newspapers. So it is likely that the matter was dealt with internally. Threats to press charges were probably talked out and the incident was smoothed over.

But it wouldn't be much of a surprise if the Zvoliner Rebbe didn't at least hold a grudge.

CHAPTER 10

URKE NACHALNIK

Fine Young Criminal

Yitzhok Farberovitsh was known as a good kid in the shtetl of Vizne, a small town in Russian-ruled Poland, in the years just before World War I. He excelled in *kheyder*, Jewish elementary school, and, when he reached his tweens, was sent to another town in the Pale of Settlement to attend a yeshiva, where he was on track to fulfill his mother's dream that he become a rabbi. But not long after his bar mitzvah, his mother died, sending the Farberovitsh household into a depression and throwing young Yitzhok's life off the rails.

Stuck as a boarding student at the yeshiva, he wrote his family letters asking about the future: Would they be able to pay his tuition and continue supporting him? No one responded. In those days yeshiva students who were boarders took occasional meals at the homes of local members of the community, for whom it was considered a duty and an honor to support them. One of these kindly hosts was a prostitute, whom Yitzhok visited on Thursdays for meals. Seeing that the boy had no means, the prostitute took Yitzhok in while he took it upon himself to convince her to quit her trade, explaining that her terrible sins would lead her straight to Hell. His reservations about her lifestyle were strong but not strong enough to make him quit eating at her house—after all, he was without family support and had no

---

This chapter was originally published in *Tablet Magazine* (January 21, 2010) and has been expanded for this book.

place to turn. With no job and no prospects, Yitzhok left school for a spell and ended up staying at her place. He had nowhere else to turn for help, and, despite her unseemly vocation, she obviously had a heart of gold.

Some months later, Yitzhok found a way to return to the yeshiva and, a few years after that, in his mid-teens, he took a job as a Hebrew teacher to a family in a nameless shtetl in the Pale. Essentially abandoned by his own family and with little money outside his meager teaching income, Yitzhok became attracted to a group of shtetl toughs who randomly stole and shook people down for cash. With nothing to show after toiling for years as a teacher, Yitzhok decided to apprentice himself to this group of local thieves. His skills as a criminal were evidently better than those as a teacher. He moved to Warsaw, where he worked his way up from a small-time pickpocket to devising well-planned heists of local businesses. Ultimately, he formalized his pursuit by taking the name Urke Nachalnik, which means "brazen master criminal" in the lingo favored by Eastern European thieves.

Like many master criminals, Nachalnik wound up in jail more than a few times. By his mid-30s he had spent nearly half his life behind bars. Bored in prison, he took up writing to while away the hours. During an eight-year stint for bank robbery that began in 1927 in western Poland's notorious Ravitsh Prison, he attended writing classes given by Stanislaw Kowalski, a graduate of a nearby teacher's college. Kowalski asked his charges to bring whatever works they had written while in prison. Nachalnik showed up with piles of paper: two finished novels and part of an autobiography, the latter of which kicks off, "Before I begin the sad story of my life, I feel bound to give at least a summary of the circumstances that led me away from the straight and narrow. I ask the reader's forgiveness for first starting with a picture of my entrance into the world."

Kowalski liked what he read and encouraged Nachalnik to keep at it. The teacher corrected and edited the autobiography and had it published in Polish as *Życiorys własny przestępcy* (Autobiography of a Criminal), under the auspices of the prison authority in 1933. The story of a boy abandoned by his family who finds a place in the seamy underworld was an instant bestseller in Poland and became the most popular book of the year, serialized in Polish and Yiddish newspapers, including Warsaw's *Haynt* and New York's *Forverts*. It was translated into a number of other languages.

Impressed by his newfound literary fame and the implication that he had
turned his life around, the prison authorities released Nachalnik in 1933, two
years before his sentence was up. He began calling himself a writer, no longer
a criminal, although he kept the name. He got married and moved to a house
in the woods outside Vilna, secluding himself to focus on his craft.

Nakhmen Mayzl, editor of *Literarishe bleter*, the most respected Yiddish
literary journal of the day, visited Nachalnik at home. He was curious about
this former thief, especially because he had begun writing in Yiddish instead
of the pidgin Polish he had picked up on the streets and in jail. What Mayzl
found was that Nachalnik knew a bit about Yiddish literature and, in particular, liked the work of writers Yankev Dinezon and Sholem Asch. He had even
read Asch's *Motke Ganef*, a tale of a Jewish thief, a story that Nachalnik, a real
criminal, had some criticisms about. "Too much literary fantasy," he said.

Living near Vilna meant that Nachalnik was relatively close to the YIVO
Institute, an organization that researched virtually all aspects of Eastern European Jewish life, especially the Yiddish language. Mayzl introduced the
former criminal to YIVO and brought him into the Philology Department,
where he showed him the institute's extensive collection of Yiddish criminal argot. More than amazed that such a collection existed, Nachalnik was
incredulous that a Jewish academic institution even existed. He wanted to
contribute however he could, and, as Mayzl and a group of Yiddish scholars
stood around him, he offered corrections and additions to their collection of
underworld slang.

But having heard that Nachalnik was revealing their linguistic ciphers,
Nachalnik's former crime buddies accused him of hiding out in Vilna like a
coward. Nachalnik claimed that he was done with a life of crime and wanted
to create a safe home in which to raise his newborn son. But he was not
able to stay away from Warsaw, and, not long after his son's birth, he moved
his family to Otvotsk, a suburb of the city. From there Nachalnik made occasional trips into Warsaw, where he would visit the famed Jewish Literary
Union, the heart of Poland's Yiddish literary life. But, even though he was
portraying himself as a writer, he was ill at ease among the literati, claiming
that he felt like a "sucker among thieves" when he was with them.

Having celebrity thrust upon him in such a way, it stands to reason that
he may have been ambivalent. The popularity of true crime stories told by

an insider was not to be dismissed, and the Yiddish papers included lots of "Urke" material, ranging from interviews to stories to bad underworld jokes.

> "Have you ever given a speech in a public forum, Mr. Nachalnik?" he was asked.
>
> "Sure, a number of times."
>
> "What did you say?"
>
> "I swear, your honor, I'm not guilty."

Nachalnik's serialized stories of the Jewish lowlife were a huge hit among the Jews of Poland, and in early 1934 actors involved with La Scala Yiddish Theatre decided to stage a play based on his tales. La Scala wasn't one of the top Yiddish theaters in Warsaw, but it always managed to snag an audience with an attractive combination of classics (such as Sholem Aleichem's *Tevye the Milkman*) and the Yiddish prurient (such as Nachalnik's *Din toyre* [Thieves Trial]). *Din toyre*, which opened just after Christmas 1933, drew big crowds not only because it brought the master criminal-turned-auteur to the premiere but also because the play portrayed the street life of Jewish pimps, prostitutes, and criminals in its own raw reality, complete with authentically foul language and nasty behavior.

The highbrow critics of the Yiddish press were aghast. They were hostile to the production and either ignored it, as they did with most of La Scala's shows, or called it low-grade trash. "They're putting on 'Urke Nachalnik' in La Scala Theater, and every serious and decent spectator is taking the play like a glob of spit in the face, as if they'd been raped," read the opening lines of the January 1934 front-page editorial in the *Yiddish Weekly for Literature, Art, and Culture*. "We are raising our voices against the degradation of Yiddish theater, against a play that spits hateful trash in the faces of a huge theater audience."

Apparently not interested in the high-flown opinions of the Yiddish press, audiences showed up in droves. After performing to packed houses for the first two performances, the actors and stagehands showed up at the theater to prepare for the third evening's show to find that all the electrical cords had been cut and that all the costumes were missing. Even the sets had disappeared. It was a mystery—the theater had been hijacked, but by whom? Word on the street suggested that members of Warsaw's underworld were furiously unhappy with the play, exposing, as it did, some of their trade secrets and, perhaps most damaging, their Yiddish slang. So, in an episode of practical criticism, they stole the entire set.

The actors and director quickly put an advertisement in the afternoon edition of *Unzer ekspres*, a popular Yiddish tabloid, and addressed it to the "Erlikhe ganovem," the "honorable thieves," asking them to return what they had taken. If they did, the ad asserted, the theater would not call the police. There was no response.

The theater managers didn't know what else to do. Without the sets and costumes, the show couldn't go on. They decided to send for the master criminal himself, Urke Nachalnik. Emerging from his suburban lair, he made things right; he contacted some of his former cronies and every costume and piece of the set was returned, enabling the show to go on as scheduled.

Warsaw's Jewish underworld was not the only group dissatisfied with the play. The socialist Bund's arts magazine, *Vokhnshrift far literatur, kunst un kultur*, fulminated angrily against what it called theatrical "trash." In a front-page editorial the theater critic whined that "when the prostitutes are on stage, spewing their filth and the thieves are doing business in their pubs and hideouts, it's ugly, it's revolting. . . . For three hours, the audience and the theater are dragged through the mud."

Yiddish theatergoers, however, seemed to enjoy the mud and didn't necessarily mind being dragged through it. The play was a minor hit.

As for Urke Nachalnik, he made good on his commitment to the literary life. He continued to write, more in Yiddish than in Polish, and he produced a number of works on crime-related topics that were consistently popular with Yiddish audiences. Among them were *Der korbn* (The Victim), *Mokotov*, and *Yosele goy* (Yosele the Gentile), all of which contain vivid descriptions of underworld characters and their lives in prison and on the outside. These were published in Polish and in Yiddish papers in Poland and in America. The Yiddish dailies also serialized the subsequent volumes of his autobiography: *Lebedike kvorim: Der letster klap* (Buried Alive: The Final Blow) and *Videroyflebung, oder der oysgeleyzter* (Resurrection, or the Reformed One). Exposing the Yiddish underworld was a tough business, and Nachalnik never received the critical recognition he craved, or even that which was on par with his popularity. On the other hand, he made a decent living, which was more than a lot of Yiddish writers could say.

Figure 10.1. Urke Nachalnik in the January 5, 1934, issue of *Literarishe bleter*. Courtesy of the YIVO Institute for Jewish Research.

With the onset of World War II, Nachalnik's publishing career was cut short. After the Nazis occupied Warsaw, he reestablished contact with the criminal underworld and began to collect money and weapons for armed attacks against the Germans. In March 1940 he and a band of Jewish gang members attacked a group of Polish collaborators who had been hired by the Germans to beat up Jews in the street. It was one of the first organized resistance attacks of this kind to be organized by Jews.

According to Leyb Feingold, a Bundist leader who would later figure in the Warsaw Ghetto Uprising, Nachalnik showed up at a meeting of Jewish underground leaders that included Mordechai Anielevitsh (a commander of the Warsaw Ghetto Uprising) and Bundist leader Mikhl Klepfish. At the meeting, Nachalnik demanded funding to organize immediate reprisals against the Nazis. Anielevitsh allegedly supported the plan, but the request was ultimately rejected. Ignorant of the mass extermination about to take place, even most Jewish underground groups didn't think retaliation against the Germans was a good idea. Dejected, Nachalnik returned to Otvotsk, where he continued to engage in acts of resistance on his own: He sabotaged the rail lines that led to Treblinka, helping a number of Jews escape from the trains and hide in nearby forests. Nachalnik was eventually caught by the Germans in 1942, and as he was being led in shackles to his execution in the center of Otvotsk, he attacked his guard and nearby soldiers shot him to death.

Warsaw Ghetto memoirist Peretz Opotshinski commented in his article on smuggling in the Warsaw Ghetto that "we ought to erect a monument to the smuggler for his risks, because consequently he saved a good part of Jewish Warsaw from starving to death." It might also be remembered that hotheaded Jewish gangsters led one of the first attacks against the Nazis, with Urke Nachalnik, writer criminal, at their head.

⌒

PASSOVER IN THE JOINT

by Urke Nachalnik
Idishe bilder (Riga), no. 16, March 1938

There were nine of us Jews in the death house. The giant stone box in which we lived contained over a thousand men, all examples of human tragedy and failure.

Young and old, newcomers and recidivists, embittered criminals, and those whose fate had sealed them in. Dead in the free world, they were just numbers in the prison system. Dead numbers representing a dead existence. The prisoners felt themselves to be a kind of living dead, their days filled with suffering.

Fate also shut me in here. As an returning resident, I was crowned king of the nine Jews in the joint. . . .

The day I told my friends that I had managed to arrange a room where we could quietly celebrate the Passover seder was the most wonderful day in my entire prison term.

The holiday room was in the back of the underground prison cellar, a section of the prison that had been built a few hundred years previous. About two meters thick, the stone walls were covered with mold and dripped thick tears of humidity.

The room they gave us had been used to store all kinds of old, broken tools that they had no use for. It took us more than a week to clean it up.

The way we figured it, the first night of Passover was to fall on a Friday evening. Earlier in the day, they moved all of us into a large room where we lived together [and prepared for the holiday].

We were in a great mood and were yelling to one another. As each arrived from his own cell, there was much to talk about after the long months of silence.

We happily doled out the meager rations we'd been given. Everyone was eager to honor one another by offering something: a piece of bread, a pinch of tobacco, a button, a needle, a piece of thread. We were all desperately poor. No one had outside help. All of us had waited for the goodhearted generosity of the "Yahudim," the wealthy Jews of Posen who we were sure would concern themselves so we wouldn't have to eat any bread during Passover.

We were already licking our chops over the treats we'd be getting. Meat, fish, matzos. And matzo balls, akh, the matzo balls!

We would drool whenever we'd describe to one another what kinds of Passover treats we used to eat at home. It was as if we were drunk on the idea that we'd get to eat meat—kosher meat!

The crummy prison food that we had to slurp down three times a day brought forth a desire to devour something—anything—delicious. A little piece of meat would strengthen a weakened body and would shore up powers in order to help make it through to the end of one's sentence.

Nobody ate lunch on Wednesday. All of us were half-full from the thought that we were about to be served some delicious Passover food. Delicacies from the free world.

The "Lifer," the one among us who had been in jail the longest, even started reciting the Haggadah, the Passover prayer book that he got from a

Christian neighbor who had taken it off the shelves of the prison library after mistaking it for a short novel.

We waited patiently as the sun descended on the horizon. The gray prison walls began to take on a gruesome, deathlike pallor. This time, the darkness weighed on our hearts like a hundred-pound stone. Each one of us, disappointed, quietly cowered in our cell corners by our crappy iron prison beds.

Everyone was silent. Everyone was surely thinking about the same thing.

We were all left shut in that narrow, moldy stone block. But our souls had broken through the bars and were wandering free over the fields to our homes, to the full seder tables where we sat during our childhood years.

I saw an image of myself as a yeshiva boy who had come home for Passover. I'm sitting at the table among my parents and my brothers and sisters, giving a fiery little speech about the holiday for my father, who calmly sat there reclining on a white pillow while tears of joy ran from my mother's eyes.

Yeah, that was how it once was . . . I had a home, a life, a Passover, matzos, four cups of wine, matzo balls, kharoyses, and bitter herbs. And now I was left only with the bitter herbs . . .

I began to nervously pace around my cell, back and forth. My cellmates also got up and mechanically followed me around.

Suddenly, I got an idea. I stopped cold in the middle of the cell and shouted, "I know! We made a mistake—it's not Passover today!"

I wanted to console my friends. They understood me and resigned themselves to collapsing each on his own hard bed.

Only the Lifer didn't go to sleep. He stood by the tiny basement window and looked out at the moon. From time to time he sent out a curse through the iron bars, a curse on the free world and it's fat, contented chumps.

I tried to convince him that this year was a leap year, that Passover was actually next month. The Lifer wasn't buying it.

*   *   *

The prison bell woke us all the next morning with its usual indifference. We crawled from our beds, tired and spent. We were too embarrassed to look one another in the face.

The righteous Jews on the outside had forgotten about us.

The door opened for breakfast. Nobody moved. The guard screamed angrily, "Breakfast! Here is your holiday food—matzos."

Everyone jumped toward the door at the same time. The guard slipped into the cell holding a basket and with great parade set out nine portions, matzos for all, two eggs with a portion of bread for each. He wished us a happy holiday with such pride, as if he were giving us some great gift. I asked him if he would take me directly to the warden.

After about a half-hour, the warden convinced me that I was unnecessarily irritated.

"You, Jewish prisoner!" he screamed. "You're not at all religious. You just wanted something better to eat. Meat, you want? There are no more Jews in town. No more that are concerned for you anyway. Someone sent these matzos in the mail for you. You should be happy. Posen is not Congress Poland!

I returned to my cell completely depressed. The Lifer gave me the stink eye, "You dipshit! This is how you organized Passover for us? This is all your fault. I've been in the joint ten years and never had to eat bread on Passover. I warned you that we should have written the *kehilla* in Warsaw this year."

All the others attacked me too. I kept my mouth shut, as if I were guilty.

Imperceptibly, the door opened again. I was being called to the warden. He welcomed me with a satisfied smile and said, "You made a pretty good haul. And from under his desk he pulled out a heavy package, tore off the wrapping and set out a few kilos of fat, meat, salami, ham, cigarettes, a cake, bread, sardines, a few different kinds of cheese and other delicacies.

"Take! It's all yours. You'll have a proper holiday!"

"Mine? . . . From where?"

"Take it and go. You got lucky. One of your former partners probably made a big haul. You wanted to press the flesh? Here it is. You won't refuse it because it's your Passover, right?

He looked at me with one of his sarcastic looks. A minute ago I was doing battle with my ravenous stomach. And now I proudly spat at him, "Give it away. I'm not allowed to eat it. Thanks anyway."

The Warden's face turned cold. He looked at me with eyes that didn't believe what they were seeing.

"You're not going to take it? . . . You?"

"Nope. . . . No . . . ," I repeated and ran out of his office as he looked at me in complete shock.

CHAPTER 11

THE STRANGE CASE OF GIMEL KUPER, MYSTERY JOURNALIST

During the early twentieth century, the New York–based socialist daily, *Forverts*, was the largest and most successful Yiddish newspaper in the world. One of the journalists who consistently provided some of the juiciest and most intriguing stories was their Warsaw correspondent, Gimel Kuper. With a biography that was somewhat of a mystery, Kuper wrote of warring Hasidic sects, Jewish pimps and prostitutes, small-time crooks, and the Jewish homeless, among many other stories of Jewish life in Poland's cities and towns. Weaving gripping tales of a Jewish lowlife, his reportage was a kind of *Fiddler on the Roof* as penned by Charles Bukowski. Kuper's stories, compelling in and of themselves, provide a fascinating antidote to the saccharine stereotypes of the Jewish shtetl that dominate the popular visions of Yiddish literature and culture that have been mediated to the English-speaking world.

But who was this journalist? In early March 1928, the *Morgn Freiheit*, a communist-affiliated Yiddish daily based in New York, launched a vitriolic attack on the socialist *Forverts* and its writer, Gimel Kuper, for publishing what they called "low-grade sensationalism," crass attempts to attract a larger readership. The *Freiheit* exposed the identity of Gimel Kuper as being none other than famed Yiddish literary figure Israel Joshua Singer, the older brother and literary mentor of future Nobel Prize–winning author Isaac Bashevis Singer.

I. J. Singer had first come on the scene with a book of short stories titled *Perl* (Pearls) in 1922. Emerging from the world of Hasidism and having dealt with the push and pull of tradition versus secularism, Singer was lauded as one of Yiddish modernity's most eloquent voices. Connected to Di khalyastre (The Gang), Warsaw's literary avant-garde, Singer would become one of Yiddish literature's brightest lights.

When Singer's *Perl* fell into the hands of Abraham Cahan, famed Yiddish tastemaker and editor-in-chief of the *Forverts*, he lavished praise on the book and on the writer, immediately hiring Singer to be his correspondent in Poland. Singer, who wanted to be a novelist, understood that he needed to support himself and his young family and that journalism would be both a reasonable and a necessary way to make a living. A novelist, as most novelists will tell you, also needs a paying job.

But journalism, for a literatus, was considered déclassé, so to distinguish his newspaper reporting from his literary output, Singer devised the pseudonym Gimel Kuper. Pen names were a common device for many Yiddish writers, especially those who wrote for competing newspapers. The readers of the *Forverts* had no inkling that the fascinating reportage of the Old

Figure 11.1. Israel Joshua Singer's press identification card for *Unzer ekspres*, a Warsaw daily that ran from 1928 to 1939. Courtesy of the YIVO Institute for Jewish Research.

World and that of the underworld provided by Gimel Kuper were written by the same famous literary figure. Not, at least, until the spring of 1928, when Singer was outed as Kuper by the *Freiheit*, which, as it turned out, had wanted Singer to come work for them. But he had refused, and exposing his secret literary identity was their way of trying to embarrass him.

As for Singer, it wasn't much of an embarrassment. The *Freiheit* had accused him of writing sensationalistic yellow journalism. Singer responded by saying that yes, he did write journalism, but that good journalism was also good literature. And so it was. From the mid-1920s to the mid-1930s Singer filed hundreds of reports for the *Forverts*, creating a journalistic oeuvre that stands as an astonishing chronicle of one of the world's largest Jewish communities as it teetered at the abyss. A window into a world that would soon disappear, the reports ceased when Singer was brought to America in 1934 by *Forverts* editor Cahan, not long after the massive success of his novel *Yoshe Kalb*, which Cahan had serialized in his paper.

Singer arrived in New York as a Yiddish novelist, not a journalist, and it was there that he would publish his greatest psychological dramas, *The Brothers Ashkenazi* and *The Family Carnovsky*. His journalistic output would disappear from the time of his arrival in New York until the beginning of World War II, when the world he knew best was being ground to dust. The reportage he delivered to the *Forverts* before he arrived in New York provides some of the best accounts of Jewish life in interwar Poland. Unusual and often startling, Singer's articles were a unique type of human interest reportage that often required copious research and delicate interview skills.

But it's tough to stand in the shadow of a younger brother's Nobel Prize, especially if you're dead and nearly forgotten. I. J. Singer has suffered just that indignity. Widely regarded as one of the greatest Yiddish novelists of the twentieth century, Singer died suddenly and young, with great recognition in Yiddish culture but little in the world of international letters. His influence on his younger brother, Isaac, however, was enormous, and it would help propel him to international literary stardom.

Like his younger brother, Israel Joshua Singer often wrote about a certain stretch of Krochmalna Street, the few blocks in Warsaw's Jewish quarter that were notorious for its criminals, its poverty, and its tough and often volatile residents. The street appears frequently, almost as a character, in the work of both Singer brothers. This stands to reason: As children, they lived at 10 Krochmalna Street on a rank stretch known as the *pletzl* (the little place, or the hangout), where gangsters and prostitutes lived among poor families and working people. The memories of the chaos and poverty remained with the Singer brothers for many years and deeply influenced their work.

Writing as Gimel Kuper, Singer delved deep into the characters produced by Warsaw's impoverished Jewish streets. This story is one among many.

WARSAW'S JEWISH CRIMINALS METE OUT SENTENCES IN THEIR OWN PRIVATE COURTROOMS

G. Kuper

Forverts, December 21, 1927

You'd be making a mistake if you thought that there was no truth and justice in the dens of thieves on Warsaw's Krochmalna Street. In fact, there is no place where truth and justice is so zealously guarded as on Krochmalna.

I'm going to tell you two stories, one about Puny Khane and Shimshon Gramophone and how they tried to con Krochmalna Street; and another about how Khaym-Yosl Jackass committed a grave sin and just how he was punished by the denizens of Krochmalna Street. In the end, you will have to admit that truth and justice reigns on Krochmalna like no other place in the world.

First off, the story about Puny Khane and Shimshon Gramophone. For twenty years, Puny Khane and Shimshon Gramophone made a living off of Thomas Edison. Out on the streets, Khane would play their gramophone and Shimshon would dance and, for many years, they earned their bread. When the device was considered to be some kind of miracle in Jewish cities throughout Poland, they lived quite nicely off the gramophone. Everyone wanted to see how this "box" played music and sang. Many believed that there was something mysterious about the thingamajig, that there was some kind of magic involved, something from the "other side."

It was later on that the business went south. The gramophone became a generally popular item and began showing up in private homes. As a result, people on the street stopped paying to hear them play. It was then that Puny Khane and Shimshon Gramophone began to wander through the smaller towns, where gramophones were few. And then, when gramophones began to appear in these smaller towns, the dancing duo was forced to relocate their trade to the really tiny villages, where the machine was still a wondrous novelty. Peasants were thrilled when they heard the box, dancing about and praising the "English wise men" who had concocted such a marvelous thing.

If not for a terrible tragedy, Puny Khane and Shimshon Gramophone probably would have lived out their years playing their gramophone:

Fortepianos became popular and began to replace gramophones, a matter that Puny Khane and Shimshon Gramophone's business couldn't survive.

"Get outta here, you idiots!" They were driven away from all sides. "Who wants to hear a gramophone when there are such wonderful, little fortepianos in the world?"

Puny Khane and Shimshon Gramophone saw that their gramophone money-making days were over. They needed a fortepiano and had to sell their gramophone to get one. But nobody wanted their old gramophone.

"For sale, cheap!" pleaded Puny Khane. "This thing is a goldmine. It made us a fine living for twenty years."

But they all laughed at her. "Why don't you just give it a nice funeral," people advised. "If not, maybe put it in an old folks home."

Puny Khane saw that nothing would come of the old gramophone, so she sat down with her Shimshon and the two decided that they would begin working the "dread disease"—in other words—epilepsy. Every morning, Khane would go out into the street and collapse in a heap, her legs shaking in an "epileptic fit."

Obviously, Shimshon Gramophone would show up right away to save her. He'd hand her a large key to grab on to, which would calm her down. People would start to congregate just as the sick woman would begin to come around.

Shimshon Gramophone would then launch into a fiery speech: "It's been three days since she's had something to eat. Have mercy on the sick!"

People would throw five cents, ten cents, twenty cents. When they would collect enough money, Khane would head over to another street to have another epileptic fit.

The money wasn't bad, even better than with the gramophone. But certain people were jealous and some of them began to spoil their new scheme.

"You see that? See?" they griped. "You just had a fit in that street over there! Now you're doing it again?!"

Puny Khane would try to defend herself. "Whatcha makin' such a big deal for?" She was furious. "I can't have more than one attack? I'm not allowed? What's it cost ya, sweetie?"

But then, the police started to take notice. The "dread disease" became too difficult to get away with. Puny Khane and Shimshon Gramophone talked it over and it was decided that Khane would have to start committing suicide.

Every morning at sunrise, Khane would sneak into a big apartment courtyard around which lived well-off Jews. She would climb up to the fifth floor, stand in an open window and start screaming, "Everybody, wake up! People, I'm going to chuck myself out of the fifth-floor window. I'm gonna do it! Help!"

Coincidentally, the first person to see her would be Shimshon Gramophone, who would start shouting, "Somebody, help! Don't do it!"

From all over the courtyard people came out and begged her to have mercy on herself.

"Lady, don't jump! We'll help you!"

"No—I don't want your help!" she would scream back. "I'm gonna jump! Enough suffering. Let me go!"

Women would rush down with pillows, bedding, comforters and begin spreading it all out on the pavement.

"Lady, don't do it!"

But there was no stopping Khane, and she prepared to jump. Women began to faint. They'd scream and shut their eyes so they wouldn't see the horrible sight.

In the meantime, Shimshon Gramophone would stealthily zip up to the fifth floor and grab the "jumper" by the arms. A battle would then ensue between Puny Khane and Shimshon Gramophone.

"Let me go! Let me die!" Puny Khane would scream.

"No, I won't let you go! You could even die—I won't let you jump!"

In the end, Shimshon Gramophone would succeed. The crowd in the courtyard would heartily applaud him and then donate money to that poor woman who had just been rescued from certain death.

This business was a goldmine! Forget Edison with his gramophones and fortepianos!

But how does the saying go? "When you are destined for tragedy, you seize it with both hands."

One day, Khane went a little nuts and got the idea to go into the courtyard of 11 Krochmalna and threatened to throw herself off the top floor.

She started screaming.

"People! I'm gonna do it! I'm gonna jump!"

The residents of Krochmalna saw her and became furious. "What's this? Why us on Krochmalna? She's going to kill herself up here on top?"

And all of them—the entire building—ran out into the courtyard, stood there, and started yelling, "Jump, jump! Faster!"

Shimshon Gramophone jumped up and started running to "rescue" the woman, but he was held back by some of the young Krochmalna hoods, who wouldn't let him through.

"Let her jump! Nobody needs to 'save' her. We know these tricks."

Standing in the window, Puny Khane figured out that things weren't going well and wanted to get out of having to commit suicide, but Krochmalna wouldn't let her.

"You wanted to jump—so jump!"

Khane began screaming for help, that she had regrets, that she wanted

to live. But the residents of 11 Krochmalna wouldn't let up. "Jump," they
yelled. "If you don't, we'll come up there and throw you off ourselves."

Now Puny Khane really yelled for help. "Shimshon!" she screamed to
her regular savior, "Shimshon, save me! They're going to kill me!"

Thrashing, Shimshon tried to tear himself away, but the Krochmalna
toughs were stronger.

"Spread out some kaftans!" some kids demanded. "The quicker this
sucker jumps, the better."

And no sooner than Puny Khane showed up at 11 Krochmalna to kill
herself, she flew out of a fourth-story window and landed on the ground with
a thump.

"There it is. Don't ever come to Krochmalna to play tricks," the courtyard's kids said to the crumpled woman.

She was treated with mercy. Puny Khane had fallen on the kaftans that
the residents had spread onto the pavement and only broke her leg. In the ambulance on the way to the hospital, Khane couldn't stop tearing her hair out.

"A tragedy! Who knows if I'll ever again be able to earn money as a
jumper? What a tragedy, what a misfortune!"

In the Warsaw papers, the only news that was reported was that, at 11
Krochmalna Street, Khane Simkholovitsh was thrown out of a fourth-story
window.

Krochmalna Street joked about the news reporting.

"Suckers," they said. "They don't know nothin'. That's not news."

*   *   *

Khaym-Yosl Jackass Moves in with Blind Rokhl Just After His Wife's Death. Krochmalna Drowns the Pair in Whiskey

Krochmalna residents meted out a second "sentence" on a local man for a
serious offense. And now that justice has been served, they are dancing with
joy.

Khaym-Yosl Jackass, who worked at a butcher shop lugging sides of
beef, lived for many years on Krochmalna with his wife and grown children.
His wife cooked and fed him and their kids until, one day, she up and died.

At the funeral of Khaym-Yosl Jackass's wife, Blind Rokhl, a beggar
from the Warsaw Catacombs, wailed horribly. On Gensha Street, by the cemetery, she was seen weeping and rubbing her one good eye. "Such a saint!
Oy, such a kosher woman! What a terrible thing!"

And just after the funeral, Blind Rokhl led Khaym-Yosl Jackass right
into a basement apartment and set a bottle of whiskey in front of him.

"Drink, Khaym-Yosl, drown your sorrows!"

Khaym-Yosl Jackass isn't the type that has to be asked to take a drink
of alcohol. He was already troubled by his wife's death, and so he quickly
drained the whole bottle.

"Rokhl, maybe you've got another bottle?" asked Khaym-Yosl, wiping his eyes from the tears produced by thoughts of his dead wife.

"It's on the way, Khaym-Yoseniu," said Rokhl, winking her one good eye.

After the second bottle Khaym-Yosl Jackass asked for a third. After the third bottle, he wasn't able to make it home to Krochmalna Street alone.

In his drunken state, he couldn't remember that he was on his way home from his wife's funeral. And he yelled to the woman with the key to the front gate, "Take me home! Nu, why don't you answer?"

"Stay right here, Khaym-Yoseniu," said Blind Rokhl, and she helped him lie down on a couch.

The next morning, after Khaym-Yosl had sobered up, he said he wanted to go home and sit shiva, but Blind Rokhl wouldn't let him.

"Whaddya wanna go home for, Khaym-Yosl? Who's gonna cook for you? You should stay here!"

"I'll stay here!" Khaym-Yosl decided. In mourning for his wife, he sat down on the floor in his socks and started nipping at the bottle of whiskey that Blind Rokhl had set in front of him.

After the seven-day mourning period was over, he returned to work, carrying dead oxen. Blind Rokhl told him, "Khaym-Yosl, take me with you. I can make you some dough singing my songs in the street, maybe 10 gilden a day. Let's be together. I'll give you all the whiskey you want, just be my man."

"I'll do it!" replied Khaym-Yosl Jackass, and he went off with Blind Rokhl to Krochmalna Street.

When he walked into the house with Blind Rokhl and showed her his dead wife's bed and told her that's where she'd be sleeping, the rumblings began.

"You're giving our mother's, may she rest in peace, our mother's bed to this blind woman? It's not going to happen," his children screamed at him.

"Let's see who's gonna stop me," threatened Khaym-Yosl Jackass.

"But mama's only been dead eight days!"

"It's none of your business. Now buzz off—I know what I'm doing."

In the meantime, Blind Rokhl's husband, Scratchy Tuvia the beggar, found out that Rokhl had moved in with the "Jackass." And he showed up howling that he wanted his wife back.

There was not a moment of peace in Khaym-Yosl Jackass's home.

Krochmalna Street wasn't happy with Khaym-Yosl Jackass either. True, everyone can do as he pleases; there are no saints on Krochmalna. But to go completely off the rails is another thing. To shack up with another woman's man right after her funeral was too much, even for Krochmalna Street.

The *macher*s on Krochmalna began to complain to Khaym-Yosl Jackass, telling him that he had to dump Blind Rokhl. But he just ignored them.

In the middle of all this, one of Khaym-Yosl's sons died a sudden and horrible death. He was bending over a boiling cauldron, checking the meat inside, when he slipped, fell in, and was boiled alive. All of Krochmalna Street went to the funeral and, in the cemetery, they made a deal with Khaym-Yosl that he would no longer live with Blind Rokhl.

"It was because of your sin, Khaym-Yosl, that your boy has departed this world! Promise us that you will never allow her back in your home."

Khaym-Yosl shook on it. But right after the funeral, he went straight to her house.

And it was then that Krochmalna Street shook with fury.

"Khaym-Yosl, you made a promise!"

"But she gives me whiskey!" replied Khaym-Yosl. "Whiskey is better than promises."

"Since you're such a good guy," the Krochmalna *macher*s said, "you can drink whiskey with us until you can't see straight."

And right then they grabbed him by the collar and dragged him into a bar.

"A fifth of whiskey, here and now."

The barman brought them a fifth.

"Khaym-Yosl, drink!"

Khaym-Yosl drank.

"More!"

Khaym-Yosl drank more.

"Another fifth!"

Khaym-Yosl Jackass tried to stand up.

"Kids, I can't drink no more."

"Drink, you bastard! You wanted whiskey, so drink!"

Khaym-Yosl saw that he was trapped, so he kept drinking. He drank and drank until he collapsed. A few days later he moved in with his wife and son in the cemetery.

"He had it coming!" was what Krochmalna Street decided. And as an expression of thanks to justice and morality, the gang from Krochmalna made another boozy toast.

CHAPTER 12

SEMITIC BEAUTY DRIVES JEWS WILD

Film at Eleven

All told, 1929 was another terrible year for the Jews. Okay, it was no 1492, 1648, or 1939, but it was still full of depressing events that boded poorly for those of the Hebraic persuasion. For example, an intensifying enmity between Arabs and Jews in Palestine culminated in a slew of ugly pogroms in which dozens were killed and hundreds wounded. And Stalin consolidated his rule in the USSR, something that would turn out to be truly awful, not only for the Jews but also for pretty much everyone else.

For the Jews of Warsaw, however, all-purpose bad news such as this just sidled alongside the doses of depression, debt, poverty, bankruptcies, suicides, and anti-Semitism that complemented the day-to-day life of an unloved minority in an economically troubled country. Life as a Warsaw Jew in the 1920s was no joyride. So, when a small group of Jewish newspaper editors fell on the idea of holding a contest to choose the most beautiful Jewish girl in Poland, they felt the event was bound to bolster the spirits of Europe's largest Jewish community. And it did. Sort of.

In February 1929 the editors of Warsaw's Polish-language Jewish daily newspaper *Nash Psheglond* (*Nasz Przegląd*, meaning "Our Review") began to publicize the Miss Judea Pageant, a contest to crown the most beautiful Jewess in Poland. Young Jewish women across the country were invited to send their photos to the editors, who would print them and, anticipating *American Idol* by a good seventy-five years, let the readers choose the ten they liked best. Those ten finalists would then participate in a gala event at which a winner would be determined by a crack team of experts in physical beauty: Jewish journalists.

The idea to organize a beauty pageant wasn't very original, but it did manage to generate a lot of press. *Nash Psheglond* publicized it heavily. Every day it printed articles related to the pageant: interviews with artists on the nature of beauty, commentary on female poise, discussions about whether blonds or brunettes were more attractive. A number of articles focused on the notion of "Semitic beauty" and the need to promote it. This desire on the part of the editors to create an iconographic Jewish beauty was an important element of the pageant: They knew that a Jewish girl would never win the national Miss Polonia title, and they were attempting to create a national female Jewish icon, which, in the mix of Jewish cultural heroes, was relatively uncommon.

For their part, Warsaw's larger-circulation Yiddish newspapers thought the pageant was something between the idiotic and the asinine. First, they said, beauty contests were a Gentile custom, an outgrowth of choosing a Mardi Gras queen. For them, there could be nothing Jewish about such contests, despite the Queen Esther beauty contests held each Purim in Tel Aviv. Second, the pageant was conceived by a Polish-language newspaper, which was seen by the Yiddish press as a tool of assimilation out to destroy *real* Jewish culture (meaning *Yiddish* culture). Third, it exploited women. Fourth, and most important, they hadn't thought of it themselves. That the Miss Judea Pageant was a well-organized, well-publicized affair really annoyed them, especially because some of their writers had somehow been duped into participating as judges.

Maybe a bit of context would be useful. In 1929 about 350,000 Jews lived in Warsaw, making up more than one-third of the city's population. The Jews' significant numbers, as well as their unique culture (expressed primarily in the Yiddish language), irritated nationalist Poles, who wanted to create a Polish nation-state in the wake of 150 years of Russian domination. As a result, the minority rights promised to Jews under the 1919 Treaty of Versailles were never instituted in Poland. Jews had a certain degree of cultural freedom—Yiddish newspapers, literature, and theater were permitted to flourish, as was increasing Jewish activity in Polish-language spheres—but they were economically, politically, and socially disenfranchised. And because Poland's economy was a disaster, the Jews of Poland lacked the funds to create, build, and serve their community whatever nominal freedoms they may have had. It would be asking a lot of a beauty contest to correct such widespread discontent.

Nevertheless, hundreds of young women from all over Poland, ranging in age from 18 to their early 20s, responded eagerly to the editors' request and sent their photos to the offices of *Nash Psheglond*. Every day from the beginning of February to mid-March of that year, the paper printed the photos—just over 130 in total. Photos of the young women also filled the paper's weekly supplement, *Nash Psheglond Ilustruvani*. Little information was supplied about each contestant: just name, city of residence, and job, if she had one. By the end of the first round, more than 20,000 readers had sent in their top ten choices, young women generally identified by Jewdonymous first names such as Amra, Hadasa, and Rebeka (only a few of the top vote getters had given their real names). Most of them looked remarkably similar: black hair parted in the middle and pulled back tight; oval faces with heavy, arched eyebrows. They were examples of Jewish orientalism at its raven-haired, swarthy best. It seems that the paper's desire to promote Semitic beauty was taken seriously by the public; they ultimately chose quite exotic-looking women who notably did not look very Polish.

The contest increased *Nash Psheglond*'s circulation dramatically, and the finals of the pageant took place at a gala in Warsaw's fabulous Hotel Polonia. The crème de la crème of Warsaw's Jewish journalistic, literary, and theatrical society attended. In the end, when the finalists were judged by the group of "experts" (expanded to include authors, artists, and even a doctor, along with the larger group of journalists), the winner turned out to be a young woman who had entered under the name Judyta. Little was known about 20-year-old Warsaw-born Judyta, whose real name was Zofia Oldak. A Frida Kahlo look-alike, she was the best-traveled contestant, having visited France and Algeria, and she seemed to have come from a reasonably well-off family. She may have looked familiar to readers, not only because she was one of those with the pulled-back black hair but also because her photo had appeared in the newspapers after she had been crowned the winner of the Yiddish Press Ball just a month earlier.

Figure 12.1. Sample page of contestants competing in the Miss Judea Beauty Pageant. Source: *Nasz Przegląd Ilustrowany*, January 1929. Courtesy of the YIVO Institute for Jewish Research.

Figure 12.2. Contest finalists. Source: *Nasz Przegląd Ilustrowany*, February 1929. Courtesy of the YIVO Institute for Jewish Research.

It wasn't long before some began grumbling that the pageant had been fixed. After all, Oldak had come in fifth in the popular vote, behind other Semitic beauties such as Amra and Liza Harkavy. She may have had previous pageant experience, but Harkavy, the runner-up, had also been featured recently in a "beautiful Jewish girl in Poland" spread in New York's *Jewish Daily Forward*. None of that mattered, though. Oldak had evidently impressed the judges with her erudite answers to their queries, including her assertion that she hoped to be both a modern, emancipated woman and a mother.

As the winner of the pageant, Oldak was showered with prizes donated by some of Jewish Warsaw's premier boutiques. The booty she received included a fur coat, salon treatments, snazzy undergarments, dresses, shoes, perfumes, and a record player. But with *Nash Psheglond* touting Miss Judea as a national Jewish icon, people began making noises that the swag she received wasn't enough, so the paper started a Miss Judea Fund, to which readers could—and did—contribute to help pay for "educational opportunities" for the winner.

NASZ PRZEGLĄD
ILUSTROWANY

MISS JUDEA".

P. ZOFJA OLDAKÓWNA OTRZYMAŁA TYTUŁ „MISS JUDAEI" NA KONKURSIE PIĘK-
NOŚCI ZORGANIZOWANYM PRZEZ „NASZ PRZEGLĄD".
P. Oldakówna nosiła suknię ze srebrnej lamy i sortie gronostajowe z firmy M. Apfelbaum (Marszałkowska 128)

Figure 12.3. The winner of the Miss Judea Pageant, Zofia Oldak. Source: *Nasz Przegląd
Ilustrowany*, March 1929. Courtesy of the YIVO Institute for Jewish Research.

At first, Oldak carried out her initial duties as Miss Judea without incident. She was carted around to all the important Jewish organizations in Warsaw, where she was feted, fed, and photographed, usually along with the editors of *Nash Psheglond*. A few events were huge, such as a reception and concert by the Warsaw Philharmonic. Others were smaller banquets and photo ops, including sit-downs with such VIPs as leader of the Polish Zionists and member of parliament Yitzhak Grinboym; the widow of eminent Yiddish writer Y. L. Peretz; the famed pediatrician and pedagogue Janusz Korcak and his orphans; actors from the Yiddish theater; and members of a practice kibbutz and their two cows in Grokhov, a nearby suburb. Many of these photos were published in the paper's weekly supplement.

Then the new beauty queen made her royal visit to the Warsaw Kehila. Each city in Poland with a significant Jewish population had a Kehila, an elected, quasi-governmental organization to which Jews paid taxes. In return, the Kehila represented them at the local and national government levels, ran Jewish schools, provided a rabbinate, oversaw issues related to kosher food certification, funded the Jewish hospital, took care of homes for the aged,

Figure 12.4. Miss Judea and farmers on a practice kibbutz outside Warsaw. Source: *Nasz Przegląd Ilustrowany*, March 1929. Courtesy of the YIVO Institute for Jewish Research.

Figure 12.5. Miss Judea posing with the editors of *Nasz Przegląd*; the leader of Poland's Zionists, Yitzhak Grinboim; and the widow of Yiddish writer Y. L. Peretz. Source: *Nasz Przegląd Ilustrowany*, March 1929. Courtesy of the YIVO Institute for Jewish Research.

Figure 12.6. Cover of *Film velt* (Film World) magazine, featuring Miss Judea, 1929. Courtesy of the YIVO Institute for Jewish Research.

and ran soup kitchens, cemeteries, and the like. In short, the Kehila filled in where the Polish state was unable or unwilling. A wide variety of Jewish political parties were represented in the Kehilas, from the socialist Bund to the religious right and everything in between. Needless to say, the representatives didn't much get along.

Warsaw Kehila president Heshl Farbstein, in his infinite wisdom, decided to hold a lavish banquet in honor of Miss Judea in the stately Kehila building at 26 Gzhibovska Street. During the banquet, Farbstein, who was also the head of Mizrahi, the religious Zionist party, praised the beauty of Miss Judea and sang her selections from the Song of Songs.

The Song of Songs is, of course, that anomalous chapter of erotica found within the grab bag of battles, genealogies, land wars, and legalistics that make up the Bible. Attributed to King Solomon, The Song of Songs is essentially

Figure 12.7. Cartoon of Miss Judea pulling the editors of *Nasz Przegląd* around town. Source: "Der seder fun mis yudeya" (The Seder of Miss Judea), *Humor Magazine* (Warsaw), April 1929. Courtesy of the YIVO Institute for Jewish Research.

a dialogue between a woman and a man deeply in love, expressed by way of horny poetics. It has been presented by some as a paean to God, but that seems pretty unlikely, unless Adonai also has a nice rack. To wit:

How graceful your steps in those sandals
O nobleman's daughter . . .
Your belly is a mound of wheat
edged with lilies.
Your breasts are two fawns,
twins of a gazelle.
Your neck is a tower of ivory.
Your eyes are pools in Heshbon,
at the gates of that city of lords.
Your proud nose the tower of Lebanon
that looks toward Damascus.
Your head crowns you like Mount Carmel,
the hair of your head like royal purple.
A king is caught in the thicket.
How wonderful you are,
O Love, how much sweeter than all other pleasures!
That day you seemed to me a tall palm tree
and your breasts the clusters of its fruit.
I said in my heart,
Let me climb into that palm tree
and take hold of its branches.

When the news came out that 60-something married-with-children Farbstein had sung the Song of Songs at the Kehila banquet to 20-something single-with-a-plunging-neckline Miss Judea, the Agudas Yisroel, the largest ultra-Orthodox party in Poland and a major player in the Warsaw Kehila, went berserk. Not exactly known for their reticence when it came to internal Jewish politics, Aguda representatives began complaining loudly and bitterly that Farbstein had not only abused his power as president but had also shamed the Kehila and desecrated holy texts. With one of their political opponents now in the mix, the Aguda led the charge against Miss Judea. They railed against the pageant, its promoters, and Heshl Farbstein himself in their own paper, *Der yid*. They also brought the students out of their yeshivas for anti–Miss Judea demonstrations in the streets; these were met with counterdemonstrations in support of her.

Eventually, after a few weeks of bitter recriminations, the scandal involving Farbstein, the Kehila, and Miss Judea began to dissipate. After all, the episode could be stretched only so far. The press began to move on to other matters. But then, Rabbi Yeshaye Rozenboym died. Rozenboym was the leader of Warsaw's Aguda contingent and vice-president of the Warsaw Kehila. Because of his leadership role in both the Aguda and Warsaw's large Hasidic community, his funeral was to be a massive affair, attended by thousands of people; it was held in Warsaw's Gensha Street Cemetery on April 1, 1929.

The huge funeral procession, led by Warsaw's Hasidic dignitaries, wound its way through Jewish Warsaw's crooked streets for two hours before arriving at the cemetery, which was packed with Hasidim. A gaggle of important rabbis stood on the dais waiting to offer their eulogies. Rabbi Yitzhok-Meyer Kanal gave the first eulogy in the name of the Warsaw rabbinate.

Also waiting nervously among the assorted dignitaries was Heshl Farbstein, who, as president of the Warsaw Kehila, was scheduled to eulogize his deceased colleague. Farbstein suspected that the Aguda might make trouble for him, so the night before the funeral he had visited the Rozenboym family to ask their permission to speak. They agreed it would be the honorable thing to do. Although Farbstein and Rozenboym were political opponents, they were also known to have been on good personal terms. After giving Farbstein their blessing, the family even contacted the Aguda to let them know that they wanted Farbstein to speak and that he should be able to do so unmolested. But when Farbstein took the podium, the foul aftertaste of the Miss Judea affair still lingered and shouts began to be heard.

Oddly, the first screams were "Bar Kokhba! Bar Kokhba!"—a strange chant, seemingly a non sequitur, considering the circumstances. Few understood what the hecklers were yelling about; to the crowd of thousands, it just seemed like a lot of anti-Farbstein blather, and many began to join in. The "Bar Kokhba" cry, which got the crowd going, had its origin ten years earlier, when the Kehila had rented an office to the Bar Kokhba sports club in the same building as a *bes medresh*, a religious study hall. This disturbed one particularly excitable study hall denizen by the name of Mordkhe-Mendel Bal-Tshive, who authored a ten-year-long stream of letters to the Kehila complaining about the "horrible things" he had seen the sports club members do, mainly transgressions such as smoking and writing on the Sabbath. Bal-Tshive decided that the funeral was a good opportunity to go straight to the head of the Kehila and give him a piece of his mind.

But Bal-Tshive's shouts of "Bar-Kokhba" were soon overwhelmed by screams of "Miss Judea! Miss Judea!" A huge throng of young men and boys began howling at Farbstein to get away from the podium. The rabbis on the dais screamed admonishments at the disruptive youths, telling them to keep quiet and respect the dead, but this was only pouring gasoline on the fire. A group of about two dozen youths positioned themselves to rush the dais and take down the Kehila president. Realizing that he would be drowned out by hecklers and that he might actually be in real physical danger, Farbstein allowed himself to be hustled away from the scene. As he left the cemetery, it was to lasting and boisterous applause.

An Aguda representative tried to mount the dais to continue the proceedings, but the crowd was too hot to return to a run-of-the-mill funeral. The mourners had split into two groups: one arguing that Farbstein should have been given the opportunity to speak, and the other still screaming that they wanted him ejected from the premises. As the arguments intensified, furious disputations led to pushing, which in turn led to punches. Hats, canes, and fists flew as a full-fledged brawl ensued. Hundreds of Hasidim began pummeling one another in the middle of the cemetery. The dais was smashed and torn apart so that people could use the broken-off pieces of wood to beat their opponents. While all this was happening, someone realized there was a funeral going on and decided to bury the body. It was, after all, getting late in the afternoon, and Jewish funerals are not permitted to take place after sundown. The situation was so out of control that even the family of the deceased didn't notice that the body had been taken for burial. So, as people screamed and fought all around the cemetery and the gravesite, the body of Yeshaye Rozenboym was lowered into the ground.

Of course this brawl was the talk of Jewish Warsaw's cafés, shops, and streets for weeks. Pretty much the entire Jewish press was in agreement that the riot was a disgraceful desecration of the dead. But when life gives you

Figure 12.8. "Where are you going with that stick?—To a funeral." Cartoon commenting on the violence at Yeshaye Rozenboym's funeral. Source: *Haynt*, April 5, 1929. Courtesy of the YIVO Institute for Jewish Research.

horseradish, you make *khreyn*. With Passover only a few weeks away, Yiddish humorists went into high gear, dedicating their columns and magazines to the Miss Judea affair. A bevy of Yiddish satire magazines were hastily published, among them *The Seder of Miss Judea* and *Miss Judea's Matzah Balls*. Warsaw's premier Yiddish satirist, Yosef Tunkel, performed his *Haggadah of Miss Judea* live in the Warsaw Jewish Writer's Union. The Yiddish cabaret troupe Sambatyen wrote and performed a musical send-up of the Miss Judea scandal called *Miss Jewess*. The humor journals and weekend humor sections of the dailies filled with satirical material related to Miss Judea.

Numerous cartoons related to the affair were published, many of which caricatured Miss Judea with an omnipresent unibrow. Much of this satiric fare combined the Miss Judea affair with the Passover holiday. Nearly all of it had some sort of Haggadah (Passover prayer book) parody that revolved around the pageant. The Four Questions were set as though asked by Miss Judea. The four sons of the Haggadah became the four daughters. That season's Passover reading material centered more on Miss Judea than on the Exodus from Egypt. The general consensus was that the whole thing was a tragic embarrassment for the community, but Shmuel Yatskan, founder of *Haynt*, the largest Yiddish daily in Warsaw, saw it differently. He realized that the importance of the pageant lay in its sheer unimportance. He wrote that Jewish Warsaw, with its worries, fears, high taxes, bankruptcies, and suicides, had never been so much fun. The Miss Judea pageant had helped everyone forget their troubles. For a community that lived between a hammer and an anvil, being able to overlook the grind of the quotidian, however briefly, was valuable in and of itself.

Figure 12.9. "Ay yay, look at those matzo balls!" Source: "Mis yudeya's kneydelekh" (Miss Judea's Matzo Balls), *Humor Magazine* (Warsaw), April 1929. Courtesy of the YIVO Institute for Jewish Research.

The Miss Judea incident, as dramatic and consuming as it was, was forgotten only months later. By year's end, Poland, along with every other country, had sunk into a worldwide economic depression, making the scandal a distant memory. The fireworks surrounding the pageant and its subsequent scandals disappeared from history. No one seemed to know what happened to Zofia Oldak. An octogenarian cousin of hers who lived near Tel Aviv said she couldn't remember if Oldak went to Australia or to Treblinka. But she was pretty sure Miss Judea ended up in one of those two places.

(CHAPTER 13)

EVER FALLEN IN LOVE WITH SOMEONE
(YOU SHOULDN'T HAVE FALLEN
IN LOVE WITH)?

Feivel Goldshvartz, a 21-year-old worker in a Warsaw clothing factory, was a stand-up guy. He and 18-year-old Reyzl (also known as Ruzhe) Shulkley-not had been an item for six months, and in the summer of 1927, they were engaged to be married. Reyzl, a poor, motherless girl who lived in a poverty-stricken and dangerous neighborhood, happily accepted the thin engagement ring Feivel offered her. Feivel's family, however, was firmly against the match; they thought Reyzl was low-class trash and didn't want her in the *mishpokhe*. They weren't entirely wrong; Reyzl's mother had died when she was a baby, and her father, Kalman, who was well known to Warsaw police as a fence, raised her alone on a particularly rank stretch of Volinska Street, a road in one of the city's poorest and most crime-ridden neighborhoods.

Feivel loved Reyzl and didn't seem to care what his family thought. But his family began to pressure him, complaining that it was a bad match and that he'd be sorry in the end. Eventually, the pressure grew too strong and Feivel was persuaded to dump Reyzl. He didn't want a bitter breakup but decided to tell her the bad news on a hot July night. They took a walk. Perhaps because it was a family heirloom, Feivel wanted to get his ring back and didn't quite know how to go about asking. He awkwardly offered Reyzl

This chapter was originally published as "Manhood, Interrupted" in *Tablet Magazine* (November 19, 2009) and has been expanded for this book.

20 zlotys for it. Reyzl knew that his family had been on his back about her and seemingly understood. Realizing that their engagement was over, she took the money and gave him back the ring.

The breakup seemed amicable, and Reyzl asked if Feivel would walk her to her apartment building, which not only was in a dangerous neighborhood but was also adjacent to a low-end brothel run by Rivka "the Cow" Linderbaum and her son, Khatzkel, a notorious Warsaw pimp. Feivel agreed to escort her to the front steps of the building. When they got there, the two began to kiss. Despite the breakup, or, perhaps because of it, things began to get hot and heavy. In the shadows to the side of the stairs, Reyzl began slithering downward on Feivel's body, descending to her knees. Though they were supposed to be splitting up, Feivel didn't stop her as she opened his pants. Suddenly, he felt a sharp pain like none he'd ever felt before. He collapsed onto the paving stones and looked up at Reyzl, who cackled as she made her way up the stairs, her face and blouse spattered with blood. Feivel looked down. She had bit his penis in half.

Feivel screamed. A dark pool of blood had already begun spreading around him. People came running after hearing his cries. An ambulance was called. Someone who recognized him ran to Feivel's house and told his sister Golda that he had been attacked. She raced to Volinska Street, bumping into Reyzl on the way; Reyzl's face and neck were flecked with blood. "Your brother got stabbed at the whorehouse! He was there to find another bride-to-be," Reyzl snapped at Golda angrily. But realizing she wore incriminating stains, Reyzl quickly blurted out, "I got all this blood on me when I tried to help him."

Feivel was rushed to the Jewish Hospital on Tshista Street. Although emergency room doctors were able to stanch the bleeding, they were concerned that the young man would contract blood poisoning, which could kill him. Meanwhile, word about the attack spread in Jewish Warsaw, and the hospital was deluged with curious gawkers who had heard about the bizarre attack on the street. The crowd situation became so bad that doctors were forced to hold an impromptu press conference announcing that Feivel Goldshvartz was expected to survive and that although he would have to live with a defective penis, he'd still be able to produce children. What a relief.

Warsaw police arrested Reyzl and her father that night. It is not clear why the father was arrested, but he told the cops that he didn't know any-

גרויסער טומעל אויף דזיסא און
סטאוקי ארום דער געשיכטע
אויף וואלינסקא גאם.

צו דער יונגערמאן לעבט.

נעכטמען, ארום האלב 11 פריה איז רו •
זישא, אין דער בענקליימונג פון איינינע
פאליציאנטמען, איבערגעפיהרט געוואַרעַן
צום אויספארשונגם • ריכטער פון 7 • מען
ראַיאָן. אויף דער נאס האט זי זי אַבע •
וואַרעם צ המוז, וועלכער האָם זי בענע •
נעגם מים אַ קצעַן אַ מזיק.

איבער'ן וועג צום אויספארשונגס • ריכ •
פער האָם זיך דער חמוז מערנרעסטערם
אויף מאר דער קאנצעלאַריע פון אויס •
פארשונגם • ריכמער אויף מיאַרטאָו
האַם זיך מערזאַמעלם אַג'עולם איינואַ •
נער פון וואַלינסקא, אָבואַרמעגדיג גיי'
גירינג אויפ'ן בעשלום פון אויספארשונגם
ריכמער.

אַ גרויסער פומעל קומם אויך פאַר
אויף דזיקא 46 פאָר'ן קרעמעל, וואַס
געהערם אָן צו רוזשאַ'ם עלמערן.
דארם מערזאַמעלם זיך כסדר אַ המ'ן
פון הונדערמער מענשעַן.

ארום האלב 12 בייטאג, וועז רוזשא
איז נאַך געזועַעַן אין וואַרמע • זאָל ביים
אויספארשונגם • ריכמער, האַם מ'אַ פאַ •
ליציאַגע נעפיהרם אין אַ דראַזשעַ פום
קריז • נערירם אין באַד • אַנשמאָלם
עפעם אַ יונגע מערמסמאַנסמין, וועלכע איז
געטומ אוימערליך עהנליד צו רוזשאַ'ן.

אויף דזיקא און וואַלינסקא האַם זיד
דעריבער פערשפריים אַ קלאַנג, אַז דאַם
פיהרם מען רוזשאַ'ן. במשך פון איינ •
נע מינום האַם זיך אויף דזיקא און סמאַ •
קי מערזאַמעלם אַג'עולם פון הונדערמער
מעַנשעַן הרי אנצנהנמז רינת בוווים•

רוזשא שולקלייננאַם
די "העלדין" פון וואַלינסקא גאַס

(X) דער צושמאַגער פון יונגעגמאַן
מיזועַל נאַלדשוואַרץ אין דערמייל צהן
עגדערונג. ער איז ביי'ם בעוואוסמזין
און פיהלם זיך נישם קשה, הגם דאַם אום •
נליק מים איהם האַם איהם אַריינגע •
בראַכם אין גרוים פערמומליונג.

די עקסמערימשם • אַפעראַציע, אַז
נאַלדשוואַרץ זאַל נאַר אַסאַל קעגעַן זיין
אַ מאַמער, האַם זיך דערמייל איינגעגעַ •
בעַן.

Figure 13.1. Article on the Goldshvartz-Shulkleynot affair accompanied by a photo of Reyzl after another woman was misidentified as her and attacked. Source: *Moment*, July 11, 1927. Courtesy of the YIVO Institute for Jewish Research.

thing about the attack and that he was sleeping soundly at home when the young man's tragedy occurred. Reyzl also hotly denied that she had anything to do with the incident, telling the police that she was on her way home when she saw that Goldshvartz had been "done." The police released Reyzl's father from custody, but Reyzl was held in the local precinct's clink.

Adding insult to injury, detectives came to the hospital and charged Goldshvartz with corrupting a minor after Reyzl informed them that she was not actually 18. Even worse for poor Feivel, *Haynt*, one of the city's Yiddish dailies, published a report—allegedly based on rumors spread by the girl and her family—that claimed the boy did not bear "any ill will toward Reyzl and still wanted to marry her." The same paper reported that it was he who had attacked her that night on the stairs and that she had bitten him in self-defense. How that version transpired was never made clear. Infuriated, Feivel was forced to give an exclusive interview to a competing daily, *Moment*, in which he vehemently refuted these claims.

All of this exhausted poor Feivel and his condition worsened. While he languished in the hospital on Tshista Street, Reyzl sat in jail, though she was occasionally brought to court for hearings. When she was brought out, huge crowds gathered to howl at her during the perp walks. Once, a herd of angry rubberneckers attacked some other female hood who had been misidentified while being escorted to jail by police. As a result, *Moment* printed a photograph of the real Reyzl so that people could see her likeness and refrain from violently attacking random female criminals who just "might be her." So offended by this bizarre sex crime, a huge chunk of Warsaw Jewry was out for blood.

Reyzl waited fearfully in prison while Feivel's condition vacillated. After all, if he died, she would be tried for murder. Fortunately for her, the penis repair department at Warsaw's Jewish Hospital was a good one and they succeeded in saving Feivel. In the end, she was charged with assault and was forced to serve a relatively short sentence.

No one knows what became of Reyzl Shulkleynot or her victim, Feivel Goldshvartz and his defective penis. As the fury of the street dissipated, the press and their readers lost interest and moved on to the next scandal. Part of a sometimes nasty, violent, Jewish underclass, Reyzl and Feivel were but two of the urban denizens who disappeared into the Jewish urban maelstrom that was interwar Warsaw.

CHAPTER 14

MY YIDDISHE DIVORCE

Yesterday, a case in Warsaw's Rabbinical Court between Berel Sh. and his bride, or, more accurately, the bride's father, was to be heard.

The issue, which should have easily produced a quick judgment, should not even have been worth talking about, but lately, the situation has been that the petitioners decide to make up their own judgments. And that is something worth talking about.

As soon as the case began and the litigants began lodging their complaints, the groom ran over to his father-in-law and began cursing him. The bride couldn't stand it and ran over to the groom and gave him a fiery slap. The groom's father and brother and the bride's mother and father came running with chairs and canes flying from all sides, the result being that the bride and her father both ended up with bloodied faces, chairs ended up with broken legs, and the rabbis ran out.

Moment, November 29, 1926

It is doubtlessly a tragedy when a marriage or a long-term relationship ripens into an angry knot of hatred and acrimony, when fury and venom are spit from lips that only recently touched in tender embrace. Horrible, unless, of course, you get to watch it happen.

Such was the luck of the Yiddish journalists who were assigned to report from the Warsaw *beyz-din*, the city's storied rabbinic court, which functioned

This chapter was originally published as "Divorce Court" in *Tablet Magazine* (February 18, 2010) and has been expanded for this book.

Figure 14.1. "A new machine being set up in the Rabbinate: When you put in a boy and a girl, out pops a ready-made divorce." Source: *Haynt,* October 29, 1926. Courtesy of the YIVO Institute for Jewish Research.

as a kind of Las Vegas–style divorce court where couples could show up without an appointment and request an instant divorce. With relationships unraveling and tensions running high, the proceedings would often devolve into pitched battles between appellants, in which chairs and fists would fly on a *sheitel* trigger. And because litigants knew that journalists would be present to report on the cases, starting in the mid-1920s, the court began to take on the flavor of a Yiddish Jerry Springer show.

The Warsaw rabbinic court was housed along with dozens of other administrative offices at 26 Gzhibovska Street, the stately building that served as the seat of the city's Kehila, or Jewish community council. A quasi-governmental agency to which Jews paid taxes, the Kehila funded Jewish schools, homes for the aged, hospitals, clinics, food kitchens, and the like. As a department within the Warsaw Community Council, the rabbinic court functioned as a subdivision of the city's Rabbinate, which itself was composed of ten appointed rabbis, one each from the city's ten districts. Among their varied clerical duties, these rabbinic appointees were required to serve on the court on a rotating basis. But serving on the court apparently was not a particularly choice assignment, and in the 1920s and 1930s certain rabbis appeared regularly in the rotation, whereas other, better known, and more politically connected rabbis did not spend much time in pursuit of such pedestrian issues as conversions, divorces, and small-time disputes brought by the city's *amkho*, or common rabble.

The rabbinic court was a come-as-you-are kind of affair, one at which petitioners could simply show up unannounced, plead their case before the court, and receive a near instant resolution. As a result, the court was often mobbed with supplicants, as well as their witnesses and families, who often came to provide emotional and moral support. Most cases were initially vetted by the court's indefatigable *shammes*, Reb Dan, whose job it was to suss out whether petitioners had a legitimate case.

Essentially an administrative assistant, Reb Dan Volkenbrayt was the person responsible for handling the logistics of settling marital and legal disputes at the Warsaw Kehila. When couples and other litigants arrived at the Rabbinate to settle their disputes, Reb Dan was the one who greeted them and explained the proper procedures. Only after speaking to Reb Dan would litigants be allowed to plead their cases before the rabbis.

Figure 14.2. Reb Dan, portrait from the series "Popular Jews," photographed by M. Kipnis. Source: *Haynt*, March 30, 1937. Courtesy of the YIVO Institute for Jewish Research.

It was common knowledge that Reb Dan, a clerical celebrity among all of Warsaw's Jews, would try to get litigants to mediate and settle their cases beforehand, instead of having them come to trial before the rabbis. His ability to settle these disputes was so legendary that one reporter facetiously announced that Reb Dan had won the Nobel Peace Prize. Reb Dan also appeared more than once in cartoons, which showed him on his way to solve intractable political disputes in the Polish parliament, an indicator of his persuasiveness in creating compromises for settlements. These cartoons are an indicator of his renown as a figure of cultural and administrative importance. Many cartoons portray divorce proceedings at the rabbinic court, but not one caricature or cartoon specifically names any of the rabbis of the Warsaw Kehila, just Reb Dan. Not only did he mediate legal disputes, but also on numerous occasions he was forced to intervene and negotiate between angry groups of witnesses, spectators, and the rabbis of the court. Reb Dan was also much sought after by Warsaw's Yiddish journalists for the lowdown on the many violent episodes and nasty scandals that occurred in the Rabbinate, and apparently he was happy to give it to them.

One of those journalists was a young Isaac Bashevis Singer, who wound up basing his own autobiography on the conceit of reporting cases from his father's private rabbinic court from the perspective of a child. Singer, who probably encountered Reb Dan as a cub reporter working for the daily *Moment*, quietly immortalized the famed *shammes* with a quiet cameo in his memoir *In My Father's Court*.

In a 1937 column in the Warsaw daily *Haynt*, titled "Popular Jews," the writer, musician, musicologist, and photographer Menakhem Kipnis wrote that Reb Dan was, after Shepsl Rotholtz (an enormously popular Jewish boxing champion of late 1930s Poland, also a forgotten character), the most popular Jew in Poland. "After all," he wrote, "who's never heard of Reb Dan?"

Sadly, no one today has heard of Reb Dan. Like most of Polish Jewry, he simply disappeared into a historical void. He was not considered an important figure by historians, but in the popular imagination of Warsaw's Jews, he was a figure of great significance. Outside of the Warsaw Yiddish press, the only historical work in which he receives mentioned is in Hillel Seidman's *Warsaw Ghetto Diary*, where the "legendary Reb Dan," as Seidman called him, was seen getting caught by the gestapo during a roundup in the ghetto in September 1942, near the tail end of the mass liquidation of the city's Jews. Although an attempt was made to extract him, Reb Dan is described as being shoved into a cattle car and shipped off to Treblinka, the death camp where the famed *shammes* of the Warsaw Kehila was exterminated. No one ever heard of Reb Dan after that because, quite literally, he went up in smoke.

All that remains of Reb Dan are the brief press reports of the stream of cases before the Rabbinate. We are lucky that Kipnis had the foresight to photograph Reb Dan and that the journalists of the Warsaw Yiddish press were resourceful enough to record the enormous pool of human interest stories that came out of his heroic work as a facilitator and mediator at the Rabbinate.

The Warsaw rabbinic court saw thousands of divorce proceedings during the interwar period. Outside of raucous blurbs that appeared in the back pages of the papers, divorce and its related issues were considered weighty social matters and were dealt with in the Yiddish press in serious news articles that typically lamented a perceived increase in marital dissolution. However, the topic also appeared in the realm of lighter fare, an indication of a widespread awareness that divorce had become a common form of marital conflict resolution among urban Jews.

The reporters of the Yiddish press understood that divorce court was a guaranteed winner when it came to providing fodder for a sensational article. The humorist and journalist Ber Kutsher was the first to report regularly from the court and was followed by brothers Israel Joshua Singer and Isaac Bashevis Singer. Many reports from the rabbinic court were also filed anonymously. They became popular fare in the Warsaw Yiddish press beginning around 1924 and were published until Warsaw's Rabbinate committee banned journalists from their proceedings in early February 1927.

However, in a remarkable turn of events, the rabbis who sat on the court refused to comply with the order; in an interview in the Yiddish daily *Moment*, one of them noted that "under the current progressive societal conditions, it is simply not possible to shut the door of such an institution like the Rabbinate on the Jewish public."

Despite the rabbis' protest, journalists did begin to suffer from restrictions. The Rabbinate found the reports of violence—usually accompanied by quotes such as "and the rabbis crept out through a side door"—abhorrent and terribly embarrassing. But the intrepid journalists of the Yiddish press continued to report on the constant barrage of *beyz-din* scandals. To do so, they turned to an inside source, the aforementioned Reb Dan.

The Jewish public seemed to love the explosive stories that pocked the back pages of Warsaw's Yiddish dailies. For the most part, the reasons for the rash of breakups—sexual affairs, poverty, irreconcilable differences—were the same laundry lists of marital dissolution that one sees everywhere. But some men insisted on a divorce because they didn't like their wives' cooking. Other complaints were based on political issues. Some appellants were there before they got to the chuppah and sought engagement divorces. Because marriages were contracted and involved dowries, engagement breakups were permitted by Jewish law and were adjudicated before the court—with damages.

Possibly the most unexpected—but oddly one of the most common—type of case that came before the three-rabbi panel dealt with what seemed like an endemic problem among Warsaw's Jews: bigamy. Banned in the eleventh-century ruling by Rebbenu Gershom, the taking of multiple wives became a phenomenon in twentieth-century Warsaw mostly because men were leaving their wives and then remarrying without bothering to obtain a *get*, or Jewish writ of divorce.

To wit:

"Why did you marry two women?"
"My father always told me that I should marry a beautiful woman and an intelligent woman."

Haynt, November 1926

Not only was bigamy illegal and immoral (though not necessarily fattening), but it also left first wives trapped in a kind of judicial limbo, because they were unable to remarry without proving they had been divorced from the husbands who had left them. As a result, men who had abandoned wives and children were often called before the court. Sometimes they showed up, and sometimes they didn't.

Violence broke out frequently during these cases, a fact that challenges the stereotype that Jews, particularly in prewar Eastern Europe, had an aversion to physical aggression. The stark reality was that with its large, uneducated, urban Jewish underclass, Warsaw's Jewish neighborhoods saw a great deal of small-scale violence in daily life. Brief outbursts were not at

Figure 14.3. "The morning walkabout on Gzhibovska Street: And just like the sun rises from behind the walls, little Jews come walking on Gzhibovska Street." Fragment from a new poem, "The Plague of the Two-Wived Jews." Source: *Haynt*, November 19, 1926. Courtesy of the YIVO Institute for Jewish Research.

all rare. If anything, pushing and slapping were a common component of social intercourse and even more so among the *amkho*.

Even those who were educated and more financially secure, including culturally and politically engaged members of the community, were known to explode into physicality in a way we might find alien today. For example, cultural activist, politician, and scholar Noyekh Prilutski and Zionist leader Yitshok Grinboym once got into such a furious argument in the Warsaw Jewish Literary Union that they began hurling ashtrays and paperweights at one another. The poet Meylekh Ravitsh, who reported on this event in a memoir of Yiddish literary figures, wrote that what made it clear that these two men were highly educated was the fact that they did not aim for the head.

Among those with little or no education, violence was often integral to conflict resolution. As a result, a moralizing tone sometimes crept into the texts of articles about the goings-on at the rabbinic courts. These stories of *amkho* gone wild were finely honed examples of how *not* to behave. The press, of course, had it both ways: They were able to editorialize on these behaviors while exploiting them as fodder for their reporting. As for their readers, it was just good, clean schadenfreude.

Figure 14.4. The title of this cartoon is "This Place Is Ready for Violence." The caption reads: "What's going on here, another Kehila meeting?—No, it's just another divorce case in the Rabbinate." Source: *Moment,* April 16, 1926. Courtesy of the YIVO Institute for Jewish Research.

Figure 14.5. The title of this cartoon is "Gas Masks Are a Means of Protection in the Rabbinate," and the caption reads, "Nu, we can start. Call in the couple who wants a divorce. We are fully protected." Source: *Haynt*, December 30, 1928. Courtesy of the YIVO Institute for Jewish Research.

PANDEMONIUM AND A BRAWL AT DIVORCE HEARING IN THE RABBINATE

Moment, April 12, 1926

Yesterday, after a long break, the Rabbinate again began to deliberate divorce proceedings. During the first case a scandalous fight broke out that left the walls of the Rabbinate shaking.

Reb Dan the *shammes* had not yet appeared to put everything in order for the case when about fifteen people abruptly broke into the room yelling. Suddenly, everyone was talking and screaming. With great effort, the rabbis managed to calm the crowd and learned exactly what was going on.

Forty-three years ago, Mr. Fishl Tsukert married his current wife, Hendl. Apparently, he was not destined to have a happy retirement, and as they entered their golden years, they began to have terrible arguments at home.

But, little by little, they got used to having these disputes and didn't bother resolving them.

Recently, however, the arguments have become more intense and violence has broken out at home. According to the wife's testimony, Tsukert attacked his only son with a knife after being slapped by him. Later, the man accused his older daughter, a midwife, of performing abortions. With tears in her eyes, Hendl Tsukert asks the rabbis to take pity on her and grant a divorce.

Tsukert, naturally, denies everything and doesn't want to hear about a divorce. Suddenly, someone from the crowd grabs a chair and heaves it at the old man. The rabbis quickly run out of the room, leaving the crowd to God's mercy! Now chairs really begin to fly, one of which smashes the oven. . . . In the meantime, someone takes out a bottle of vitriol and starts splashing it left and right. There is a huge commotion. No one knows against whom the acid is directed, since everyone is a sister, a son-in-law, or a son of the old man.

Miraculously, the vitriol didn't do much damage. Only the old man got some poured on his neck. Wounded by the punches and the vitriol, he was left lying in the Rabbinate.

The green tablecloth of the rabbi's table was completely burned by the acid.

In the end, the police arrived and didn't find anyone except for the old man. One clobbered Fishl Tsukert was brought to the 7th Precinct house, where a complaint was written up. The old man accuses his children of wanting to burn him. The police are investigating.

BEFORE THE COURT

Moment, January 21, 1927

43-year-old Tsalke Kamashnmakher of Stavki Street was married three years ago to his wife, Reyzl. They got on well with one another, and since Tsalke is a big fan of fish, Reyzl always filled him up with plenty of it.

In time, a child was born.

Yesterday, Reyzl came running into the Rabbinate wailing that her man threw her out. With that, she proceeded to tell no more and no less the following story:

Last Shabbos, when she served him his fish, he began to gripe about how the fish was no good and also started to threaten her, saying that she and the child should get out of the house.

"I came home that evening and he wouldn't let me in because he says he doesn't need me anymore."

"What do you mean, 'He doesn't need you anymore?'" the rabbis ask.

"It was just like turning on a light," she says. "He went off with our neighbor Anya, put up a chuppah and got married."

"By a rabbi?"

"Who needs a rabbi?" she says as she wipes away her tears. "He went to Harshl Treger, and Harshl married them . . . Now I wander around with the child and he doesn't need me anymore."

"Bring your husband here," she is told. "Bring him and we'll ask him what he's got against you."

The woman is humiliated.

"Bring him? How? And if he doesn't want to come?"

"We can't offer any other advice." She drags herself out of the *beyz-din* in tears. A tragedy. She has to bring him in.

BEFORE THE COURT: TSALKE IS BROUGHT IN!

Moment, January 23, 1927

Reyzl from Stavki Street shlepped her fish-fresser husband Tsalke, along with his brand new wife, Anya, to the *beyz-din*. This love triangle, and Reyzl in particular, with her shrieking soprano, made such a ruckus that she had to be sent out.

First she screamed at him; then she spat at him. But Tsalke is also no sucker—he started to pummel her and they could barely be pulled apart.

"Why did you dump her and marry another one?" the rabbi asks Tsalke.

"She's deadly; she's already had four husbands," Tsalke says, "and all four are dead. She's evil."

"You have to divorce the second wife and return to the first one," says the rabbi.

"I can't do it," says Tsalke, "because my wife put the apartment in her name."

"Which wife?"

"Anya!" answers Tsalke.

"So you have to divorce both of them."

"Jews—children of Israel!" screams Reyzl. "Where will my child and I go?"

They leave and Tsalke is pleased, since he will be able to get rid of "the evil wife" and can stay married to Anya.

A MUTE COURT

Haynt, July 18, 1927

In the Rabbinate, the rabbis sat with furrowed brows while the litigants poured out their bitter hearts. But it was a situation in which no one heard a single word.

It can't be said that the litigants were in a happy mood or that they were calm—because they can't speak a word—they are mutes.

They stood before the bench: he, a young man of about 25–26 and she, 2–3 years younger. And they "complain."

"Officially," they don't even have to complain, since both of their parents have come to do so. But the couple doesn't let them and attempt to do it themselves.

The wife runs up to the rabbi, makes a fist and begins to wave it up and down above the rabbi's shoulders. This is her way of telling the rabbi that he treats her badly and beats her. But the husband doesn't sit still either. He grabs his beard, puts his hand to his cheek and leans to one side, as if he were sleeping. This is his way of saying that his wife betrayed him and sleeps with other men.

The witnesses from both sides—all mutes—also get into the act and begin to throw their hands about in the air, stamp their feet, and move around in such a way that the rabbis stand up and begin to look for a way to get out of there.

Finally, someone gets the crowd to calm down and only then do we discover from the parents what this is all about.

The couple, Yosl P. and Khane L., met four years ago in the home for deaf mutes on 28 Shliska Street. Both are children from fine Jewish homes and both are well educated. They immediately liked each other and a love developed. They were married two years ago, moved into a rented house, and lived happily together.

Suddenly, however, the man began to suspect his wife of disloyalty and began to beat her. This continued for a few months, until finally, they split up. He went back to live with his parents, and she went back to hers. Now the young man has called his wife to the Rabbinate and requested a divorce. The wife is willing to grant the divorce, but first she wants him to return what she claims he stole from her.

The complaints last over an hour, and the rabbis don't understand a word. They look closely at the litigants and keep an eye on the door too.

In the end, the rabbis decide to postpone the divorce for four weeks, during which time both sides must return what each took from the other.

RIVKA TSADIK WANTS TO SHOW THE RABBINATE THAT SHE CAN COOK UP POTATOES AND EGG DROP SOUP

Moment, August 26, 1927

Yesterday, Rivka Tsadik of the Old City came into the Rabbinate and asked that her husband, Beynesh, be called to the court because he refuses to live with her peaceably. The little woman, who is still quite young, told the following, unusual story:

Her husband is a craftsman, a quiet and kind person. But he has one flaw: He doesn't like the lunches she cooks. If she cooks him potatoes and egg drop soup, he yells that he'd rather have potatoes and borsht. If she cooks him potatoes and borsht, he'd rather have potatoes and egg drop soup . . . In short, they start fighting and the husband eventually runs out of the house with an empty stomach.

"Anyway," she says, "I would forgive him all that. It's probably my destiny to suffer in this world. But my husband gets up and goes to a restaurant. He goes to work and gives the money he earns to the restaurant where he eats lunch."

Certainly, she says, her neighbors can be queried as to the quality of her cooking, or she will be willing to take an exam to see if she can cook a good lunch or not.

But since the rabbis were not in the Rabbinate, Rivka Tsadik filed her complaint and went home to wait for the rabbis to call her for her cooking examination.

HE "CHARACTERIZES" HER, SHE BEARS A CHILD
Moment, July 24, 1928

Lipa Kamashenmakher is a man with a "standing in society," and he stood this Sunday before, as he calls it, "the highest representation of religious standing"; in other words, the *beyz-din* table of the Warsaw Rabbinate.

The story of this case was detailed for *Moment*:

Lipa, a small soul with beady, black eyes, went on strike after eighteen years of marriage with his Tshipe.

What happened?

She is religious and he, as a "professions commissioner" and member of the "union," cannot agree with her "superstitions."

Not long ago, during a lecture at the "union," he fell in love with a comrade. She "checked him out," he "checked her out," and a child was born.

Lipa showed up dressed up like a dandy and arrived with one of his comrades. Seven or eight women showed up with Tshipe as witnesses.

Lipa gave a fiery speech about how no one can threaten his "male rights" and about how, from a "democratic standpoint," he is allowed to take care of the newborn child.

"A bastard," Tshipe argued, "will not come into my home under any circumstances."

"But what is this tiny soul guilty of?" cried Lipa.

Both scream and yell for a while until the rabbi bangs on the table and gives the judgment [to Lipa]:

"You may not live with the second one!"

"But I won't live with Tshipe, either," answers Lipa. "I will leave her entirely."

One of Tshipe's witnesses chimes in, "You'll get married to a third one."

"That is my own personal prerogative," yells Lipa.

The rabbi determined that Lipa must pay Tshipe 6 zlotys per day and under no circumstances may he live with the second woman.

Lipa agrees. He yells to Reb Dan, "I offer my humblest thanks to you: We have sinned, we have betrayed. More of the same, I won't do."

MEN GO LOOKING FOR WORK AND "MEANWHILE" GET MARRIED A SECOND TIME

Moment, July 30, 1928

Yesterday, Gitl Akerman came into the Rabbinate and told the following "new-fangled" story:

She has lived with her husband, Avrom, a tailor, for sixteen years according to the laws of Moses and even has a Polish marriage certificate and birth certificates for their two children.

In Radom, she stopped working while her husband went to work in the big city, in Warsaw, where there is a need for artisans.

And he was quickly snatched up. Mademoiselle Feyge of 63 Gensha street, a girl, a gold digger, was really looking for a solid man for a husband, not one of these young Charleston dancers. Such a man she found in Avrom, who introduced himself as a stable man and a complete gentleman.

Gitl saw that it was already a few months since Avrom had forgotten their address. Without thinking long, she left the two kids with a neighbor and came to Warsaw. Once here, she inquired at the address bureau and went to 63 Gensha Street. When she got to the address, she happened to arrive exactly one hour after her husband had been led to the chuppah.

Gitl didn't want to disturb the wedding party and said to him quietly, "Avrom, come home."

"What? Who are you?" he yelled. "A crazy lady just walked in."

Her arguments didn't help, and Gitl ended up getting slapped around too.

Because Avrom refuses to go to a rabbi and not to anyone else either, Reb Dan suggested to her that she take the Polish marriage and birth certificates directly to the government commissar.

Gitl left the Rabbinate in a despondent state: How can one make one's own husband unhappy and bring him to a criminal trial!

BLACK SABBATH ON KROCHMALNA STREET BETWEEN BERL TREGER AND HIS WIFE— ALL BECAUSE OF SOREH THE PLUCKER

Moment, August 21, 1928

Not all the rabbis have returned from their summer vacations. Officially, the *beyz-din* is not hearing any cases. But their door is still swinging.

On Sunday, about a dozen people poured in, men and women, trailing a number of children behind them. Everyone talks at once; there is a huge racket and a tumult, and no one can make any sense out of it.

What happened?

Berl Treger and his wife, Matl, from the Okopova came into the Rabbinate to "complain" about each other. The others are in-laws from both sides and some of their neighbors who came with just to "help out."

The crowd was greeted by Reb Dan and the following story was told:

The couple was married seventeen years ago. Up until a year ago, everything was fine and good. Berl was an ideal husband and a good father. Everything he earned he gave to his wife, and one couldn't complain about him. But when Berl started work as a porter in the Halyes marketplace, their good family life came to an end.

There, in the Halyes, sits a feather plucker by the name of Soreh. This plucker quickly became the heat in Berl's heart, and instead of going home to his wife and kids after work, he began to "get lost" on Krochmalna at Soreh's.

Berl's parents are siding with their daughter-in-law and aren't cheap with their three-story curses. Berl's 15-year-old daughter also testifies that she caught her father with Soreh the Plucker in not too pretty a pose.

Berl denies the whole story and says that Soreh is not more than a good friend. Reb Dan tries to resolve the issue, and Berl states categorically, "I'm still gonna go see Soreh. If Matl still wants to be my wife, that's fine; and if she doesn't, she doesn't have to. I'll give her a divorce and that's it!"

This past Saturday, the whole family, including Berl's parents, took a walk over to Krochmalna to raise a little hell with Soreh the Plucker. By the time night fell on Krochmalna Street, everyone was talking about how they made a "Black Sabbath" for Soreh. Berl was so furious that he grabbed his wife and beat her black and blue from head to toe. His wife strips down and it really is horrible to look at the nasty bruises that Berl gave her.

But Berl doesn't let it cool down and—cursing and screaming—he flees from the Rabbinate.

Now one sees that nothing will work with Berl, and his father hands the case over to the police. Matl goes straight from the Rabbinate to the doctor, who will bandage the wounds her husband gave her, and then she will also go to the police.

KROCHMALNA 'AMKHO' THROWS PUNCHES IN RABBINATE

Moment, November 2, 1928

On Wednesday the Rabbinate heard a case from Krochmalna Street: The bride and groom showed up with about fifteen people from the real *amkho*, who came as witnesses.

Upon seeing such an "army" entering the court, Rabbis Ritshevol, Poyzner, and Sheyngras began to tremble and started to look for a door.

The bride and groom met about eight months ago and set and signed conditions for their future marriage and even set specific dates for the event, but the groom doesn't want to go under the chuppah because "the bride isn't an honest one . . ."

So they came to the rabbi to get a judgment.

The rabbi asks, "What do you mean by 'not honest'?"

"I'm certain that she already has a child," he answers.

Upon hearing the word "child," the prospective bride whacked the groom with a fiery slap. The groom didn't want to "owe" her and paid up with a sizzling "reply." The Rabbinate filled with screams as turmoil ensued. The witnesses also began fighting, and when the rabbis saw what was coming, they slowly crept out.

Once again, Reb Dan had to run out to get a policeman. By the time the policeman arrived, things had already calmed down. Both sides turned to Reb Dan and asked him to convince the other rabbis to consider the case, that earlier they had been agitated and that they won't "brawl" anymore.

But it didn't help.

"You can't fight in the Rabbinate. You'll have to come another time," he told them.

The group went away with the intention of returning.

"Krochmalna" doesn't know any tricks: Either get married or don't. "Just don't hassle a Jewish girl!"

PICANTE AND TRAGIC
(The "Little Packages" with Which They Come into the Rabbinate)
At Least He Could Give Something for the Child . . .

Moment, November 16, 1928

Yesterday in the Rabbinate, everyone's attention was drawn to a 20-year-old *shikse* who cradled in her arms a tiny child with two beautiful black Jewish eyes.

During this time, in the courthouse, a case followed that took more than two hours. With pathetic eyes she sat the whole time in the hallway looking at the door of the courtroom waiting for a "Rabbi."

No one from the Rabbinate administration so much as said a word to her. Moreover, it was clear from the pain in her eyes that she is—doomed.

At last the door of the courtroom opened and Rabbi Kanal appeared. The girl jumped up noisily, ran to the rabbi and began to tell him:

"I was seduced by a young Jewish man, an actor who is now working in one of the Yiddish theaters in Warsaw. For a while this actor, the father of the child, gave a bit of money for support. But lately he completely stopped making payments, and I'm ready to simply throw myself into the Vistula River."

She requests a small amount: 15 zlotys per week from the seducer and she'll figure out what to do with it.

The tragic case was sent to the Jewish "Women's Support Group" at 20 Panska Street. If the Women's Support Group can't compel the seducer to pay up, the case will revert to the Rabbinate and will be heard there.

The answer that the Rabbinate would take the case if need be was received with great thanks.

"Slitshnye dzhankuye [kind thanks]."

ON ACCOUNT OF TWO ZLOTYS
Moment, November 16, 1928

The Nobel Peace Prize goes to none other than . . . Reb Dan from the Warsaw Rabbinate . . .

How many distraught couples and marital disputes has this Jew settled or repaired!

He had a tough piece of work yesterday with a couple who had been engaged for two years. Only eight weeks ago they had such a fight that they're already sending back the engagement gifts.

And why?

The bride, a pretty girl of about 22, learned from her "cronies" that her husband doesn't know Polish very well: He said "dvie zloti." She doesn't want a man like that, one with whom she can't show up in the "right social circles."

Reb Dan doesn't get upset and calls the bride over to the side and makes her understand that, in these times, a boy and, more so, one who can provide (he is a wallet maker and makes 100 zlotys a week) is worth his weight in gold . . . So he doesn't like her friends, so what?

But the bride won't hear of it. What is that—can't speak Polish? What's that—"dvie zloti"?

Finally, Reb Dan threatens that she will have to pay half her dowry as a penalty.

In short, it helped. The couple makes up and on the spot they talk about getting married this weekend.

A "JEWISH CHRISTIAN"
Moment, November 16, 1928

A Christian woman with four children (two boys and two girls) came to the Rabbinate yesterday with the request that she and her children be converted to Judaism.

Initially, it was thought that the woman was not entirely rational . . . But all were astounded when this Christian woman began to speak to her children in a beautiful Lithuanian Yiddish.

The story turned out to be this: She is the daughter of a wealthy Count from Grodno. During the first year of the World War, she fell in love with a young Jew. During those hard times, she gave aid to the young man and he swore to take her as his wife. Because the young man did not want to convert, they lived together without getting married. The house was run as a traditional Jewish household: She maintained all Jewish regulations and the children pray every day and even speak Hebrew.

Now she wants to convert and get married according to Jewish law.

However, because the government has legislated that the Rabbinate may not convert Christians to Judaism, she was given the address of the Rabbinate in Danzig where she can complete the procedure.

The "Jewish Christian" happily left the Rabbinate.

WIFE POURS VITRIOL ON HUSBAND
DURING A CASE IN THE RABBINATE

Moment, November 26, 1928

For the first time in the history of the Rabbinate chronicle: a woman pours vitriol on her husband and burns herself in the process.

Yesterday at noon, the many petitioners at the Rabbinate who were sitting and waiting for their own cases to be heard were suddenly shaken by a hard bang on the door accompanied by screams of "Help, save me!"

The frightened bystanders opened the door that leads from the petitioners' room to the Rabbinate, where they saw the following:

A young man writhing on the floor in terrible pain and a young woman, the guilty party in the tragedy, also screaming for help herself. The young man was the approximately 30-year-old Yankev Adelfang (Mila 24) and the woman, Feyge Shtshutshiner, Adelfang's wife.

Twenty months ago the couple were married, and it's been a year that they've been fighting each other. Adelfang came into the Rabbinate a week ago and petitioned Reb Dan with a request to subpoena his wife, Feyge, to the court. A date was set for Sunday and she appeared. But as they entered the Rabbinate, a bitter dispute broke out between the couple and she pulled out a container of acid and splashed it in his face, burning her own hand in the process, and [thus she] began screaming. The Rabbinate administration brought both of them to the hospital.

IN THE SHADOWS OF JEWISH FAMILY LIFE:
A WOMAN OF VALOR

Moment, January 3, 1929

The door of the Rabbinate is thrust open and in falls one Tshipe-Kayle Yagora of Black Street, shlepping her husband Borekh Einbinder behind her. About two dozen Jews, men and women, pour in after them. Some of them are "helpers" planning to testify and the rest are simply curious.

The *shammes* asks, "What do you want?"

Tshipe-Kayle is in the mood for a song and starts off on a high note: "I gotta get to the Rabbinate. What I want is none a ya business. For once and for all I want my Borekh should have a carcass, right now. I'll light a candle in shul!"

One of the rabbis steps in: "Briefly, what's this all about?"

Tshipe-Kayle starts her tune. Oy, does she pour out a hail of accusations on her husband's head, among them that at the time they were married, she, a divorcée, gave him $300 as dowry and in only a short time he wasted all of it. And on top of that he's got a lover and doesn't come home for nights at a time.

Borekh, a scrawny Jew with a scratchy little beard and red eyes, stands there and doesn't utter a word. When the rabbi asks him if he is guilty of what Tshipe-Kayle accuses him, he simply shrugs his shoulders without making a peep.

"You idiot!" yells one of her supporters, shoving him. "Now that you're not with Tshipe-Kayle, you have to tell the rabbi everything. Nu, talk!"

Borekh finally gets the courage to say something and begins to describe the troubles that he suffers from his "woman of valor."

"It's true," he says, that Tshipe-Kayle gave him $300, but what could he do if business was bad and his own money was also lost? "That she is a malicious woman I learned right after the wedding, but because she was mine 'according to the laws of Moses and Israel,' I didn't want to ridicule anyone and suffered in silence. And did I suffer. Just when business started to take off, my bread landed butter side down. She began to make all kinds of scandals, driving me out of the house and refusing to cook for me even a spoonful of food. I was forced to go to my 68-year-old aunt's house to get something to eat. And my nag calls that a 'lover.'"

"Rotten little Borekh!" Tshipe-Kayle can't take it any longer. "You should live as long as you speak the truth! Why don't you tell the rabbi where you spend your nights?"

"Yes, rabbi," answers Borekh meekly, "that's also true. I purposely try to avoid having to listen to her curses by spending half the night in the study house reading Psalms or studying a bit of Mishnah. I can't take any more of her. Rabbi, please grant us a divorce. Maybe it's still possible for me to have a few comfortable years."

"What?!" booms Tshipe-Kayle, like a cannon. "You wanna divorce? I'll dress you in a shroud first and send you express mail into the next world!"

The rabbi decides that the couple should try to live together in peace for two weeks. Tshipe-Kayle is warned not to pester Borekh—because if she does, they will force her to accept a divorce.

"Ha, ha, ha," she laughs to herself. "I'd like to see the Cossacks that will force *me* to get a divorce."

Tshipe-Kayle is dragged out of the Rabbinate by force and, for a long time, her screams and curses reverberate in the stairs.

TWO WIVES, BLAZING PUNCHES, AND—THE COPS
Moment, April 14, 1929

A scandal occurred on Thursday in the Warsaw Rabbinate, which resulted in the participants being hauled off to the local precinct.

Avrom A., a young man from an extremely religious Hasidic family, was married six years ago to one Royze Frenkel from Plotsk.

The couple lived in Warsaw. Royze bore him a little girl, who is now 5 years old. The couple lived together happily.

To make a long story short, a "colleague" of Royze's named Rivke Shniadov used to drop by to visit. The "colleague" caught Avrom's eye and convinced him to leave Royze. Avrom subsequently traveled to Kalish "on business" and married Rivke there.

That was six months ago. Royze, still in Warsaw, knew nothing about it and did not even notice any changes in Avrom. The only thing she could figure out was that her "colleague," who used to drop by nearly every day, had stopped showing up lately. However, a few months ago, neighbors started talking about how Avrom was in contact with Rivke. Avrom's brother, a fanatical Hasid and a son-in-law to the rebbe's court, decided to put an end to the affair and bring his brother into line. It was then he discovered the tragic story that his brother had married Rivke and was living with her.

On Thursday, this same brother dragged Avrom into the Rabbinate. The two wives were there, as well as about thirty family members, mostly women.

The judgment was given by Rabbi Shakhne Ritshevol, whose verdict was that Avrom must divorce both women.

After Rabbi Ritshevol read the verdict, Avrom's brother ran over to him and punched him in the face. If that wasn't enough, the remaining women threw themselves on Rivke and began to beat her. A huge fight broke out, accompanied by spasmodic wails. When those in charge of the Rabbinate were unable to handle the situation, the police were called, who arrested all involved and brought them to the 7th Precinct station house.

A STORMY ESCAPADE WITH A "SACRIFICE"
YESTERDAY ON KROCHMALNA STREET
Moment, September 29, 1933

Krochmalna Street went black yesterday on account of a discussion of "principle" about a white rooster.

It had to do with the following:

On the so-called "Pletzl" (7, 9, and 11 Krochmalna Street) lives the well-known Reb Zorekh of the Shabbos Enforcer Jews. This Jew is terribly meticulous regarding everything that has to do with the holidays. He also performs a sacrifice with a large white rooster, which must be bought by his wife Pesl eight days before the eve of Yom Kippur.

This year, too, Pesl prepared such a rooster, which has crowed at dawn for an entire week, not letting the neighbors get their sleep.

Therefore the neighbors decided to get their revenge on Reb Zorekh and did it like this: Yesterday morning, just after he performed the sacrifice, a few of the neighbors went to Reb Zorekh and announced to him—with serious faces—that today he had sacrificed not a rooster, but a hen.

Reb Zorekh was left sitting as if he were frozen. A bit later he called in more neighbors to check, but all of them agreed unanimously that this was a hen. Without thinking too long, Reb Zorekh grabbed his wife by the arm and shlepped her to the rabbi to get a divorce. On the way to the rabbi, to whom Reb Zorekh brought the unfortunate chicken as "corpus delicti," there trailed after them a strange train of people from the entire block, running to see what would happen at the *beyz-din*.

The rabbi considered the chicken but announced that he was no expert because "that's a job for women."

This got Reb Zorekh boiling, and even when the rabbi's wife arrived and asserted that the chicken was indeed a rooster, he still requested a divorce.

The children who came with broke out in wailing cries. At this point, the rabbi strongly reproached the man, informing him that the famous Rabbi Khayem Soleveytshik wanted to do away entirely with the sacrifice as an unnecessary ritual. Now, however, because he is an elderly Jew, he was scared that he would die the same year and this would strengthen the tradition even more.

These very words convinced Reb Zorekh to remain with his wife, and he and his whole train returned to Krochmalna Street with great joy.

A HOT AND BLOODY DAY IN THE RABBINATE

Moment, February 12, 1934

Yesterday in the Rabbinate was a hot one—and bloody too. Good sense was butchered and the blood flowed like water. And rest assured that the rabbis ran out in the middle of these cases. All of the disputes broke out in connection with divorce proceedings, which, unfortunately, have occurred all too often as of late.

The first fight occurred between the owner of the Garden Restaurant, 45-year-old Masha Becker, and her second husband, 25-year-old Yitshok Lerner, an employee in her restaurant.

Five years ago, Becker's first husband died and she took Lerner the waiter as her husband. But in the restaurant she still treated him like a servant. Lerner refused to put up with that and called his wife to the Rabbinate and asked to have her sign the business over to him.

Words were exchanged and Lerner slapped his wife. This didn't seem to bother her at all, and she blackened his face with the contents of an inkwell.

No agreement was reached.

A second couple beat each other up over a heated issue. A certain Leybl Nayman was a frequent guest at his fiancée's house, where he would come to eat and occasionally sleep over, until his fiancée ended up with "a bun in the oven."

But in front of the rabbi, he said he didn't know anything about it.

"What?" the girl screamed. "Now you don't know anything? Here, now you'll know something!" And she punched him in the mouth so hard that she knocked two of his teeth out and he was completely soaked with blood.

A third case did not even make it into the courtroom—it played out in the hallway.

A young man with four women—two wives and two brides—showed up in the hall. They pounded one another so badly before the trial that the police had to be called, who were able to pull the combatants apart only after great effort.

What a hot day it was yesterday in the Rabbinate.

HE WANTS A DIVORCE BECAUSE HIS
WIFE REFUSES TO BE A MARXIST

Unzer ekspres, March 1935

Among the interesting cases that have recently entered the Kingdom of Reb Dan (a.k.a., the Rabbinate), one finds a woman, a certain Tshipe Vaynepl, the wife of one Sholem Vandel, a shoemaker, who lives on Leshno and Pzheyzd. The woman complained to the Rabbinate that her husband beats her mercilessly and forces her to keep an unkosher home and to break the Sabbath. It was with this chunk of information that she managed to grab the interest of the rabbis and convince Reb Dan to have them consider the case.

Last Friday, the couple paid a visit to the Rabbinate, but seeing as the rabbis were not in, they were greeted by Reb Dan, to whom they gave an earful. The bratty husband launched into a real sermon, all about Marxism. He declared that, as a socialist and atheist, it was inappropriate for him to even enter the Rabbinate, but he did it in order to express his perspective on all these "played out" issues.

In regard to the main complaint, that he beats his wife, he didn't deny it, but he says he's convinced that by beating her, he is fighting a battle with superstition. He also said that he will never forgive her for embarrassing him in front of his colleagues by having had their son circumcised. Plus, he added, he is unwilling to live with her. He demands that they get a divorce according to the laws of Marx.

Reb Dan told them to come back when the rabbis are there.

TWO COUPLES GO TO A RABBI TO GET DIVORCED BECAUSE THEY WANT TO SWAP WIVES

Moment, January 10, 1938

A sensational "transaction" occurred recently before a Warsaw rabbi. The plot of the story sounds a lot like a novel.

A number of years ago, a young man, M.P., from the shtetl Piontitse came to Lomzhe looking for a job. Things worked out for him and he started to earn a good living. In the meantime, P. [that is, M.P.] met a local woman, Frumet G. The two young people became friends and soon a love flared up between them. P. wanted to marry Miss G., but when his father heard about it, he came to Lomzhe and split the couple up by sending his son to Radzimin, to live with a brother. Not long after, P. was married to the daughter of his uncle in Radzimin, with whom he lived.

In the meantime, Miss G. found another candidate in Lomzhe, one Moyshe Fr. of Lomzhe, whom she married.

A few years passed. To make a long story short, at a wedding in Warsaw in the house of Rav Ozherov on 27 Gensha Street, the two couples met, Miss G. and her husband and Mr. P. and his wife.

The two couples became fast friends and at a certain point in the conversation began to remember "the good old days."

The result of this hearty conversation was that the two couples returned to the house of Rav Ozherov. They told the rabbi that they decided to swap wives and asked him to perform two divorces and then two weddings.

To their great disappointment, they did not achieve their goal, since the rabbi declared that divorces cannot be performed in the heat of the moment.

Chained Heat in the Rabbinate

Agune, meaning "anchored" or "chained," is a Jewish legal term referring to a woman whose husband has gone missing and who cannot grant her a divorce, or a woman whose husband refuses to grant her one. According to Jewish law, a woman whose husband has not granted her a divorce may not remarry. This was extremely problematic for the thousands of women whose husbands had been killed or had gone missing during World War I or during any other conflict or pogrom. Without proof of death, these women could not get on with their lives. Shackled to what appeared to an immutable

Jewish law, the Warsaw Rabbinate created a special *agunes* department in 1928 that was supposed to deal with the problem. Their success was limited. For example, of 200 women who, in 1928, sent in documents to prove that their husbands were dead, only 3 were granted divorces. In addition to the thousands of war *agunes*, approximately twenty new ones approached the Rabbinate each year. The statistics here are important, because although they do not seem like large numbers, they are additions to an increasing pool of *agunes*, a pool that did not include women who, for whatever reasons, did not come forward and register and who, according to an article in *Moment*, numbered in the thousands by 1928. And this was only in Warsaw.

As one might expect, this was a social problem of significance that was difficult to resolve and devastating for the women who suffered from it. Journalists understood that the stories about *agunes* were important, not only because of the sometimes dramatic events connected to them but also because they exposed a serious problem that required resolution.

DEAD JEW BAKES BAGELS IN WARSAW

Moment, October 19, 1928

Yesterday, an elegantly dressed young woman walked into the Rabbinate and told the following story:

Her father, a Hasidic Jew from Rave, near Warsaw, disappeared into the night eleven years ago on *Hashone rabo* [the seventh day of Sukkot]; he had gone into the sukkah to bind *heshaynes* [willow twigs for a holiday ritual] and never came back. The forlorn family, a mother and three children, began to search for him and went to local Hasidim to ask advice, but no one had answers for them and everyone concluded that the father was no longer among the living.

Her brother said Kaddish for the father and lit a memorial candle each year on the night of *Hashone rabo*.

Last *Hashone rabo* night, the girl's grandfather appeared to her mother in a dream and said, "Your husband is not dead—he lives in Warsaw. Remember!"

Many people who heard the story simply laughed, said the young woman. But the dream caused a lot of grief for her mother. She decided that right after the holidays, she would send her daughter to Warsaw to find out if her husband was alive or not.

Yesterday on the streets of Warsaw, the woman found many people she knows who, to her great surprise, told her that her "dead" father is working as a bagel baker, is married to another woman, and had even had children with her.

Shaking with fear, the young woman began to ask if someone would take her to her father's address, but no one knew where it was. Because the woman suspected that no one wanted to tell her the address to prevent a scandal, she turned to the Rabbinate to bring these people to justice and to tell her where she can find her father.

Reb Dan advised her to first go to the Bakers' Union and if she does not receive a concrete answer from them, the Rabbinate will then call in the people in question.

A JUDGMENT ON THE STEPS OF THE RABBINATE
Moment, April 2, 1929

Among the patrons of the Rabbinate, one finds many women who cannot be considered to be among Reb Dan's official "guests" but who may be called "permanent residents."

These are the unfortunate *agunes*—victims of the war, or of such men who left them and disappeared into the wide world, leaving them "on the meat rack."

These women show up almost every day in the waiting room of the Rabbinate and sit there for hours with no ostensible purpose; every day they are taken care of in the same manner: Either the Rabbinate secretary or Reb Dan tells them with a shrug of his shoulders, "Nothing, no news about your husbands." And they, the abandoned and forsaken women, are so used to the answer that they no longer even sigh when they hear this well-known "incantation."

Sitting there in the Rabbinate waiting room, they remember little of their own personal tragedies and instead interest themselves in the situations of others. And there's an expression for it: "A *shikse* who has worked in a rabbi's house for a year can also answer religious queries." So these *agunes* sit and give advice to other women. They advise them on what to do and how to lodge complaints in the court in order to receive a better judgment for themselves.

Because of the Christian holidays, all departments of the Kehila were closed. The Rabbinate was also not functioning. But that did not stop its "permanent residents" from coming and waiting outside for a few hours in front of the locked doors of the Rabbinate. There are also a number of "visitors," or couples who have arrived to get divorced. And since the Rabbinate doors were locked, this circle of people continued to get bigger. The potential petitioners begin to lodge their complaints among themselves, in front of the *agunes*— and the judgments take place on the steps which lead into the Rabbinate.

Zelda Piekarek, a skinny, greenish woman, like a *lulav* with a squeaky voice, begins to testify: "My mother warned me not to marry him. Now he beats me up and I'm black and blue all over my body . . . "

The *agune*s listen intelligently, like "judges," and Khaye Melman, with her disheveled *sheytl* pulled down over her eyes, spits out, "Yeah, yeah, they should be branded already. They'll lay down like sheep. They should stand up like lions."

Feivel Piekarek, Zelda's husband (a porter by trade), is insulted by Khaye's remark and yells out, "Only you're good, right? A plague on all of youse. Get married and take care of your man, who needs it . . . Ask mine if she can cook a soup . . . You could puke!"

A commotion begins. The female judges take it on for the honor of the woman. A few women help out with Zelda's complaint and come out singing their own "tune." Feivel won't let it slide and throws back an answer; the women don't remain innocent and a series of three-story curses is exchanged which echo in the empty yard of the Kehila building and, in the end, the gang of women throw themselves on Feivel with fist and nail.

It turns into a real fracas. Feivel, hero that he is, flails punches left and right. Throughout, one hears women scream, "Gevalt, my head," or "Oy, my teeth," or "Save me," or "Oy, my eyes," or "Okh, my side," and so on and so forth.

The women aren't doing so well, like the lions [they thought they'd be]. Blood is pouring out of Feivel's nose and his whole face is scratched up. And the women's screaming keeps on going . . .

Suddenly, the deep, bass voice of a Pole is heard: "Wynosić się natychmiast! Dziś święto! [Get out of here immediately! Today is a holiday!]"

The janitor lumbers out of the basement holding a heavy teacher's whip. He wants to bring things into "order" in honor of Khane. For a moment, the courtyard is empty.

One woman is left on the stairs unconscious with bruised, puffy eyes. The janitor takes a full pail of water and dumps it on the woman, who is unable to move.

"Akh, akh, akh," she wakes up terrified, "where is my husband? Help! Jews, save me!"

This was Zelda, Feivel's wife. Totally soaked, like a cat after a hard rain, Zelda takes off. Only the janitor remains, laughing so hard his sides shake.

FIVE YEARS AS AN *AGUNE*
AND FINALLY CATCHES HER MAN

Haynt, June 11, 1936

For fifteen years, Menakhem Rozenboym lived happily with his wife, Leah Boymgarten. He received a large dowry from her, bought a knitting factory on Mila Street, and also had two children.

But suddenly he began to disappear for entire nights and the two began fighting. The end came one summer when Rozenboym sent his wife to live in a summer house. He rented another apartment and disappeared.

For the past five years his wife has been looking for him and, according to reports she received, he left for Canada.

The unhappy *agune*, through the intercession of the Warsaw Rabbinate, turned to Canadian rabbis to help look for her husband, but it was useless—he had disappeared without a trace.

Yesterday morning, Leah Boymgarten recognized her husband on Zamenhof Street in the company of a woman. She quickly jumped on him and refused to let him go.

All of his arguments, that he didn't know who she was, that it must have been some kind of mistake, didn't help. The crowd that had begun to gather also did not let him go. Only after receiving a number of slaps from his wife did the two of them go to a rabbi, where he gave her a writ of divorce and paid her 600 zlotys on the spot for the children.

CHAPTER 15

SHOMER FUCKING SHABBOS

The holiest of Jewish holidays might be Yom Kippur, but the Sabbath is a holy day so important, that it's the only one that ranks on God's top ten list. Keeping the Sabbath is mentioned at least a dozen times in the Torah, far more than any other commandment. Remembering the Sabbath and keeping it holy is, according to the Talmud, like observing all 613 commandments at once, which is why, as we learn in *The Big Lebowski*, observant Jews absolutely, positively do not roll on Shabbos.

For those dedicated to the commandment's full implementation, the Sabbath is something that must be protected against any infraction, no matter how minute. This means that nothing defined by the sages as work can be performed. Moreover, these same sages delimited exactly thirty-nine specific types of work that you're not permitted to do. Although most people are concerned about the lighting and extinguishing of fire (i.e., using electricity), the other thirty-seven items on the list include chores such as planting, plowing, reaping, gathering, threshing, winnowing, sorting, and grinding. You can't weave, trap, cook, cut, warp, or spin. Don't even think of skinning a fish or trapping a beaver. Those activities and a number of others are strictly forbidden on Shabbos.

This chapter was originally published as "Enforcers" in *Tablet Magazine* (April 15, 2010) and has been expanded for this book.

The problem is—and has always been—that there will always be Jews who need to comb wool or cure meat on the Sabbath. And this little fact infuriates a fair number of other Jews who assiduously refrain from all thirty-nine types of work prohibited on the Sabbath. Those troubled by Sabbath desecration created an organization called the Shomrey Shabbos, "Guardians of the Sabbath," or, perhaps more accurately, "the Sabbath Enforcers," and they were well known for bringing the Shabbos ruckus. The enforcers have their distant origins in the medieval character known as the *klopper*, the man in the shtetl whose job it was to walk about the town and bang on the Jews' houses with a block of wood to let them know it was time to close up shop because Shabbos was about to begin.

This form of public communal cultural preservation was particularly tested by the urbanization of the late nineteenth and early twentieth centuries. When Jews opened their own businesses, there were always those Shabbos enthusiasts who made the rounds on Friday evenings to make sure that Jewish shops were closed before sunset. Infractions were often met with threats of boycott, public reprimand, and even violence. From the enforcers' perspective, the holy day was not something to trifle with. But if you were a baker or a grocer and wanted to sell out of your perishables before your day off, you sometimes did what you could to stay open. And with increasing levels of secularization among Jews, meaning those Hebrews who no longer cared about keeping the Sabbath exactly as prescribed by the sages of old, a fair amount of antagonism was generated.

As secular Yiddish groups—for example, women's rights organizations, literary clubs, and sports associations—established themselves in the early twentieth century, so too did Orthodox groups begin formalizing their unions. Chief among them was the establishment of an official Shomrey Shabbos organization, the official address for those who don't roll on Shabbos and who thought no one else should either. In Warsaw the group was informally organized by the local rabbinate before World War I. But German Jews made it an international affair. At a conference held in Berlin in 1929 and organized by a group of German rabbis, an "official" Shomrey Shabbos organization was created, drawing observant Jews from many countries, all of whom agreed that desecration of the Sabbath was on the rise because of the nature of modern life: Forced store and factory closures on Sundays often required Jews to work on Saturdays. Rabbis at the conference sought a way to ensure Sabbath observance among Jews who had no choice but to work on the day of rest. Among their proposals they considered petitioning governments to allow a day off on Saturday and to work on Sunday instead. All fairly reasonable demands—for Jews, anyway.

In 1930 a second, much larger Shomrey Shabbos conference was held, also in Berlin. Some 2,000 people attended. By then, Shomrey Shabbos organizations were active in more than twenty-one countries, an indication that their platform was making headway. Among ideas floated at the conference was a proposal to approach the League of Nations about making Sabbath rest an international priority and the suggestion of creating a Shabbos encyclopedia, which would examine the history of Saturday work stoppage from biblical times to the present. They allegedly convinced famed poet Chaim Nachman Bialik to contribute an article, though the project never came to fruition.

Figure 15.1. Participants at the Shomrey Shabbos conference in Berlin. Source: *Nasz Przegląd Ilustrowany,* September 7, 1930. Courtesy of the YIVO Institute for Jewish Research.

Geared toward helping working-class Jews who wanted to but who couldn't observe Shabbos because they were forced to work, the conference did not take into account people who cared nothing for the day of rest or those who might purposely break it as part of their political or social ideologies. To the enforcers on the streets of Warsaw, this was indeed a matter of national security. They had no qualms about cracking skulls for the sake of Shabbos and, occasionally, breaking it in order to keep it whole. As Jewish ideologue Ahad Ha'am once quipped, "*Shabbos* keeps the Jews more than the Jews keep *Shabbos*."

The Warsaw Yiddish press is full of incidents involving the enforcers. In August 1927 the Yiddish daily *Moment* regaled readers with the story of a young Jew riding a bicycle through a heavily Hasidic neighborhood of Warsaw on a Saturday. It was just after noon, when synagogue services typically concluded and thousands of congregants spilled onto the city streets. As the young rider approached the corner of Tvarda and Marianska Streets, a Hasid saw him and screamed "Shabbos breaker!" at the top of his lungs. With that, the Hasid hurled himself off the sidewalk and block-tackled the cyclist, sending him and his bicycle clattering to the ground.

"A bitter holy war began to play out," *Moment* dutifully reported. Furious at being smashed to the ground, the cyclist got up and began to argue with his assailant. The Hasid, meanwhile, was equally angry at the public flouting of the holy day. The two began throwing punches. Other Hasidic bystanders began to join in, taking their own swings at the biker—to protect "the honor of the Sabbath," said *Moment*. The Hasidim even "saw fit to settle the score with the young man's bicycle, breaking spokes and bending the frame and wheels until it was transformed into a formal heap of junk."

Eventually, the police showed up to drive the large crowd away. They arrested the cyclist and his attackers and lugged the smashed bike back to the precinct as evidence. Although riding a bike doesn't technically break any Sabbath rules, rabbis frown on it because if a tire pops or a chain breaks, the cyclist might have to fix it and thereby transgress the holiday's dictates. Warsaw's Hasidim didn't care either way. They just wanted to kick some Shabbos ass.

Fear of arrest did not deter these Sabbath day watchdogs. About a year later, *Moment* reported on roving gangs who performed pre-Shabbos street crawls every Friday evening to make sure the local Jews had shut down their businesses. One particular Friday evening in August 1928, they happened upon a Jewish boy at the corner of Gzhibovska and Granitshna Streets in Warsaw shouting, "Buy 'em ladies, roasted pumpkin seeds, fresh out of the oven, buy 'em now!"

One of the enforcers walked over and calmly alerted the young salesman that Shabbos had begun and that he should stop selling his wares. The boy roundly ignored him. What began, according to *Moment*, as "moral advice from the enforcer, quickly turned into a threat of physical violence." While the enforcer was angrily chewing out the young entrepreneur, a crowd began to grow. On one side of the crowd were Jews on their way to synagogue who were poised to drag the "Shabbos breaker" into an alley and pound some sense into him. The other side consisted of people who defended the alleged transgressor.

As in the earlier incident, emotions got heated and the fight escalated. Screams began to sound and people began smashing their canes over one another's heads. *Moment*'s reporter doesn't say what happened to the peddler boy during the fracas but does tell us that when the police arrived, they arrested half a dozen people, all of whom wound up spending Shabbos in the clink.

Despite the post-melee arrests, other enforcers continued to prowl that evening, and, "after determining that the Jewish-owned seltzer stands on Tvarda Street were indeed closed," one of the gangs happened upon a young Jewish couple out on a date. While a Shabbos rendezvous does not qualify as a transgression, it just so happened that the young man was smoking a cigarette—an act that doubtlessly necessitated the lighting of a match, one of the thirty-nine types of work strictly prohibited on the day of rest.

Still furious from the pumpkin seed episode, one of the enforcers flew into a rage upon seeing the smoker. He snatched the smoker's hat off his head, threw it to the ground, and stomped on it. The victim, *Moment* explained, "was baffled and didn't quite know how to react" to this maniac who had just stolen and stomped on his hat. "His date, on the other hand, was a real *eyshes khayel*—a woman of valor," the newspaper said. "She knew exactly what was happening and pounced on the enforcer, scratching his face like a cat, and tearing out a hefty chunk of his beard." The enforcer, *Moment* continued, let out a "blood-curdling scream," which brought "hundreds of people into the street, crowding it so much that the tram was unable to get through." The police finally arrived and arrested everyone involved.

As is evident, not all Jews appreciated the ostensibly helpful actions of the Shabbos enforcers. Plenty of simple businesspeople wanted to open their stores or sell in the markets on Saturdays, and scores of other people merely wanted to grab a smoke without being harassed or molested by these pesky God-botherers. In some places, for instance, Praga, a heavily Jewish neighborhood in Warsaw, a small group of businesspeople banded together to fight the enforcers' attempts to keep Jewish-owned shops closed on Saturdays. But their will was no match for the Shomrey Shabbos. In 1935 the three leaders of the anti-Shabbos contingent in Praga were all found to have died under mysterious circumstances. Bar owner Yitzkhok Sumek was found to have suffocated after someone left a gas pipe open in his bar; another Praga store owner, a Mr. Likhtenshteyn, was found dead of an alleged "heart attack"; and the lifeless body of a third member of the anti-Shabbos group, Moyshe Tsukerman, was found with his throat slashed. What remained of the anti-Shabbos group collapsed and disappeared in the wake of these fearful murders. Although no one was ever arrested for these mysterious deaths, what is clear is that some of the Shomrey Shabbos were deadly serious about Sabbath transgression.

While business owners may have withered in the face of the enforcers, politically engaged Shabbos breakers did not. The Free Thinkers, as they were known, had bureaus all over Poland, clubhouses for nonbelievers where lectures and meetings were held (see Chapter 6 for the Yom Kippur activities of the Free Thinkers). Willing to fight at the drop of a hat, the Free Thinkers and the Shabbos enforcers often came to fisticuffs, or worse; in 1935 the enforcers tried to bomb a Free Thinker office on Warsaw's Krulevska Street.

But the enforcers' animus wasn't reserved only for Jews who flouted religious law. Occasionally they used their powers to deal with internal affairs, moral issues that plagued their own religious communities.

Take, for example, the May 1933 case of Yoel Vayderfeld, a Warsaw Hasid who was also a wealthy landlord. According to *Moment*, Vayderfeld had evicted a family with six small children from one of his apartments, literally throwing them out into the street. Although neighbors and other local Hasidim tried to get Vayderfeld to reconsider his decision, the landlord remained unmoved.

Not so the Shabbos enforcers, who sprang into action. On a Friday night, while Vayderfeld was at his *shtibl* greeting the Shabbos, the enforcers moved the poor family, "together with their meager belongings, back into their apartment," a kindly act if there ever was one.

When Vayderfeld found out about it, he was livid and vowed to initiate new eviction procedures. But the Shabbos enforcers remained on the case. So did other local Hasidim: "When the landlord went to pray the following Shabbos morning, the other worshippers asked that he allow the poor renter back in," *Moment* reported. They also tried to delay the Torah reading until Vayderfeld agreed to allow the family to remain, a public attempt to shame the cruel landlord. But Vayderfeld was a stubborn sort and steadfastly refused their entreaties.

Without other recourse, the enforcers' next move was to enter the synagogue, grab Vayderfeld's prayer shawl, wrap it around his head, throw him over a bench, and start beating him viciously on his back and buttocks— a Yiddish underworld tactic known as *aroysnemen a mashkante*, or "taking out a mortgage" on someone. Despite what was clearly a serious shellacking, Vayderfeld managed to extricate himself and fled the synagogue to a nearby pharmacy, where he called the police—himself violating the Sabbath. Instead of returning to synagogue, he engaged the services of the law, who again, *Moment* continued, "threw the poor family out of the apartment—on Shabbos, no less." Not a victory, but a valiant effort on the part of the enforcers.

More than anything the Shomrey Shabbos saw themselves as being on a mission of morality. Although the Shabbos enforcers were not always successful and although they were often a bit too hotheaded, their actions were nonetheless condoned by the most important rabbis and legitimized by an international organization. Unsurprisingly, the street-level tactics of the enforcers remain a violent inheritance among some contemporary Jews. Although the contradiction inherent in their aggression seems to elude them, their desire to protect, defend, and enforce the Sabbath remains paramount: So long as they're around, they'll see to it that nobody rolls on the day of rest.

CHAPTER 16

625-POUND JEWS

AND OTHER ODDITIES

Reporting for the *New York World-Telegram*, renowned journalist Joseph Mitchell called Martin "the Blimp" Levy "the most meat which ever stepped into a ring." Other papers used such phrases as "The Miniature Mastodon" and the "Boston Pachyderm." Discovered by wrestling impresario Jack Pfefer in the mid-1930s while working as the fat man in a Coney Island sideshow, the Blimp tipped the scales at somewhere between 600 and 700 pounds. Nobody knew exactly how much he weighed because normal scales couldn't contain him. Allegedly, he had to be weighed on livestock scales and was brought to matches in baggage cars. With the larger men in the mat game weighing in at 250–300 pounds, the morbidly obese Blimp, with his ample corpus and bug eyes, was one of the first freaks in professional wrestling.

Freaks were Pfefer's specialty. He made wrestlers in his stable shave their heads or grow huge antennaed mustaches. He also brought in grapplers such as the acromegalic Swedish Angel, christening him "the ugliest man in the world" and guaranteeing that ladies in the audience would faint, men would shout, and children would cry upon laying eyes on him.

Veteran newsmen like Joseph Mitchell and A. J. Liebling loved Pfefer and the strange characters he brought to wrestling. "I am da orginator of

---

This chapter was originally published as "Big Man" in *Tablet Magazine* (December 17, 2009) and has been expanded for this book.

Figure 16.1. Martin "the Blimp" Levy promotional photo, c. 1939. Reproduced from the original photograph held by the Department of Special Collections of the Hesburgh Libraries of the University of Notre Dame. Courtesy of the Jack Pfefer Collection, Rare Books and Special Collections, Hesburgh Libraries of Notre Dame.

da freaks," Pfefer himself said in a 1961 *Denver Post* profile that featured his
heavy Yiddish accent. "Whatcha call careactors. I bring over Ivan the Terrible Poddubny from Russiam, Sergei Kalmikoff from Siberia, Fritz Kley
from Germany, Ferenc Holuban from Hungary. Also I am bringing in the
original Blimp, who weighs 650 pounds. And da original Swedish Angel,
the ugliest man in da vorl—unless you count me in da ugly contest. Also the
Lady Angel, dis bald-headed broad. Now I am having for da nice pipple of
Denver on Friday night some of my new vuns. Like Big Splash Humphrey,
Ali Singh, Haystack Muldoon, Big Daddy Siki."

Pfefer himself was somewhat of a oddity. Having arrived in the United
States in 1921 as part of a Russian opera company, he swapped one kind of
drama for another and got involved in wrestling, a profession in which he
was known as the "Plotter from Pinsk," "the Smirker from Smolensk," and
"the Halitosis Kid," among other, less complimentary appellations. Pfefer
hailed from Warsaw and initially specialized in importing hulking Eastern

Figure 16.2. Jack Pfefer, wrestling manager extraordinaire, c. 1935. Reproduced from the
original photograph held by the Department of Special Collections of the Hesburgh
Libraries of the University of Notre Dame. Courtesy of the Jack Pfefer Collection, Rare
Books and Special Collections, Hesburgh Libraries of Notre Dame.

European grapplers. A player in the industry from the 1920s through the 1960s, Pfefer was probably best known for outing professional wrestling as a form of spectacle as opposed to pure sport. "I've never seen an honest wrestling bout in my twenty years in the game," he told Jack Miley in a 1938 *Collier's Magazine* interview, "Maybe there was one, but I wasn't there." When Pfefer's competitors tried to shut him out, he began to provide sports writers with the results of wrestling matches before they happened. For this, journalists loved him, but within his own industry he was regarded as the ultimate double-crosser.

Described as standing 5 feet tall with his hat on, wearing pants pulled up to his armpits and wielding an ivory-knobbed cane, Pfefer commanded one of the fiercest stables of professional wrestlers in the industry. A former pianist in a traveling Russian opera company, he loved the performative aspect of pro wrestling and was very much responsible for the promotion of the grotesque in the industry. "Freaks I love and they're my specialty. I am very proud of some of my monstrosities. You can't get a dollar with a normal-looking guy, no matter how good he can wrestle. Those birds with shaved, egg-shaped heads, handlebar moustaches, tattooed bodies, big stomachs—they're for me!" he explained.

Goldie Ahearn, another wrestling promoter of similar origins, concurred. Speaking to the *Washington Post* sports columnist Shirley Povich in 1941, he said, "I'm tallink you the poblic wants its rasslers should be ugly, und I am giving them ugly rasslers with two pair pants, yet. I am showing my mother-in-law a picture from the Swedish Angel and tallink her if she gets fresh I will invite him home to dinner, already. Myself, I am a toff guy but I look at the Angel and I haff a bad dream. Soch ogliness I did not see in the zoo, yet. It is vonderful." Reporters loved quoting promoters like Ahearn (whose real name was Isadore Goldstein) and Pfefer in Yiddish dialect. There was something about Yiddish and wrestling that went well together.

And many of the wrestlers themselves were either immigrants or came from Yiddish-speaking homes. Jewish toughs such as Harry "Jewish Bad Boy" Finkelstein, Abie "Hebrew Hercules" Coleman, and Max Krauser were mixing it up in rings across the country, sporting the Star of David on their trunks. Pfefer maintained multiple stables of ethnic wrestlers: Greeks, Russians, Poles, and Jews among them. Of all his ethnic giants, he was especially

Figure 16.3. Martin Levy's bar mitzvah picture, c. 1919. Courtesy of Liz Levy.

proud to have debuted Martin "the Blimp" Levy in 1937. At that time in professional wrestling, Levy was unique. Pfefer likened the 625-pound wrestler to
a wall. "Can you throw the wall? Can you pin the wall to the mat?" he asked.

Raised in Boston by immigrant parents, Levy was a big boy from early
on. He allegedly weighed 200 pounds at his bar mitzvah and was over 350
by the time he got to high school. He played football for a short time but
was asked to leave the team after falling on and breaking the legs of several
opposing linemen. In a 1946 *Washington Post* interview, Blimp described his
unusual dietary regimen: "Some mornings I eat a dozen eggs, and then again,
sometimes only two. Sometimes I eat six pounds of steak, and then I might
eat a pound." He also admitted to going on an occasional mashed potato
binge, which required a half bushel of spuds, two quarts of milk, and a pound
of butter.

Despite his massive bulk, the Blimp was surprisingly athletic, even nim-
ble, an example of a big boy who could really move. Paul Boesch, one of
the only wrestlers of the golden era of the 1930s and 1940s to pen a cogent
autobiography, wrote that his first impression of the Blimp was that he was
simply a pituitary case who won his matches by falling on his opponents,
immobilizing them with his enormity. That may be partly accurate. But
Boesch noted that the Blimp suspected that the other wrestlers considered
him a no-talent fat man, and one day in a locker room, he was challenged to

Figure 16.4. The Blimp is flexible. Source: "Special 'Turkey Stuffing' Section: The Fattest Wrestlers of Our Generation," *Sports Review Wrestling,* January 1990, pp. 27–28.

kick a small metal can which dangled from the ceiling about 6 feet off the ground. In an attempt to show off his athletic prowess, the Blimp gingerly approached the can, brought one of his monstrous, fleshy legs up high into the air and tapped the can with his foot. The other wrestlers were amazed because they couldn't do it themselves without falling on their asses. It became evident that Levy wasn't a run-of-the-mill morbidly obese wrestler: He had skill. He was, as his manager insisted, "a freak with class."

Outside the ring, the Blimp was said to have a voracious sexual appetite and he often regaled peers with stories of his conquests. Boesch described Levy as "a seething volcano of sexual passion," evidently some kind of Semitic Pantagruel. Although Levy's conquests were not elaborated upon (thankfully, perhaps), he married multiple times, usually women far younger than he. And like flies to honey, the ladies were all over the Blimp. In 1940, 24-year-old Juanita Thomas was so eager to hitch her wagon to the Blimp that she neglected to obtain a divorce from her previous husband or to inform her newly betrothed that she had even been married. This little fact came in handy

Figure 16.5. The Blimp and Tiny Wickham in court, 1945. Wire service photograph.

when, in 1945, she tried to squeeze alimony payments out of poor Mr. Levy. Moreover, he testified in court—after having been shoehorned into the witness stand—that little Ms. Thomas physically abused him. In the end, the court had mercy on the Blimp and ruled against Juanita. Back in the saddle a year later, he wed 18-year-old Charlotte Jones, a woman half his age, in the Dallas Sportatorium in front of 6,000 adoring fans.

Despite his courtroom victory and his sexual conquests, bad luck seemed to trail the Blimp. In 1946 the Connecticut State Athletic Commission revoked his license on the recommendation of physicians, who claimed he was in poor health. Even his manager opined that Levy was so fat that he would probably drop dead in the ring. But all was not lost; the Blimp could still wrestle abroad. In Malaysia a Singapore-based promoter lined up Harnam Singh, Son of Kong, and the 6'10" Da Ra Singh, among other famed South Asian behemoths, and offered the Blimp $2,000 plus travel expenses and accommodations. But perhaps the most attractive clause in his contract had to do with an unlimited supply of food to throw his weight around the subcontinent for six months.

Even though the Blimp endured his share of mockery, he was actually a pretty decent wrestler. He tended to lumber around the ring, but he nonethe-

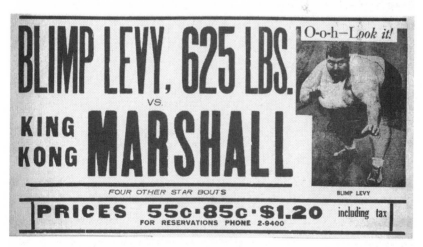

Figure 16.6. Detail of a poster featuring the Blimp vs. "King Kong" Marshall, c. 1940. Reproduced from the original poster held by the Department of Special Collections of the Hesburgh Libraries of the University of Notre Dame. Courtesy of the Jack Pfefer Collection, Rare Books and Special Collections, Hesburgh Libraries of Notre Dame.

less fought some major opponents and defeated such famous grapplers as Tor Johnson, the Swedish Angel, and Nature Boy Buddy Rogers, names familiar to anyone who followed the mat game in the 1940s and 1950s.

But by the end of his career in the early 1950s, the Blimp's health truly did begin to fail. Not surprisingly, the incidental exercise provided to him by his profession had helped to keep him somewhat trim. When he retired from the ring and dropped from sight, he really ballooned. Adding insult to injury, he was forcibly retired from wrestling because of his poor health and had no choice but to return to playing the fat man in the "World of Mirth" traveling circus.

On a somewhat less mirthful note, the Blimp weighed 900 pounds when he died at age 56 in the aptly named Sunset Motel in Prattsville, Alabama. By then he had a 120-inch waistline. Take ten steps, turn around and look at the spot where you started: that was the final measurement of Blimp Levy's waist. His massive corpse was brought by train back to Boston, where he was buried in a family plot.

It may not seem so, but in a certain time and place Levy was famous, world famous. He performed in front of thousands of people regularly, fans gasping upon seeing his blubbery mass as he lumbered up the steps into the wrestling ring. They howled when he did the splits or when he, quite literally, crushed an opponent. He was a major attraction that brought in legions of fans. But like many such characters who inhabit the liminal world between sport and entertainment in which abnormality is a virtue, the Blimp has been lost to history. With Jews of this magnitude so few and far between, it is a value simply to know of him.

CHAPTER 17

BAD RABBI

Bigamy, Blackmail, and the Radimner Rebbetzin

This is a quaint little story about a small-town Hasidic rabbi in Poland who, in 1923, left his wife and nine children to travel to New York, where he tricked a wealthy widow into paying him a large sum of money to marry him and then hightailed it back to the old country with the loot to live the Yiddish high life.

But maybe that's not the story. Perhaps it's about a slightly unhinged but crafty widow who tried to reach the highest echelon possible for a woman in traditional Jewish life—that of a rabbi's wife, or *rebbetzin*—by duping a naïve Hasidic rabbi who was visiting New York into marrying her for a cash reward.

And then it could also be that it's some combination of the two or, quite possibly, neither of them. Either way, in the early spring of 1927 readers of the Yiddish press in Poland were treated to a flood of daily reportage on a strange story of bigamy and blackmail between a Hasidic rebbe and a bombastic American woman. As the opening lines of many an article in the Yiddish papers once asked, "What's this all about?"

It all started when Shmuel Shapira,* also known as the Radimner Rebbe, decided to take a trip to New York in 1923. A descendant of the Dinov

---

* The spelling of the rebbe's last name had a number of variations in newspapers and other documents: Shapira, Shapiro, Spira, Szpira, and so on.

Hasidic dynasty, he was one of hundreds of small-town Hasidic rabbis who were scattered throughout interwar Poland. Based in Redem (Radymno in Polish; Radimne in the Yiddish papers, a hybrid created by journalists that evokes the Polish Radymno spoken with a Yiddish accent), a small town in southeastern Poland, he was a solid enough rebbe for a Jewish backwater but truly nothing spectacular on the rabbinic front. That he never published anything may or may not have been indicative of a lack of scholarly ability. More telling, perhaps, is that he didn't manage to inherit his father's post as the rebbe of the larger town of Lantzut—a job that went instead to his brother-in-law, Rabbi Khaym-Ruvn Vogshol, a fact that had to hurt, at least a little. Shapira may simply have lacked the charisma to make it as a big-time rebbe, or, for that matter, even a mediocre-time rebbe. So instead of attracting numerous followers and creating a big Hasidic court, he wound up ministering to the Jews of Redem, a Galician shtetl whose Jewish population hovered at about half of the grand total of the town (which was just a few thousand people). In other words, he was Hasidic small potatoes.

Situated on the main road that connected both Warsaw and Krakow with Lemberg (subsequently Lvov, currently Lviv), Redem was mainly a small market town, a spot where traveling merchants and traders stopped to buy and sell their wares. It wasn't a particularly rich town, and maintaining a Hasidic court there was not an easy business. As a result, the Radimner Rebbe did what most Hasidic rebbes did and relied on selling *kvitlekh* (blessings and queries) and accepting donations from his followers, a fiscal policy that, in small towns, tended to yield weak results. And with Poland in constant economic crisis, the rebbe decided that it would be a good idea to travel to New York to raise funds from fellow townspeople who had moved there and who were better off financially than his local congregation. By no means a spring chicken, the rebbe, who was older than 65 at the time, still had three unmarried daughters for whom he needed to provide dowries—in addition to having to maintain his Hasidic court. So in 1923 he traveled to Le Havre, where he boarded the S.S. *Rousillon*, a posh ship with a chapel and a theater—even third class had a nifty smoking lounge—for a ten-day journey to New York.

It is not entirely clear what the rebbe was up to during his stay in New York. The Yiddish press did not take note of his arrival, as they did when

European rabbis of note washed up on America's shores. While in New York, Shapira shifted between the homes of old acquaintances and distant relatives. Although there were active Hasidic communities in the New World, most Jewish immigrants were eager to take advantage of all of America's modern conveniences at the expense of maintaining more austere religious practices. Even if they did remain within the warm folds of traditional life, immigrants who had come even as little as five or ten years earlier were already culturally different from the Jews who had remained in Poland, most of whom had also hitched their wagons to modernity. But there was still enough of the Old World clinging to Poland's small towns to make New York look like a different planet.

The rebbe's sojourn in New York meandered for nearly two years, perhaps a result of a less than successful fundraising appeal. Or, possibly, a really good time. One wonders what Shapira did all day while he sponged off his landsmen. It's likely that he spent his days in one of the city's dozens of *shtiblekh* (small Hasidic synagogues) or in a *bes medresh* (a religious study hall), discussing the intricacies of talmudic legislation. Evenings were probably spent doling out advice and blessings to his *landslayt*, or fellow townspeople, in return for cold hard cash. He appears to have spent a fair amount of time with a distant relative in the Bronx by the name of Betsalel Rubin, who himself had emigrated from Redem around 1890. Rubin, who started out in America as a tailor and clothes presser, was by then in his 50s and had settled in a community of near middle-class Jewish strivers in the Bronx. One of millions of Jewish immigrants from Eastern Europe who seemingly made no mark on the world, virtually nothing is known about him.

About a year and a half into the rebbe's stay, Rubin expired from a coronary at the age of 56, a death that would set terribly strange events into motion, making him a kind of *presser ex machina*. Shortly after the shiva, the seven-day mourning period, Rubin's widow, Zlate, told the rebbe that he and his assistant could move into their large apartment and that she would move into the smaller one next door. It was considered a great honor to host the rebbe, and Zlate, despite officially being in mourning, was willing to do anything to accommodate the great sage from the old country. Out of a sense of duty, she helped out around the house, cleaning and cooking for the two scholars.

One day, seemingly out of the blue, Zlate approached the rebbe with an unusual suggestion: that the two of them get married. After all, she was now a widow, and what's more, she had inherited her dead husband's estate, which included some real estate and, apparently, tens of thousands of dollars. The rebbe was mildly flabbergasted and told Zlate that there was just no way. First of all, he already had a wife and nine children back in Poland. Second, on account of his advanced age, he wasn't much interested in women anymore.

Evidently a woman who did not like to take no for an answer, Zlate's first move was to accuse the rebbe of getting her pregnant. Her second move was to tell him not to worry—that the situation was under control because she had already gotten an abortion. Complicating matters, however, she claimed that the doctor who performed the procedure knew the identity of the father (she said that she had groaned "Oy, Shmuel" multiple times while under anesthesia) and, as a result, he demanded a payment of $11,000. Otherwise, he would go public with the news that the rebbe was Zlate's baby daddy. The good news was, she paid the doctor off. But, as far as she was concerned, Shapira could make good on this debt by making an honest woman out of her.

The rebbe was absolutely mortified. Here he was, a foreigner in New York with a limited command of English and no idea how to defend himself against this seemingly bizarre charge. Even if he hadn't knocked up Zlate, he had been living with the Rubins for at least a year—circumstantial evidence that could make it appear to outsiders that, just maybe, he and Zlate had been bumping uglies. Either the rebbe was paralyzed with fear or his grip on reality was somewhat weak. How could it be possible that a woman of her age could get pregnant? She had told him herself that she was 50, even though the reality was that she was already in her early 60s. At either age it's fairly astonishing that the rebbe thought anyone might actually believe the story.

Matters escalated quickly. The rebbe alleged that after he refused to make any kind of deal with Zlate, she pulled out a revolver and threatened to blow a hole in his Hasidic head if he didn't agree to step under the chuppah and marry her. It was under this pressure that he devised a neat compromise. He proposed to Zlate that if his wife back in Poland died, he would marry her and he even drew up a contract in Hebrew to seal the deal. Zlate, however, was illiterate and alleged that she was told that the contract was a promise to marry her if she paid him a certain sum of money. Despite the confusion, she chewed on this idea for a while, but it turned out it wasn't what she was looking for. She wanted to be a *rebbetzin*, the wife of a rabbi. And she was willing to pay to become one.

One complication was the fact that the rebbe had served as the executor of Zlate's dead husband's will, so he knew exactly what she was worth. Zlate claimed that after estate matters were settled, the rebbe asked *her* to marry *him*. The rebbe said this was a lie, but he also subsequently admitted to having accepted cash gifts from her during the mourning period in the wake of her husband's demise.

The rebbe, as we know, needed money. And Zlate wanted a rabbinic husband. In the end a plan was hatched for the two to get married in a civil ceremony, a procedure that the rebbe did not see as legitimate in any way but which satisfied Zlate's desire to marry a rabbi and become a card-carrying *rebbetzin*. In return, the rebbe would get a pile of cash.

At the time, it seemed like a good compromise: Zlate would fulfill her wish to become a rabbi's wife and the rebbe could return to Poland with a windfall. So on June 25, 1925, Zlate Rubin and Shmuel Shapira, the Radimner Rebbe, were married in a courtroom in the Bronx. According to the marriage certificate, both had been widowed and both were entering their second marriage. The rebbe was clearly lying about both aspects, but Zlate also lied about her age, which is listed as 50, giving her a backward leap of at least a ten years.

Zlate was finally a *rebbetzin* and, what's more, the wife of a small-time but sort of esteemed rebbe from a genuine Hasidic dynasty. For his part in the charade, the rebbe got a heap of cash, allegedly $16,000, which in 1925 was not small potatoes, especially for someone from a poor town in Eastern Europe.

Shortly after the ceremony the rebbe hightailed it back to Poland with the loot. Great success: His trip to America yielded a sum that would not only help him pay the dowries of his three unmarried daughters but also run his court in style. Upon his return, he assumed his usual activities and attempted to forget about the whole sordid episode. He also, apparently, didn't bother to tell anyone about his little matrimonial escapade. But, as the saying goes, it's tough to be a Jew. Sometimes it's tough to be a Hasidic rebbe. In

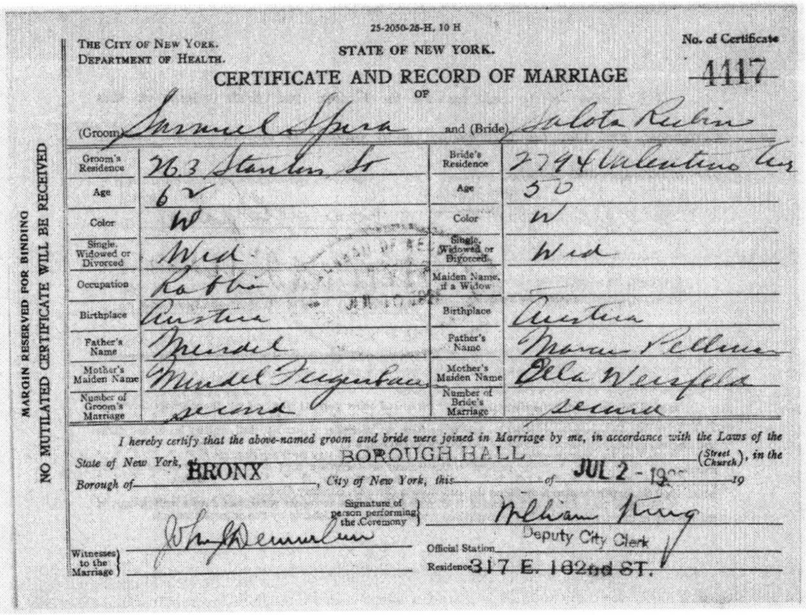

25-2050-25-H, 10 H

THE CITY OF NEW YORK.
DEPARTMENT OF HEALTH.

STATE OF NEW YORK.

No. of Certificate 4417

CERTIFICATE AND RECORD OF MARRIAGE
OF

(Groom) Samuel Spira and (Bride) Salota Rubin

MARGIN RESERVED FOR BINDING
NO MUTILATED CERTIFICATE WILL BE RECEIVED

Groom's Residence	163 Stanton St	Bride's Residence	2794 Valentine Av
Age	62	Age	50
Color	W	Color	W
Single, Widowed or Divorced	Wid	Single, Widowed or Divorced	Wid
Occupation	Rabbi	Maiden Name, if a Widow	
Birthplace	Austria	Birthplace	Austria
Father's Name	Mendel	Father's Name	Marcus Pellman
Mother's Maiden Name	Mendel Feigenbaum	Mother's Maiden Name	Ella Weisfeld
Number of Groom's Marriage	second	Number of Bride's Marriage	second

I hereby certify that the above-named groom and bride were joined in Marriage by me, in accordance with the Laws of the State of New York, BOROUGH HALL (Street / Church), *in the Borough of* BRONX, *City of New York, this* JUL 2 - 19 *of* 19

Signature of person performing the Ceremony: William King
Deputy City Clerk

Witnesses to the Marriage: John J Demmler

Official Station

Residence 317 E. 182nd ST.

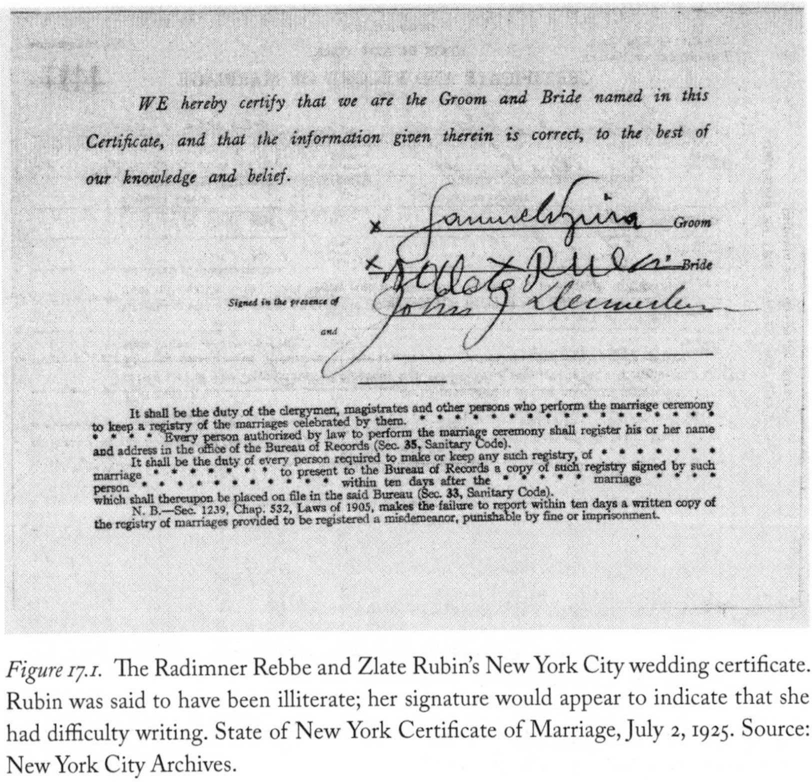

WE hereby certify that we are the Groom and Bride named in this Certificate, and that the information given therein is correct, to the best of our knowledge and belief.

x Samuel Spira Groom

x Zlote x Rubin Bride

Signed in the presence of John J Demmler

and

It shall be the duty of the clergymen, magistrates and other persons who perform the marriage ceremony to keep a registry of the marriages celebrated by them.

Every person authorized by law to perform the marriage ceremony shall register his or her name and address in the office of the Bureau of Records (Sec. 35, Sanitary Code).

It shall be the duty of every person required to make or keep any such registry, of marriage to present to the Bureau of Records a copy of such registry signed by such person within ten days after the marriage which shall thereupon be placed on file in the said Bureau (Sec. 33, Sanitary Code).

N. B.—Sec. 1239, Chap. 532, Laws of 1905, makes the failure to report within ten days a written copy of the registry of marriages provided to be registered a misdemeanor, punishable by fine or imprisonment.

Figure 17.1. The Radimner Rebbe and Zlate Rubin's New York City wedding certificate. Rubin was said to have been illiterate; her signature would appear to indicate that she had difficulty writing. State of New York Certificate of Marriage, July 2, 1925. Source: New York City Archives.

this case, however, everyone seemed to wind up with what they wanted. For a while, anyway.

Then the letters began arriving. It turned out that Zlate was simply not satisfied with the deal they cut and decided that she wanted to marry the rebbe in a genuine Jewish wedding with all the trimmings. Among the missives she sent was one that claimed he had impregnated her just before he left for Poland and that she had given birth to a boy. Included was the baby's photograph, in addition to the bonus prize of a bloody wad of cotton containing a small blob of dead skin, allegedly a souvenir from the boy's bris. A subsequent letter included a packet of pills for the current *rebbetzin* to take and a message to the rebbe to put up a tombstone for her.

Figure 17.2. Zlate and the rebbe's alleged baby. Source: *Moment, March 8,* 1927. Courtesy of the YIVO Institute for Jewish Research.

Although clearly unpleasant, this long-distance postal harassment was nonetheless tolerable, and the rebbe burned the letters as fast as they arrived. But in the late summer of 1926, Zlate Rubin suddenly appeared in the flesh at the rebbe's house in Redem. She confronted him and demanded that he divorce his wife and marry her in a real Jewish ceremony, either that or he would have to return the money she gave him. If he didn't, she said she would walk right into the sanctuary of the town's biggest synagogue on Saturday morning and start singing. The rebbe freaked. He had apparently already spent a fair portion of the money. He did have some left, though, and he began to give it back to her in dribs and drabs.

But the money didn't come fast enough for Zlate and she kept demanding more, and faster. In lieu of cash, the rebbe gave her his wife's and his daughters' jewelry. He also got some of his relatives to try to broker a deal, but that didn't work out either. They tried to find a man who would marry her, but it was also to no avail. With nowhere to turn, the rebbe secured the services of an attorney, who promptly had Zlate arrested for blackmail and extortion. But Zlate was also no dummy: She lawyered up from the confines of her jail cell and had the rebbe charged with bigamy. Though charged with a crime, the rebbe managed to stay out of the clink and remained under a kind of Hasidic house arrest in Radimne.

Zlate was incarcerated for about six months in Pshemishl (Przemysl), the nearest big city to Radimne, which was so small it didn't have either a jail or a courthouse. During this time, an investigation ensued in preparation for a trial. Zlate's trial began on February 28, 1927, in a courtroom packed to the rafters. The Yiddish daily *Moment* described the crowd as "an army of women" who not only filled the gallery but also jammed themselves into the benches reserved for journalists. The atmosphere was described as dank and stifling, with the attorneys dripping sweat even at the tail end of a frigid Polish winter.

After the charges against her—blackmail and extortion—were read, Zlate was permitted to make a statement. In it she described her tragic life. Born in the shtetl of Nay Santsh to a poor family, she was married off at age 15 to the shtetl water carrier, a man by the name of Shmuel Krops, who was probably one rung above the village idiot. The marriage lasted about a week. At age 22, Zlate was married again to one Shaul Adler, a well-off horse trader from Bukovina. The two left Poland for America but eventually split because Adler couldn't get her pregnant. Using the $4,000 she received in the settlement as a personal dowry, she married Betsalel Rubin and together they used the money to invest in real estate. Rubin couldn't get her pregnant either, but things seemed to go reasonably well until Rubin bit the dust during the rebbe's visit.

Zlate's testimony took place in a strange mix of Yiddish, English, and a smattering of Polish, all of which had to be translated by her attorneys. Despite the linguistic mishmash, she managed to keep the courtroom riveted with her description of how she came to marry the Radimner Rebbe after losing her third husband and how she gave birth to his child. Her testimony was feverish and, as one reporter described it, came "streaming out of her mouth like burning hot lava from a volcano."

In spite of her intensity, not everything she said was taken with great seriousness. In particular, her insistence that she gave birth at the age of 50 was met with no small amount of incredulity. That she was actually 63 years old rendered the idea absurd, and her persistent attestations to having become a mother at such an overripe age were met with a fair amount of ridicule in the courtroom. Zlate doubtlessly realized this, but, in for a penny, in for a pound, she reached into her purse during her opening statement and pulled out a glass breast pump. Thrusting it into the air, she screamed, "Here it is! Look at the pump I used before my child died!" Needless to say, this gesture did not elicit the empathetic response she'd intended. Instead, the courtroom exploded with laughter.

After the atmosphere calmed a bit, Zlate completed her statement and the trial began in earnest. The lead judge on the panel of three asked if she understood that she had been "accused of the serious crime of extorting a clergy member and blackening his good name?" This time it was her turn to burst out laughing. The judge scolded her and asked that she refrain from laughing at his questions. "But I'm innocent," she responded coyly, a comment that brought forth even more snickering.

The judges spent much of the trial's first day grilling Zlate about her relationship with the rebbe. According to her, the story began when the rebbe drew up a will for her ailing husband, Betsalel Rubin. On his deathbed, Rubin had asked that the rebbe to take care of his wife after he passed. In subsequent testimony the rebbe corroborated this, saying, "I figured that, as a rabbi, I felt I could promise her husband that I could advise her after his death. After all, she was already 56 and had a glass eye." For her part, Zlate claimed that in the moments following her husband's death, the rebbe tried to molest her. What's worse, it was while the man's corpse was still lying on the floor of the apartment. She said she pushed him away so hard he fell on the body. "I'll swear on a Torah that I never touched her," was the rebbe's response.

Zlate's testimony took the better part of two days, and she more or less ruled the roost. Showing up in a sumptuous fur coat and wearing thick, plastic "American" glasses, she howled at the prosecution and constantly interrupted the judges. She played to the journalists assembled to cover the story, commenting directly to them when she felt it necessary. She also struck poses for the courtroom photographers. "Zlate conquered the courtroom, the judges, and the attorneys as only a brilliant actress could," was one of the assessments of her performance during the early days of the trial.

דער ראדימנער רבי.

Figure 17.3. The Radimner Rebbe, Shmuel Shapira. Source: *Moment*, March 1, 1927. Courtesy of the YIVO Institute for Jewish Research.

זלאטא רובין

Figure 17.4. Zlate in court. Source: *Moment*, March 2, 1927.

Another Yiddish journalistic assessment was that she was a modern in-
carnation of Brayndele Cossack, an early Yiddish theater character, a brash,
snarling female archetype from the traditional Jewish shtetl. A stock character in Eastern European Jewish life, *Brayndele Kozak* referenced a particular
kind of woman who, in a deeply patriarchal society, kicked ass and took
names. Essentially a female Jewish Cossack, she was named after a violent
regional military and political figure that struck fear into the hearts of Jews.
Brayndele Kozak was tough as nails, stood her ground, and fought and got
what she thought she deserved.

The term became a colloquialism, and when Yiddish speakers referred
to a woman as a Brayndele Cossack, they were talking about a woman who
was to be feared and respected but also denigrated as a *klafte*, a crazy bitch.
She wasn't an *eyshes-khayl*, a proper, dignified woman who knew her place
and did the right thing, but someone who mainly looked out for herself.

The original *Brayndele Kozak* was the main character of an eponymous 1887 play by Avrom Goldfaden in which Brayndele was married six times, all to weak-willed men driven to suicide by way of her heavy-handed antics. But life imitates art and every shtetl had its own real Brayndele.

Describing the phenomenon in the March 18, 1927, edition of *Moment*, journalist Yosef Heftman wrote:

> She is like the "Brayndele Cossack" from times gone by; the type of Brayndl who set the shtetl shaking, who, when she turned the screw and started in with her unique vulgarities, sent everyone packing. But this Brayndl has evolved and progressed. She's been emancipated. The Brayndl of the past has been civilized, become modern, traveled the world, and has lived in America—and therefore she is much more dangerous.
>
> The Brayndl Cossack of the past spoke differently: Her lips were blue and she had bits of spittle sitting in the corners of her mouth. And when her little lips began to speak, the world around them was inflamed. Brayndl's eyes shot out fire, her wig went askew, and her whole face was twisted. Today's Brayndl—Zlate Rubin—speaks in a more refined manner; she has a pair of slightly thicker lips that maybe have a touch of lipstick; she wears glasses and supports her case with documents, official pronouncements, and photographic evidence. The way she speaks also isn't like the Brayndls of old; she speaks ten times more, and it may be here that we see the progress of this woman of valor. The Jewish female Cossack of the past babbled pathetically with such a feverish intensity that the head of steam she produced caused her to become hoarse and tired, and she thus would have to depart the battlefield; the modern Brayndl Cossack can talk for 24 hours without getting tired and not exhausting her listeners either. Modern Brayndl throws in some spicy language, tells a story from the bedroom, stunning every man in the room, making them swallow mouthfuls of spit. . . . Today's Brayndls feel their power . . . and all of us male bystanders should pay attention. Brayndele Cossack has been weaponized.

It bears mentioning here that many of the journalists of the Yiddish press, although they relished the opportunity to report and comment on such a sensational story, stood pretty firmly in the corner of the rebbe. As a result, the reportage is generally skewed against Zlate. This probably has something to do with the fact that, although she was born in Poland, she was considered a foreigner, an American, and she had dug her claws into a local. Reporters who went to Redem to interview the townspeople found that even those who didn't like the rebbe at all, those from heavily politicized secular youth groups—the diametric sociopolitical opposite of the Hasidim—also wanted him to win the suit.

When the rebbe showed up to give his testimony on the second day of the trial, he arrived with a phalanx of Hasidim who filled the courtroom behind him. He first took the stand to be put under oath, but one of Zlate's lawyers protested, saying that a man who married two women couldn't be trusted, even under oath. As a result, the rebbe testified without actually being sworn in. Just before he began to speak, he shot Zlate an angry look of bitter hatred.

The rebbe was first questioned about the nature of his trip to New York and what he did there. "To serve as a rabbi and to earn some money," he said. He was asked if he ever slept over at Zlate's apartment. He said no and that, in fact, he was only in her apartment a few times and was always with his assistant.

"Shmulke, tell the truth!" Zlate shouted.

The rebbe responded, "With God as my witness, I am innocent."

Zlate refused to take it sitting down and screamed, "You liar!"

Trying to get to the bottom of it, the prosecutor asked why he had gotten involved with Zlate in the first place. The rebbe said that after her husband died, Zlate invited him to stay in her apartment and that she would move next door. In fact, she helped cook and clean for him and his assistant. Cutting quickly to the chase, the prosecutor asked why Zlate had a marriage contract with his name and signature on it. The rebbe responded that she tormented him with the idea of getting married even though he told her he couldn't because he was already married. He claimed Zlate offered to pay his real wife a separation fee and that later on, she claimed to be pregnant by him and if he didn't marry her, she'd blacken his name.

The prosecutor asked flat out, "Why didn't you just spit in her face?"

"I wanted to prevent a scandal," said the rebbe. "She was saying all kinds of things. Later on she told me she got an abortion that cost $11,000 and demanded that I pay her for it. At the same time, she said that, during the abortion while she was under sedation, the doctor heard her murmur, 'Shmuel.' When she came to me afterward, she showed up with the doctor, who knew who I was and where I lived. I saw that all was lost and begged her with tears in my eyes to leave me be," sobbed the rebbe.

"I should go blind if he's not lying," screamed Zlate.

"I couldn't get her to leave me alone," said the rebbe. "In the end," he said, "she threatened to shoot me if I didn't marry her."

And so he went through with it. As the rebbe sat on the stand telling his tale of woe, Zlate punctuated his testimony with screams of "liar" and "thief." It got so bad that the judges threatened to throw her out and jail her for contempt.

By the fourth day of the trial, the rebbe was still on the stand being peppered with questions. He explained how in the aftermath of his departure from New York, Zlate sent him a stream of letters among which were the aforementioned missives containing a bloodied foreskin and pills for his wife to take with a special note to put up a nice tombstone for her.

Inexplicably, one of the judges on the panel of three expressed an abiding interest in the breast pump that had appeared on the first day and asked the rebbe if he had seen it. Amazingly, the story had legs—short ones, but legs nonetheless. "She didn't show it to me," the rebbe responded, "although she told me that 'Goldstein,' a friend of mine in New York, accidentally saw her extracting milk from her breasts and, as a result, she had to tell him the whole story—that she allegedly gave birth to my child. Goldstein, in fact, wrote me a letter saying that Zlate purposely wanted to show him that she was still lactating but that he quickly turned away because he didn't want to see. When he turned back [after he was sure she had finished], she handed him a glass of milk that she allegedly extracted." The courtroom exploded with laughter.

Amid the absurdity of some of the testimony were also many severe, serious moments. Neither the judges, the prosecutor, nor the defense attorneys could seem to figure out the rebbe's rationale for having gone through with the civil marriage. He said repeatedly that he wanted to prevent a scandal.

"Among the Jews there are two kinds of death: moral death and physical death," the rebbe attempted to explain to the court. "A moral death is worse because it remains a stain on one's children and their children. One word from Zlate Rubin would have been a moral death for me."

It wasn't clear how many moral deaths the rebbe could die, but his on-going attempts to "prevent scandal" simply amped up the affair until it reached intolerable levels. The effects on him and his family were devastating.

Among the things the rebbe admitted doing under duress was having signed a contract with Zlate stating that if his current wife died, he would marry her. He said he had to act the part, to "make sure she remained pleased"; otherwise, he feared she might have him iced. Another of his admissions on the stand was an emphatic no when asked by Zlate's attorney if he ever "got close" to her. But when asked if she ever "got close" to him, he said, "I can't take responsibility for that. I won't say no." Although he clearly stated that he never initiated anything with Zlate, he seemed to admit that a Zlate-initiated hookup of some kind may have actually taken place.

The defense saw an opening here but tried a bit too hard to pry it open. "Which is a bigger disgrace," asked Dr. Frim, one of Zlate's attorneys, "to produce a bastard, or to be a bigamist?" On tenterhooks, the gallery eagerly awaited an answer to this provocative question, but the prosecutor immediately asked to have it tabled, and it was.

At this point, Zlate returned to the stand. "Rebbe Shapira testified that he never even came close to you," said the prosecutor. "Is that the truth?" As she delivered her response, claiming that "Jews on the street are saying that the rebbe swore falsely in court, claiming he never got close to me," she began to move about in her chair, eventually standing up and roaming around the courtroom. Screaming her testimony in a long crescendo, she began to move in the direction of the rebbe. As her shrill voice surged and peaked, she lunged at the rebbe and tried to grab him. She didn't manage to get ahold of him, but he was forced to hide under a table until things calmed down enough for her to restart her testimony. The gallery went wild.

As may be evident, Zlate's antics in court often did not help her case. Taking advantage of her mercurial behavior, the rebbe's attorneys continued their full court press to discredit her. Among the documents they produced was a notarized letter from New York written by one Rivka Unger, who claimed that Zlate was well known in New York as a blackmailer and had pulled a similar stunt on Unger's father thirty years earlier, claiming she'd had a child out of wedlock with him. How they found Unger is unknown. Another letter came from one Meylekh Zilberman, the man in New York who wrote Zlate's letters for her (she was illiterate). He chimed in with a note that Zlate had also asked him to marry her and even offered his wife $4,000 to take a hike.

Seeing the danger for his client, Dr. Peiper, one of Zlate's attorneys, suddenly requested that Zlate deliver a portion of her testimony behind closed doors. Why, asked the court. She intends on describing a variety of marks on the rebbe's body in addition to those on his male organ. The courtroom convulsed and nearly burst. Exasperated, the judges demurred and decided to call it a day.

As the next day's session was about to commence, the judges received an urgent letter from the head of the Pshemishl courthouse informing them that, because of the excessive number of people in the courtroom, the ceiling of the room below theirs was sagging heavily and was in danger of collapse. To the chagrin of the spectators, the judges were forced to limit the number of people in the gallery.

After a portion of the horde was excised from the courtroom, proceedings continued. Subsequent testimony included that of two of the rebbe's sons-in-law, Rabbi Zalmen Yehuda Halberstam of Nay-Sandz and Mendel Klingberg of Krakow, both scions of famous Hasidic dynasties, who had been drafted into a number of failed schemes to try do something with their in-law's Zlate problem.

Figure 17.5. Lawyers and judges serving on the Zlate Rubin trial. Source: *Moment,* March 9, 1927. Courtesy of the YIVO Institute for Jewish Research.

Both men explained that the rebbe and his family wanted Zlate out of Radimne. At the time, she was still demanding that the rebbe divorce his wife and marry her in a fully Jewish ceremony. Either that, or he had to fork over the money she had given him in America. Desperate to get her out of town, where she continually threatened to go public with all the sordid details—real and imagined—she was promised a meeting with the rebbe, but only in Krakow, which was about an hour away by train. She was convinced to go there with Dovid Weiss, a friend of both Halberstam and Klingberg. Weiss was also a kind of reluctant insider whose father-in-law was Zlate's brother and whose family she had visited in the nearby town of Oshpitzin.

Although Zlate was mainly focused on her relationship with the rebbe, she also seemed open to other options. According to a number of these and other witnesses, Zlate was desperate to get married, mainly to a rabbi or talmudic scholar, but almost anyone would do. Well aware of this, the rebbe and his circle tried to find a match for her. If they succeeded, they would finally be rid of her. So the rebbe and his family did what they could to make her a match. One of these ill-fated potential mates, a man named Avrom Dominik, who lived in a small village not far from Radimne, wound up on the stand.

Dominik, a widower, explained that the rebbe's daughters approached him with a potential mate who, they claimed, was a relative from America. In interwar Poland the phrase "relative from America" was Yiddish code for "cash money" and even though 62-year-old Dominik said that he wasn't initially interested in marrying anyone, he took the bait and decided to go to Radimne and meet Zlate. Miracle of miracles, it turned out they liked each other and, after a few dates, they decided to get hitched. Zlate, however, already had a trip planned to go to the famed mineral baths in Marienbad, so a wedding would have to wait a few weeks. But stoking the fire just before she left, Dominik said she approached him and stroked his beard, saying, "You'll see, Avromtshe, baby—we'll have some children yet."

Shortly after Zlate left for Marienbad, Dominik happened to meet the rebbe in the ritual bath. The rebbe asked how things were going. Dominik told him he hadn't heard from Zlate for a few weeks, but, as far as he knew, the wedding was still on. And when Zlate returned a few weeks later, Dominik told the court things were hot and heavy. But Zlate couldn't shake her obsession with the rebbe and the arrangement with Dominik fell apart shortly thereafter. Just when the rebbe thought he was out, she pulled him back in.

Throughout the months that Zlate Rubin could be found perambulating in southeastern Poland, the rebbe and his extended family tried whatever they could to mollify her. Shuttling between Radimne and Krakow, both the rebbe and his family tried to make various deals with Zlate to keep the story out of the papers. They gave her a silver box and two valuable strands of pearls. Zlate countered with an offer to the rebbe's wife, Rokhl, that if she'd pack up and leave for Palestine, an extra $4,000 would be deposited in the family's coffers, but she refused. Zlate later told the rebbe he could make the whole sordid thing go away by giving her $4,000. But when they all met in Krakow to seal the deal, Zlate jacked up the price another $1,000 and swore on a mezuzah that she wouldn't take a dime less than $5,000 to pack it up and go back to America. The rebbe and his family were completely exasperated by these antics. It was at that point that the rebbe and his family called a lawyer, who had Zlate arrested for blackmail and extortion—and the moment that marks the beginning of the legal saga of Zlate the *rebbetzin*.

As is evident, the trial riveted Yiddish newspaper readers and was the major story for Poland's Jews during the early spring of 1927. All the Yiddish dailies carried full-page reports from the trial, and as it got heated, even the Polish-language papers took up the story. As noted, most of the Yiddish press was biased in favor of the rebbe, but some papers took the opposite tack. Lemberg's morning paper, the aptly named *Morgn*, published wild rumors about the affair, among them one about a secret midnight make-out session between the rebbe and Zlate in the lobby of Radimne's one little hotel. This charge was so serious that the hotel's owner was sworn in as a witness to testify that yes, Zlate and the rebbe met in the hotel but that, no, there was no sucking of rabbinic face.

Sensationalism was the order of the day, and lawyers from both sides got in on the act as well. The rebbe's team tried to call a mysterious witness by the name of Pinkhes Luks who would swear that Zlate Rubin not only once ran a whorehouse but also had previously been arrested for similar fake civil marriage and unborn child scams. Luks, however, never materialized. But that didn't stop the lawyers from talking about the issues in court. Anything was done to try to blacken Zlate's name.

The Yiddish press was having a field day. Everyone from humorists to serious commentators wanted to chime in on the Zlate Rubin case. *Moment* sent a special correspondent, Leon Karpovski, to do the heavy journalistic lifting on the case. *Haynt*, whose reportage had multiple authors, peppered its articles with sensationalistic subheadings throughout its pages of text:

"I WON'T ANSWER THAT *SHEYGETS!*"

"WITH GOD AS MY WITNESS, I AM INNOCENT!"

"THE REBBE AGAIN BURSTS INTO TEARS!"

"SHMULIK YOU'RE A COSSACK!"

"NOT JUST ONE KISS, BUT MANY!"

And so on and so forth. The Friday humor sections were full of Zlate poems, dialogues, and cartoons.

Warsaw's Rabbinate, the seat of Jewish Poland's religious establishment, even saw fit to discuss the trial during an official meeting. Some of the rabbis defended the rebbe, saying anyone could be tricked in such a way. Others agreed but also argued that there was clearly some rabbinic monkey busi-

Figure 17.6. An American rabbi trap with Zlate as the bait. Source: *Haynt*, March 11, 1927. Courtesy of the YIVO Institute for Jewish Research.

Figure 17.7. The rebbe being offered to Zlate as a Purim holiday gift. Source: *Shalekh mones*, March 1927. Courtesy of the YIVO Institute for Jewish Research.

ness going on. Rabbi Ritshevol, one of the Rabbinate's leading figures, did not mince words and said that, based on the fact that he participated in the civil wedding ceremony, the Radimner Rebbe must be an idiot: "Was he really powerless against the threats of Zlate Rubin? He had many friends in America. It would have been sufficient had he simply told them. They would have helped him free himself from her grip."

Echoing the basic sensibility of the Rabbinate, popular religious columnist Hillel Tseytlen lamented, "Never in the history of the Jewish settlement in Poland have we lived through such a shameful episode as the trial that is now taking place between the Radimner Rebbe and Mrs. Zlate Rubin. This trial has shrouded us in shame. Where are we headed? What has happened to our leaders and our religious figures? A strange entanglement: a woman who mostly speaks obscenity in front of the judges and the public."

The daily newspaper *Moment* even sent in the humorist Bontshe (Yosef-Shimen Goldshteyn) to lighten the mood with comic descriptions of the trial.

> The gallery was full of women and girls. It's a good time: They sit and eat candy, even dinner—and they drink straight from the bottle. You could easily forget that you're not actually in court, but at the Azazel Cabaret watching a skit in rich Galitsianer Yiddish dialect with its "ekh" and "mekh" all translated into "their language" for the judges. The judges have learned a lot about (Jewish) women's issues and try to say "khipe" [wedding canopy], but it comes out "kipa," "shipa," and almost "glipa." All the while, the "Rebbetzin" groans. It's a bitter scene, though one cannot help but laugh.

Bontshe's comment about cabaret would turn out to be prophetic. In the months following the end of the trial, Warsaw's Sambatyen Cabaret did in fact perform a hit musical comedy titled *Zlate the Rebbetzin*, in which the scandal was set to music.

Figure 17.8. Advertisement for the cabaret show *Zlate the Rebbetzin*. Source: *Zlate the Rebbetzin, Moment,* March 18, 1927. Courtesy of the YIVO Institute for Jewish Research.

But for those involved, the trial was no comedy. After seven days of testimony and deliberation, everyone was exhausted and the press was reporting that Zlate was expected to go down in flames. But no one really knew what the outcome would be. The atmosphere was electric during the final day of the trial. The courtroom was packed, and thousands of people waited outside the building to hear the verdict.

The rebbe's attorney began his closing statement by asking that the court view the rebbe simply as a person who had been blackmailed, not as a rabbi. "I have no interest in presenting the rebbe as being completely innocent. He is guilty of allowing Zlate Rubin to have dragged him into a swamp from which she could blackmail him," he said.

He then summarized all of what he called, "Rubin's lies": $11,000 for an abortion; an invitation from the rebbe to come to Radimne; giving birth to the rebbe's child. In tragic detail he described the web of lies she created: fake photographs of her posing with the rebbe, the letters he allegedly sent to her, the breast pump. He closed by explaining her insane desire to become a *rebbetzin*, the highest peak a woman could reach in traditional Jewish life, one that she could attain only by marrying a rabbi. She didn't care which one or even that he may have already been married. Finally, he asked that the court find her guilty of blackmail and extortion.

The closing statement of the defense tried to turn the tables, portraying Zlate as the victim while castigating the rebbe.

> I stand here to defend, not a demon, as the prosecutor has characterized Zlate Rubin, but an elderly, sick, and lonely woman who came to Poland not to blackmail anyone but to demand her rights. Rebbe Shapira has been idealized for no reason. He admitted here that he went to America to make money. This old rabbi went abroad not to serve God but to serve the golden calf. His relationship to Zlate was not created with pure intentions. He began taking her money from the beginning. I don't know who here is the demon, Zlate or the rebbe, who made his plans to get her money while her husband was still on his deathbed. It's not possible to characterize him as an idealist or a holy man. It is simply foolish to believe that Zlate Rubin, a wealthy woman, came to Poland to extort money from a poor rebbe. Zlate Rubin has enough money that she doesn't need to extort money from an impoverished rabbi from Radimne.

ראָס בילד פֿון רבי און "רביצין", וואָס איז צוזאמענגעשטעלם געוואָ*
רען פֿון 2 בעזונדערע פֿאָטאָגראַפֿיעס.

Figure 17.9. Doctored photograph showing Zlate and the rebbe posing together. Source: *Moment*, March 3, 1927. Courtesy of the YIVO Institute for Jewish Research.

The words of the defense hung in the air. To break the tension, the judges decided to let everyone cool down and announced that they would wait until the following day to proffer their decision, disappointing the thousands who had gathered outside the courthouse and leaving all of Jewish Poland in deep suspense.

So embittered was the rebbe that he didn't even bother to show up the next day to hear the verdict. He had evidently had enough. The only family member to appear was his youngest daughter, who was there to "hopefully" bring good news back to the family. By the time she arrived, the corridors of the courthouse were thick with people. Public interest was at its peak and the mood was one of nervous anticipation. The defense attorneys were also milling about in the corridors of the courthouse. They also seemed nervous.

At 11:30 a.m. the doors to Courtroom 26 were opened and the public was allowed to enter. There was no room to sit. The room was so packed that people could barely breathe. The gallery apparently included a number of Christians who had become interested in the circus of a case. According to press reports, they sided with Zlate and were participating in the large number of betting pools in which huge sums had been bet that she would be found innocent. Jews, who were mainly in the anti-Zlate camp, had placed their bets on the rebbe.

The lead judge stood to read the verdict, but someone suddenly noticed that Zlate was nowhere to be found. He stopped and waited while the corridors and bathrooms were searched. She was finally discovered wandering in a hallway and brought in. The judge continued.

> In the name of the Polish Republic, the 63-year-old American citizen, Zlate Rubin, is found guilty of paragraph 98, line b, and is hereby sentenced according to article 100, line 2, for threatening Rebbe Shapira and his entire family in Radimne and in other locations in Poland, and for extortion. In consideration of the standing of Rebbe Shapira and his family and the danger that these threats of extortion posed to his entire family, Zlate Rubin is sentenced to six months in a high-security prison with one day per month laying on a hard board and fasting. The six months she already served in prison will be taken into account. In addition, Zlate Rubin must return $1,035, six strands of pearls, and the silver box that she extorted. She must also pay 1,450 zlotys in court charges, after which she will be deported to America.

When the words "Zlate Rubin is found guilty" were read, Zlate began weeping quietly. But she quickly fell into convulsive hysterics, screaming that she was innocent.

The news arrived quickly to the rebbe's court in Radimne, where there was much rejoicing. Even the rebbe's enemies were happy for him. Well, most of them, anyway. A member of a socialist youth group handed the rebbe an invitation to their Purim dance and asked him to deliver it to Zlate.

One would think the verdict would have completely shattered Zlate. Perhaps she was cheered by the fact that she was not actually going to have to go to jail thanks to time served. Only a week after her debacle ended, she was still in action and showed up in nearby Lemberg trying to find a rabbi who would force the rebbe to give her a *get*, an official Jewish writ of divorce. But she was recognized as soon as she hit the street and was surrounded by enormous crowds that cursed and baited her and even threatened violence. She tried, under police guard, to go to the offices of Lemberg's chief rabbi, Leybele Broyde, but he refused to see her. Other rabbis shut her down as well. In the end, the police brought her back to her hotel, where crowds broke the doors down trying to get to her. An entire police battalion was required to break it all up. The police demanded that she leave town and forced her into a car that delivered her to the train station, from which she was returned to Pshemishl. Humiliated by the verdict and without much leverage, she nonetheless milled about the area for a few weeks, finally announcing through her attorney that she was abandoning the bigamy suit against the rebbe. She left Poland on a train for Berlin and then to Hamburg. From there she returned to New York, where she disappeared into the largest Jewish city in the world.

But Zlate had made her mark. And even though it may have been an ugly one, she lived on as an example of a strange new media phenomenon: a self-propelled sensation triggered by personal tragedy. Powered by sheer hubris, she was a perfect match for the press, which created characters like Zlate in order to fulminate against them. She was an early example of someone who both exploited the media and who was exploited by it. For journalists and readers she was a natural performer, and the whirlwind of a Yiddish drama she created was a welcome respite from the regular affairs of Polish Jewry: high taxes, unemployment, poverty, messy politics, and social exclusion.

Although she appears to have been mentally unhinged, Zlate Rubin nonetheless represents a long-standing problem of female Jewish dreams deferred. Without access to real agency or power, women like Zlate had little choice but to choose alternative and sometimes unsavory means to try to get any modicum of power whatsoever. Although Zlate may have initially burned brightly, she was eventually extinguished into shame and failure, particularly in light of the fact that the trial transpired on foreign turf. But given other circumstances, it really could have been the other way around, with Zlate coming out on top and the rebbe being strung up for bigamy.

In a way, *Moment* columnist Yosef Heftman had it right: Traditional Jewish life did have something to fear from women exerting their rights. Zlate may not have been the best representative, but her intensity and aggressiveness certainly achieved something women of the day were not supposed to.

Long live Brayndele Cossack.

CHAPTER 18

YOU THINK YOU'VE GOT TROUBLES?

Stories from Warsaw's Yiddish Crime Blotter

As usual, when I got the paper yesterday, I jumped straight to the
Crime Blotter. I like to know what's happening in the city.

Reb Yoyne, *Unzer ekspres*, January 26, 1928

Long a popular feature in many urban newspapers, the crime blotter typically features brief and sometimes lurid local stories of crime and transgression. As Jews poured into urban areas and as the Yiddish press developed
and professionalized, journalists and editors imitated what they saw around
them in their industry. This meant reporting on Jews involved in all manner
of transgressive activity, a task that Yiddish journalists were well situated to
perform.

The Yiddish crime blotter wasn't really just a crime blotter. A one- or
occasionally two-page section found in the back pages of the dailies, it contained a variety of outrageous or scandalous stories of local interest, some
criminally minded, others not. Warsaw's top two Yiddish dailies, *Haynt* and
Moment, both had their crime blotters set up the same way. Titled "What's
Up in Warsaw?" (or literally from the Yiddish, "What Does One Hear in
Warsaw?")" and "Life in Warsaw," respectively, each included explosive little
blurbs that peered into broken lives, eavesdropping and reporting on events
that perhaps weren't so appropriate for public consumption but that the
reading public eagerly devoured.

The *khronik*, or chronicle, as it was popularly known in Yiddish, made
its appearance early on, showing up sporadically in *Dos yidishe folksblat*, an
1880s-era weekly out of St. Petersburg. This paper's chronicle dealt mainly
with news of Jewish organizational life, not crime reports or unusual events.

Similarly, *Der fraynd*, the Russian Empire's first Yiddish daily, had an occasional chronicle section that also dealt with headier affairs. This paper,
founded in St. Petersburg in 1903 but relocated to Warsaw five years later,
was the first attempt at a serious newspaper of record in the Yiddish language. It wasn't until 1905 that a Yiddish daily was permitted in Warsaw.
When it did, the Warsaw *khronik* began to reflect local interest and grew into
its own little section. A popular chronicle of crime and scandal, it lasted until
World War II.

Operating on the understanding that an element of scandal and sensation sells papers, the reporters of the Yiddish press mined all kinds of sources
for this fare: street peddlers, bums and bag ladies, doctors and nurses at the
Jewish Hospital, the police, rabbis, neighborhood finks, and anyone else who
might be able to give them the lowdown on whatever freak show just happened in the vicinity. Local Jewish do-gooders and blabbermouths were a
dime a dozen, standing at the ready not only to tell all but possibly to make
some of it up as well. It was the job of Yiddish journalists to suss out which
sources gave them the most accurate or, possibly, the most interesting version,
all with the knowledge that a variation on the same story might appear in a
competing paper that could check and balance their own.

The ability of Yiddish journalists to coax these strange stories out of
their lowly sources was legion, and it was dependent, in part, on the Jewish
chattering classes, who may or may not have been forthcoming. Although
it seems remarkably common, loquacity among the Jews is a phenomenon
that hasn't been adequately addressed. On the one hand, scholars have long
argued that Jewish culture is a text-bound culture. There is certainly truth to
that. However, on the other hand, Jewish culture is also very much a talking culture. There has never been any such thing as a vow of silence among
Jews, religious or otherwise. The stereotype exists of a talkative, persuasive,
argumentative Jew; there is at least a grain of truth in that as well. It was thus
among the garrulous lower-class Jews of Warsaw that reporters found some
of their best sources. The rendering of their speech into prose is one of the
great joys of reading the Yiddish press.

Composed in short bursts for the pleasure of the Yiddish reading public, the crime blotter frequently provides a glimpse into the realm of Jewish
anger, stupidity, and lunacy. Many of the stories have no resolution, meaning

that what you see is all that was reported. Reporters and editors either forgot or didn't bother to follow up. After all, they were on to the next thing, that is, the wild stories that would continue to fill up the crime blotter.

What does fill up the *khronik* is a plethora of different topics, many of them rarely considered and practically untouched by modern scholarship. The stories touch on a huge number of issues: superstition, petty theft, smuggling, homosexuality, love affairs, poverty, prostitution, and gambling, to name just a few. Although these are what were considered the troubling details of the daily life of a once vibrant community, they nonetheless reveal aspects that are worthy of further inquiry.

One of the major threads that weaves its way through the *khronik* is violence, a form of conflict resolution that was endemic in the poor neighborhoods in the Jewish quarters of Warsaw. Violence exists in all cultures and so it does with the Jews as well. Despite a history of oppression and stereotypes of weakness, there have always been elements in the Jewish community, often the poorest and the least educated, who let their fists do the talking when patience ran out and words let them down. Slaps, punches, and kicks functioned in daily discourse as an emphatic way to get one's point across. Violence occurred not only in connection with crime but also in the sphere of interpersonal relations. The Yiddish papers of the 1920s and 1930s are full of reports of furious Jew-on-Jew violence, attacks that took place between all kinds of Jews.

The articles printed here are a fairly random sampling, taken mostly from the late 1920s, a slightly more stable period than the years immediately following World War I and the years of the Depression of the 1930s. They have been translated as closely as possible to match the Yiddish originals; grammatical errors, run-on sentences, scare quotes, and the like have mostly been left intact. Articles in the crime blotter section of the paper generally have a headline but are often followed immediately by a subhead that provides a brief description of the blurb itself. Some of the stories reference specific aspects of Jewish life or unique customs. In such cases, footnotes have been attached to elucidate the situation. Names and addresses, when available, have been left in for posterity. Who knows, maybe you'll find a relative.

HORRIBLE LOVE-TRAGEDY ON 9 SOLNA STREET
(A married father of five children throws his lover
out a third-story window out of jealousy.
His victim hangs on and drags him down too,
leaving both in a puddle of blood.)

Haynt, February 5, 1926

Early yesterday a horrible love-drama played out on 9 Solna Street.

Beyle Shvartskop, a 26-year-old cleaning woman, has worked for a number of years in the house of the fruit vendor Dovid Vaden. Avrom Vasershtand (Shliska 48), a 34-year-old carpenter, who is married and has five children but who is having a love affair with Shvartskop, used to visit her there often.

During the past few months, Miss Shvartskop met someone else and became engaged to him. This upset Vasershtand terribly and he decided to get revenge.

Yesterday, at 8:30 a.m., Vasershtand entered the Vaden home, grabbed Shvartskop and, in spite of her resistance, dragged her to the stairs and, after a struggle, threw her out of the third-story window.

But Shvartskop held fast onto her attacker, who was dragged down with her.

Shvartskop fell onto the sidewalk and was badly wounded in the head. Vasershtand tried to grab onto a first-floor window frame, but it broke and he fell directly onto Shvartskop.

Both were unconscious and brought to the hospital in critical condition.

THE LUCKY BEDSHEET AND THE UNLUCKY BOY
(A thief with a bedsheet gets chased down Pavia Street—
How a fortune teller told him it would bring luck.—
The tragic end to the tale of the bedsheet.)

Moment, February 23, 1926

Passersby in the area of 37 Pavia Street were alarmed suddenly by cries of "Stop thief, stop thief!"

At the same time, they saw a young man running quickly down the street with a bedsheet in his hand.

The young man was quickly apprehended and brought to the precinct. He turned out to be one Yosl Shlenker of 62 Nizka Street. Regarding his thievery, he told the following story:

Things were not going very well for him in life; no matter what he tried, he ended up suffering terrible failures.

A gypsy read his cards and informed him that his luck would change if he got his hands on a bedsheet that had been slept on by a 14-year-old virgin. But because luck cannot be bought, he had to get it without paying for it.

For a long time this *shlimazl* searched for his luck—until he discovered that it could be found in the dwelling of Moyshe Shvigman at 37 Pavia Street.

Waiting for the right moment, Shlenker snuck into the house, where he actually found a 14-year-old girl, along with her little old grandmother.

Without giving it much thought, he quickly threw off all the bedding, grabbed the sheet and took off running.

Unfortunately though, his luck ran out: He was chased down and caught.

The end of the story: The lucky bedsheet went directly from the thief's hands to the evidence room. And the one who tried to steal his luck, directly to jail.

BLOODY BATTLE ON 17 KROCHMALNA STREET
ON ACCOUNT OF A BRIDE
(Her lover ends up with seven wounds to his head.)

Haynt, April 28, 1926

An aspiring film actress, Mirel Volfson (Krochmalna 17), was engaged to the 31-year-old driver Yisroel Mukha (Pshebyeg 1). Her two brothers, Moyshe and Eliezer, were against the match with Mukha and wanted her to marry their friend Khaym Blokzilber. But their sister was categorically opposed to dumping her fiancé. She told the story to Mukha, that her brothers were trying to convince her to marry someone else. Because of this, Mukha stopped going to the Volfson's home and always waited for his fiancée by the building's front gate. While Volfson went out to see Mukha by the iron gate, her two brothers, together with Blokzilber, ran ahead and attacked Mukha, beating him badly. Mukha, however, fought back and in the yard of 17 Krochmalna, he stuffed one of them into a barrel of herring, another in a garbage can, and the third he left lying in a cellar. Mukha himself ended up with seven wounds to his head.

BLOODY BATTLE AT A WEDDING AMONG THE GUESTS

Haynt, November 18, 1926

A wedding took place in the home of Moyshe Toybenblat (12 Smotshe St.) on Tuesday evening. Sometime between 12 and 1 a.m., the residents of his building and neighboring buildings were suddenly frightened by the high-pitched screams of a few dozen people in the courtyard. It appeared that a terrible fight broke out between some of the wedding guests. Wigs, chunks of hair, caps and hats were flying through the air. The police took those involved in the fight into the 3rd Precinct. They included the following wedding guests:

Yankev Tzhevek (35 Panska St.); Khaym Mandel (43 Panska St.); Khaym Kriger (79 Volska St.); Efroim Fishman (46 Panska St.); Yekhezkl

Goldman (38 Panska St.); Yisroel Handelsman, Shmuel and Khaym Loyfer (72 Nizka St.); Hersh Kirshenblat (17 Smotshe St.); Malke and Regina Goldberg (75 Panska St.); and the *badkhn,*[*] Avrom Harnblikht (6 Smotshe St.).

As we have been informed, the entire fight was because of the *badkhn.*

THE MISHEBEYREKH WAR IN THE YABLONER *SHTIBL* IN PRAGA[**]

(Three parties with three rebbes—who gets the Mishebeyrekh?)

Moment, March 28, 1927

The Yabloner *shtibl* has existed for years at 11 Zombkovska Street in the Praga neighborhood. Since the Yabloner Rebbe now lives in the Land of Israel, the Hasidim that worship there have split into three factions. The split occurred in connection with the fact that the Hasidim argue that they have to have a "rebbe" to travel to. And going to the Land of Israel is out of the question. One group of Hasidim has remained loyal to the Yabloner Rebbe, and a second group decided to become "Volominer Hasidim." The third contingent chose the Kazmirer Rebbe, who actually lives in the neighborhood.

As a result of the "fracture," huge arguments break out every Shabbos among those praying. They fight over who is to say the Mishebeyrekh just before the Torah reading, since each party wants to say it for its own rebbe. The screams in the *shtibl* go on and on until they turn into fistfights.

Pitched battles have broken out among the Hasidim for the last three Saturdays and serious punches have been thrown. Yesterday also did not pass by calmly.

It's being said that these ugly arguments have interested the leading Orthodox circles, who want to extinguish this Mishebeyrekh war in a rabbinic court.

---

[*] A badkhn is a wedding jester. A traditional figure at Jewish weddings, the badkhn would often compose extemporaneous rhymes that mocked the bride, groom, and, sometimes, the guests.

[**] A shtibl is a small Hasidic synagogue. Hasidim are divided into an innumerable number of sects, each of which follows their own rabbi, or as they call him, rebbe. The rebbes and their Hasidim are often known by the town names from which they came; hence the Yabloner Rebbe and the Yabloner Hasidim, all of whom pray in the Yabloner shtibl, are all originally from the town of Yablon (Jabłoń in Polish). After World War I, dozens of small-town Hasidic rebbes moved to Warsaw, where they and their sects bumped up against one another in ways they had not previously when they were in their own shtetls. In this case, three different sects that are sharing one synagogue fight over who gets to say a Mishebeyrekh, a prayer for the health of a particular individual.

NINE ATTEMPTS TO "STOW AWAY" TO AMERICA

Moment, March 30, 1927

Mandelboym, a carpenter from Pinsk, has long dreamed of going to America, where he has well-off relatives. But because of the quota, he could not get a visa to travel there.

Mandelboym came up with an idea: to smuggle himself in with a fake passport, as well as a fake visa.

But Mandelboym has a short memory, which screwed everything up for him.

He has already been stopped nine times in Danzig, where they recognized his false documents.

This time, however, he arranged to get such good forgeries that no one would be able to identify them as false. Mandelboym might have made it, especially since he had already gotten onto the ship.

But on the fake documents, Mandelboym had used a false name and he kept forgetting it.

Just before the ship left port, he decided to get to know one of the ship's employees and accidentally introduced himself with his real name.

This aroused some suspicion with the employee, who discovered the truth.

Mandelboym was removed from the ship by a special delegation of investigators and brought from Danzig to Warsaw, where the case is being investigated.

PRE-PASSOVER LAUNDRY THEFT*

Moment, April 3, 1927

Last week, laundry was stolen from Khane Bialer (17 Nalevki St.) in the amount of 400 zlotys; Avrom Yustman (16 Dzika St.) in the amount of 800 zlotys; and Sofia Patsyak (20 Dzielna St.) in the amount of 160 zlotys.

These kinds of laundry robberies are becoming more and more common, since the "gangs," aware that a lot of laundry is washed just before Passover, have "mobilized" especially for the holiday.

CATASTROPHE WHILE BAKING MATZO

Moment, April 12, 1927

Because the holiday is nearly upon us, the matzo bakeries are working at a feverish pace.

This year's matzo season got off to a late start compared to last year

---

* It is a Jewish tradition to purchase new clothing and bedding for Passover. It is also a tradition to perform a massive house cleaning before the holiday. As a result, new clothes and bedding are washed and hung out to dry. For thieves who know this, the Passover holiday provides them with excellent opportunities.

and because of the large orders from the provinces (mostly machine-made matzos and matzo meal), the bakeries are working nonstop, by night and by day. Naturally, the workers are exhausted. There are only two shifts and they are really punching away.

Yesterday afternoon at the matzo bakery at 16 Smotshe Street a disaster occurred while the bakery was going full speed; and it cost a 45-year-old man three fingers off his right hand.

It happened like this:

45-year-old Moyshe Linder went to the kneading machine in the afore-mentioned bakery and had three fingers ripped off his right hand while trying to remove the dough.

All the workers, as well as some neighbors, came running after hearing the victim's screams.

The injured party was brought to the clinic at 52 Leshno Street, where the head doctor administered first aid.

A LADY'S COURTESY TO A BUSINESSMAN FROM LODZ
Moment, April 26, 1927

A businessman from Lodz, Mr. Berel Lipshitz, was on tramway number 14 wondering why a certain lady was very "interested" in him and was treating him a bit too "courteously."

The lady got off the tram at Granitshna Street when Lipshitz realized that together with this lady, his wallet had also disappeared. Without giving it much thought, Mr. L. jumped off the tram and, with the help of a police officer, stopped the woman at the gate of 6 Granitshna Street.

The arrestee turned out to be the well-known "artist of pickpocketry" Toybe Shvakhovitsh of Nizka Street.

When Toybe was searched, they found the stolen wallet, as well as a razor and a few banknotes, probably from a previous "performance."

Rest assured that the thief was thrown in the can with great respect.

THE DEVIL MADE ME DO IT
Moment, April 26, 1927

The Gzhibovska neighborhood is cooking with a terrible story: A board member of a synagogue who is also a member of various religious organiza-tions stumbled, and was not able to overcome temptation . . .

The 40-something-year-old leading man is called Reb Moyshele, but be-cause he used to stand at the pulpit and dole out the honors and *aliyes** every

---

* An aliye is the reading of a special blessing thanking God for giving the Torah to the Jews dur-ing which the honoree goes up on the bimah (pulpit) and stands with the Torah reader. It is considered an honor to receive an aliye.

Shabbos and holiday, they call him Reb Moyshele Gabay.* His little woman, Khanele, is about eight years younger than Reb Moyshele and has already given him four children.

A few years ago, Khanele hired a Christian woman as a housekeeper, who used to take the children out for walks. In time, Khanele, who had been pregnant, went off to a birthing center and the house was without its *balebuste*** for three weeks.

And what shouldn't have happened, happened.

A few months later, Khanele cried, fainted, and went into spasms:

"What gives? You, Moyshele, my own husband, shamed me in my own home with a Christian woman?"

If only the drama had ended when the housekeeper, already in the "high numbered months," took money from Reb Moyshele and left. In truth, though, she continued to show up every once in a while in Reb Moyshele's house asking for more "donations"—but it was always done on the sly.

For years there were no more housekeepers in Reb Moyshele's house. But it wasn't working out: Khanele was inundated with five wee kids, so they finally hired another housekeeper—this time, a Jewish girl.

The girl worked in Reb Moyshele's house for a number of months and everything was on the straight and narrow. But suddenly, the evil impulse again confounded Reb Moyshele's thoughts, and the Jewish girl, who was the real deal—Saltshe was her name—exploited Reb Moyshele's "curious predilections" and "coerced" him. And after a few "idyllic" months, the "heavens burst open." And Saltshe complained that her boss put her in an "unfortunate" position. Reb Moyshele swore up and down by his beard and *peyes* that he didn't know what she was talking about and that she had the nerve to simply harass him.

Unfortunately, it was a big lie.

And one of Saltshe's "buddies" swore that he once went over to her house and met Reb Moyshele in the kitchen.

In short, it wasn't going so smoothly for Reb Moyshele. They began talking about a "deal." But Saltshe proposed a sum that was out of Reb Moyshele's ballpark.

And now, it's already been two weeks since Reb Moyshele has disappeared. Saltshe shows up every day at her *balebuste*'s house and sings her a "tune" that fills the entire courtyard with screams. Last Friday, the scandal reached a high mark: After Saltshe showed up and sang a two-hour concert of invectives, the door opened suddenly and in walked an "old acquain-

---

* Moyshele Gabay is not his real name, which is not provided. A gabay is an administrative assistant in a synagogue.
** A balebuste is a capable housewife.

tance," Reb Moyshele's one-time Christian housekeeper, carrying her child: and the "set" was "complete."

Both "seduced women" began smashing plates and windows, and if someone hadn't called the police, Reb Moyshele's house would have been transformed into a formal heap of junk.

The policeman who arrived brought both "heroines" down to the precinct, where they were written up for disturbing the peace and destroying private property. Now the whole affair will conclude in a court of law.

In the meantime, the Gzhibovska neighborhood has something to talk about for the second day of the holiday.

ALREADY IN THE 8TH PRECINCT
AND CAN'T SEEM TO QUIT HIS "JOB"
(Yisroel Rubin, making a guest-appearance in Warsaw from Vilna.)
Moment, June 23, 1927

Gendarme-Sergeant Yan Voshinski was on tramway 18 when he suddenly felt a strange hand in his pocket. He quickly grabbed it and held fast. How surprised he was when he turned around to see whose long arm it was and saw that it belonged to a gray-haired old man who could barely stand on two feet.

The old man was taken into the precinct, where it was determined that he was 72-year-old Yisroel Rubin.

He is an old, well-known veteran of thievery from Vilna. As a "pensioner," Rubin receives a regular "honorarium" from Vilna thieves. While the money is sufficient to live a decent life, it seems the old pickpocket simply can't resign from his polite nature and is unable to go without a "bit of work." To this end, he often comes to Warsaw to make "guest appearances."

He lived on 7 Vilenska Street in Warsaw.

In the meantime, the "veteran" was handed over to the investigating authorities.

HUGE CROWD BATTLES WITH THE POLICE
FOR THE SAKE OF TWO BAGEL VENDORS
(The police win and the bagel bakers get arrested.)
Moment, August 11, 1927

Recently, the police have strengthened their battle against illegal street peddlers of baked goods. Mainly, the battle against the poor bagel peddlers has been increased. Typically, when one of them is caught in the act, his goods are confiscated immediately.

It is therefore easy to figure out under what kind of fear these poor people "handle their business."

It's also easy to grasp how worrisome it would be if one of them is caught by a policeman.

Two days ago a tragic scene played out by the Iron Tower:

Khane and Meylekh Goldberg stood there for a long time with baskets of baked goods. Whenever they saw a policeman, they ran away. And after he had passed by, they would come back and try to sell a few more bagels.

Yesterday at about 4 p.m., the couple didn't notice that misfortune was nearby and a mounted policeman blocked their way. The "encirclement" occurred so quickly that, out of fear, the peddlers let out a terrible scream. Many people who heard the scream came running and looked on as the poor woman lurched spasmodically while the policeman kicked her. As long as he doesn't confiscate all of her goods. The peddlers argued with the policeman for a while, pulling at his buttons. This increased the interest and the growing crowd took the side of the two bagel peddlers and refused to allow the policeman to arrest them. The policeman called the precinct and a large group of officers came running. After a frenzied battle with the hostile crowd, the police brought the two peddlers and their merchandise into the precinct.

Because the peddlers resisted arrest, the presiding judge placed them in prison and confiscated their bagels.

The painful incident made a deep impression in the area around the Iron Tower.

A BLOODY BATTLE BETWEEN JEWS
(That lasted 21 hours.)

Haynt, October 3, 1927

The residents of Krochmalna were disturbed by a bloody fight that took place between Jewish residents of 25 Krochmalna Street. The battle started on Saturday night at about 10 p.m. and lasted, with small breaks, until 7 p.m. on Sunday. The fight began because of "rumors" that one woman started about another. The men then had to protect the honor of their wives.

"Arguments" in this "discussion" included sticks, weights, pots, brooms, plates, glasses, hats, and anything else that fell into their hands. Accordingly, the following were wounded:

Saturday night—the carpenter Mendl Raysman, 30, and his wife, Feyge, 26; the peddler Khane Rayter, 50 (28 Tshepla Street). During the course of Sunday: the hairdresser Yisroel Zoktreger, 31, and his wife, Lola, 25; Sunday evening: Yokheved Kotsholek, 17, and her sister Khane, 20, both shipping clerks, as well as the peddler Hela Kirshenboym, 19.

This isolated fight about "women's honor" brought much activity into the street. Hundreds of people came out after hearing screams from far off.

A JEW SHOULDN'T GET DRUNK,
AND IF HE DOES, HE'LL GET CLOCKED

Haynt, October 24, 1927

In the school on 12 Krochmalna Street, Shloyme Shlenker, 50, was found laid out drunk and unconscious on Friday night. Emergency medical help was called, and he was brought back to consciousness and his stomach was pumped of all the whiskey and beer he drank. Shlenker was then taken to the police station to sober up. In the waiting room, he met up with the well-known professional drunk Josephina Ostrovska (Seymova 7), who was also being held on charges of intoxication. Upon seeing the drunken Jew, she jumped on Shlenker and screamed, "Jews shouldn't get drunk, so I don't respect you," and beat him badly. The police came in and separated the two after hearing Shlenker's screams.

WHAT'S WITH THE LEG FOUND
AT THE BURIAL SOCIETY?

Moment, October 26, 1927

In our Sunday afternoon paper, "Radio," we reported the sensational story of a human leg having been thrown into the yard of the Burial Society on Gzhibovska.

The leg had been amputated from the laborer Yankl Zilberberg, who had been in the hospital for indigents. His family had been given the leg in order to bury it in the cemetery. But because of economic hardship, they simply threw the leg over the gate of the Burial Society building.

Since Monday morning, the leg has been laying in the 8th Precinct, but, at last, it was returned to the family for burial.

But when the leg got to the cemetery, the story took on a new twist.

At the last minute, the district attorney of the court refused to allow the leg to be buried and ordered that it be sent to the morgue.

On account of the D.A.'s order, the Burial Society sent a car to take the leg from the cemetery to the morgue.

Charges are now being filed against the Zilberberg family for throwing the leg into the yard.

THE HOMOSEXUALS USED FALSE DOCUMENTS

Moment, December 9, 1927

Mrs. Khaye Anter informed the police that her 19-year-old son Aren left home and disappeared for two weeks. Because he took his mother's jewelry, an investigation was initiated.

The police arrived at the conclusion that the missing young man had be-friended one Adam Mikhalak, who was arrested last week with a large group of homosexuals. It also appears that Anter had also been arrested with the homosexuals, but had given the police a document with a fake name.

Anter had already been released and was on his way home when he was re-arrested as a result of the new investigation in order to determine who gave him the falsified documents. It became apparent that the unmasked band of degenerates maintained their own "workshop" for forging documents for their cohorts who did not want their real names to be made known in case they were arrested. The "workshop" also produced false documents for those who were transported as "merchandise" outside the country.

GANG OF WELL-KNOWN CRIMINALS
IS ARRESTED IN "YANKL BAVARNIK'S" CASINO

Moment, December 11, 1927

Police investigators have announced that criminal elements have been cheating in Yankl Bavarnik's well-known "card club" with the use of a new "invention": mechanical cards. The "trick" with these cards is that queens suddenly turn into kings, kings turn into jacks, and numbered cards change from high numbers to low according to the wishes of the cheater.

During the course of the investigation, a large number of agents visited Yankl Bavarnik's on Thursday night. A group of twenty-six people were killing at a game of *tertl-mertl* using the "mechanical cards."

The entire group, along with Yankl Bavarnik, was soon taken into the investigations bureau, where it became evident that part of the group consisted of "suckers" and the rest, clever con artists. They included: Tuvie Mlinazh (61 Gensha), who had come to Warsaw "for pleasure" from Hamburg, where he is known as a swindler and safe-cracker; Vatslav Bartshinski, a fence; Shmuel Bartsh (21 Smotshe), a well-known specialist in the art of pickpocketing; Yankev Torma (18 Solna), who has served time for fraud; Shiye Piltz (Novolipie 62) and Ber Yudashka (49 Nalevkes), both well-known crooks; Yitskhok Bronshteyn (17 Prosta) and Leyb Rafes (17 Sh. Vierska), both arrested for robbery six times; Moyshe Zalevski, also known as "Litvin" (26 Lutska), regarded as the best lock picker up until a year ago; Aren Shnayderman (10 Tseglana), a safe cracker; Leyzer Flokshtrom (50 Shlizka), a house burglar.

The most interesting character from among those under arrest is the tramway thief Avrom Vaysboym (1 Pshyebeg), who is known as "Zlota Rontshka" [Little Golden Hand].

Vaysboym is well known in the criminal world not only as an excellent "artist" but also for having managed to escape the clutches of every detective in the city. The arresting officers therefore ordered Vaysboym to be bound in chains.

The entire gang remains in custody under the auspices of the investigating authorities.

BLOOD-DRENCHED SCANDAL
ON ACCOUNT OF . . . DAVENING*
(A religious father tries to drive his freethinking son
into shul with a stick.)

Moment, September 25, 1928

A major scandal of an unusual nature occurred Shabbos morning on 63 Pavia Street.

At the above-mentioned house lives the Shvartshteyn family, the father of which, Dovid, is a religious Jew who goes to shul every Saturday. His 18-year-old son, Shloyme, a craftsman, who since joining the union became completely "freethinking," does not. Naturally, he doesn't even want to hear about shul and davening.

This created great anguish for the religious father and the two began fighting regularly.

This past Saturday morning, when the elder Shvartshteyn was ready to go to shul, Shloyme was still laying comfortably in bed.

"Shloyme, are you sleeping?" said the father, waking him up.

"I'm not sleeping and I'm not going to go pray either," answered the boy.

Words were exchanged until the father grabbed a stick and beat his "freethinking" son until the bed was soaked with blood from the boy's head and hands.

Medical help was called and the boy's wounds were bandaged.

THE TRAGI-COMIC PURSUIT OF . . . A SIDE OF BEEF
(A cop "saves" the thief.)

Moment, January 9, 1929

Yesterday, meat wholesaler Aren Bernheim (19 Vspulna) drove a wagonload of meat to 21 Faksal Street. While the workers were unloading the wagon, a thief ran by, grabbed a side of beef off the wagon, and started running.

Bernheim took off running after the thief and so did the meat packers who had been unloading the wagon. The chase caused a sensation on the street because of the unique appearance of the pursuers, who were clad in white aprons, not to mention the "bloody" heist.

The thief, a 40-year-old man, was so fast that the whole group, even the healthy and young among them, couldn't catch him. When they were so close that they could almost reach out and grab him by the collar, the thief

---

* Davening is praying.

threw the slab of meat at their legs, causing them to trip and fall and bang up their knees and hands. But they got up and continued the chase.

The attack on his pursuers caused the thief to become fearful of their revenge and he began to yell for help.

A policeman came running after hearing all the screaming. He spread out his arms and grabbed the thief, who fell on him as if he were his savior.

The perpetrator is the 40-year-old thief, "wagon-snatcher" Yosef Vshetshesh.

SCANDAL IN AN UPSTANDING FAMILY
(A wild. bash given by trendy daughters and, pardon the expression, a Hasidic son's *siyem-haseyfer*. A war between modern types and Hasidic boys.)

Moment, January 13, 1929

Vierska Street is really buzzing about a spicy story that happened in connection to the Hasidic Jew, Reb Shloyme V. of that very street.

The story happened like this:

This past New Year's Eve, Reb Shloyme's daughters, Fela and Bronia, arranged to have a party in their father's house with young people and all kinds of goodies. When the party was in full swing, Reb Shloyme suddenly cracked open the door to see what was going on.

"Get out! All of you get out of my house!" screamed Reb Shloyme. "My new year is Rosh Hashanah and not today!" The young people were confused, Fela and Bronia were upset, and the guests all left as if they had been bludgeoned.

But the scandal in Reb Shloyme's house did not yet come to an end. Saturday evening, the home was laden with the heavy atmosphere created by his loathsome deeds.

Bronia and Fela were sitting with some friends in the living room when in walked Reb Shloyme and his two Hasidic sons, Meir and Asher, together with a group of their yeshiva friends: Asher had completed the Talmud tractate *Yevamos* and had invited the yeshiva boys for a *melave-malke*.*

The young Hasidim started to party and began to scream at the girls' "high society" friends to get out.

---

* The linchpin of this story has to do with intrafamilial cultural differences. In Hasidic families, girls did not receive the same religious education as boys, whose schooling was far more intensive. As a result, girls of Hasidic families were often far more secularized and spoke far better Polish than the boys. What is evident here is that the girls have Polish names (Fela and Bronia) and the boys have Jewish names (Meir and Asher). The boys, who attend yeshiva, have completed a particular volume of the Talmud (siyum haseyfer) in school and are celebrating with their friends at a post-Sabbath meal, known as a melave-malke, which literally means "escorting of the [Sabbath] queen," in other words, bringing the Sabbath to a close.

"Scumbags! You should go to the rebbe and have your party there!" screamed Fela and Bronia.

With that, Asher ran over to Fela and punched her in the face, giving her a bloody nose. Fela grabbed a candlestick holder and threw it at her brother's head. Both "communities" began to mix it up and fists started to fly. The Hasidic boys, of whom there were a larger number, took the belts off their silk robes and began to beat the secular kids over their heads. They grabbed one secular kid by the name of Felix and dragged him into another room, where they "took out a mortgage"* and paid him back one punch at a time. The result was that, after hearing his screams, the rest ran in and it became a real war, during which Felix took out a knife and stabbed a Hasidic boy, Avrom F., wounding him.

All were written up by the police and will meet in court to lodge their complaints. Avrom F. was taken to the hospital.

TRAGI-COMIC SCENE, JUST LIKE IN THE "THEATAH"
(Why did Mr. Greenberg beat the postman with a broom?)

Moment, January 9, 1933

In a house on *Hamokem* [The Place] the great-grandfathers of two neighbors, the Greenbergs and the Futtermans, had lived next door to one another for a long time.

But not all neighbors are created equal. Greenberg and Futterman, however, are an exception. They are remarkable in their "eternal" mutual hatred of one another, which has been handed down from generation to generation.

Who knows today what the source of the neighbors' hatred is? Even the "enemies" themselves don't know. Old-timers say that the animosity began with a military contract from the time of Ivan [Russian rule]. Other old folks assured us that the great-grandfathers of the current neighbors fought over a spot on the eastern wall of the synagogue.** And so it went—the fact remains that the neighbors never forgave one another.

When it came time for the angel of death to arrive and take the grandfather, the son had to swear to maintain the grievance against the neighbor and, God willing, another son would be born who would suckle drops of this hatred of the neighbor in his mother's milk.

And now, Greenberg is in the dock.

He is there as a result of the fact that the Futtermans tortured their neighbor with strange pranks.

---

* "Taking out a mortgage" on someone is a Yiddish expression indicating that the victim is held down and beaten.
** Because most Jews pray in an easterly direction, toward Jerusalem, it is considered a great honor to have a seat on the eastern wall of the synagogue.

Every other night there would be a knock on the door. They would say it was the police. The next time they would say it was an ambulance; a third time they'd say it was the burial society; and, occasionally, and worst of all, they would knock and say it was the repo man.

Futterman made Greenberg's life so miserable that the latter decided to hide behind the door and wait with a broom for his neighbor to knock.

He didn't have to wait long until he actually heard a loud knock. To the question, "Who's there?" he received the response "Telegram."

Shloyme Greenberg, who was sure that he had caught his nefarious neighbor in the act, quietly reached for the door and with a quick pull, yanked it open and, before he saw who was standing there, he began to beat his "neighbor" over the head with a broom.

"Kogo pan bitsh [Who are you hitting?]," he suddenly heard a scream in Polish.

Greenberg was left standing in shock. He saw standing before him not his bitter enemy, but a real postman with silk buttons and a mailbag slung over his shoulder.

All of his entreaties were of no help, and yesterday Greenberg stood before the court, accused of attacking a government employee attempting to fulfill his duty.

The defendant wept bitter tears as he poured out his heavy heart to the judge and told of the frightful troubles he suffers at the hands of his neighbor and that what occurred with the postman was a misunderstanding.

The judge had mercy on the accused and allowed him to go free.

11-YEAR-OLD JEWISH GIRL GOES FROM PINSK TO WARSAW TO PURCHASE LIVE MERCHANDISE
(Police are holding the girl together with a number of Warsaw pimps.)
Moment, June 21, 1933

A month ago, an 11-year-old girl named Malke Sherman came to Warsaw from Pinsk. She didn't go to friends or relatives, nor did she seek work or admittance to any schools.

She arrived—it's hard to believe—as a representative of a certain Halina Liberman, the proprietor of a whorehouse in Pinsk.

When she left the train station, she went up to an old wagon driver and asked where she could find a "salon." The driver gave his passenger an odd look and gave her an address: 5 Smotshe Street.

Eleven-year-old Sherman spent the day running around the streets, tired and hungry, until she arrived at the address.

No one was in the brothel, except for the cook, Khane Laksman, who engaged her "guest" in conversation.

It was then that the girl told her that she had been sent to Warsaw from Pinsk in order to buy "two dark, hairy girls."

The cook then sent her "guest" to her boss, one Yisroel Mosak, of 58 Novolipie Street.

Although it was also strange for him, dealing with this little "pimpette," he nonetheless went along with her request and arranged for her to get two "dark, hairy ones."

Little Sherman sent a letter back to Pinsk about the deal and was awaiting a reply. In the meantime, the girl revealed that this wasn't her first time working as this kind of representative.

A few days passed, a week, two weeks, and no reply was received from Pinsk. She was thus thrown out of the "salon."

Again the little girl shlepped herself around the streets all day and, when it was good and late, she went to the police and told them the whole story.

There it was learned that 11-year-old Sherman comes from an unlawful union and doesn't even know her parents. Until the age of 5, she was in an orphanage. After that, she was taken on as a servant to wash clothes for a certain Khaye Liberberg. Recently, she has been working as a representative for the aforementioned Halina Liberman, who runs a brothel.

The police became interested in this original story and immediately initiated an investigation. The proprietors of the brothel, Yisroel (Srulik) Mosak and Khane Toltshinski, were arrested, as was the madame, Khane Leyzerovitsh.

It is alleged that they dealt in the sale of women.

The 11-year-old girl was sent to the newly opened home for girls on Okentsha Street.

"BLIND YANKL" OPENS A "UNIVERSITY" FOR THIEVES
(A story of a thief who became a "professor" in his old age.
The police have already caught this professor,
along with young "students.")

Moment, January 3, 1938

The successful but elderly pickpocket Yankev Pomerantz (11 Krochmalna), also known as "Blind Yankl," is very popular in the world of thieves. Mainly, he is regarded as an excellent "professional" but has also "retired" and is living off the advice he gives to the youngsters while they attempt to go to "work."

The advice business has done quite well, but since in today's business world one can't simply charge money for simple "words," Blind Yankl came up with another idea. He thus opened a school for young thieves, where he teaches his "students" both the theory and practice of the "profession." "Professor Yankl" even prepared a lesson with mannequins, which the beginners worked on with straight razors. Afterward, he would bring his young students out on the street. The practical street lessons would take place in the markets and in the Muranover Halyes where there is always a lot of noise and action.

Instead of taking tuition, Blind Yankl was paid with his students' first "earnings," which they made in the Halyes.

The school business would have gone quite well, if not for the police. It didn't take long for them to discover his "institution of higher learning." Professor Yankl and his two assistants, Shloyme Mandelboym and Yoyel Pasternak, landed in Paviak Prison. Also held were a number of "young talents," also students of Blind Yankl.

DRAMATIC STREET SCENE BETWEEN TWO WOMEN
(What did her man do when she caught him red-handed?)

Moment, January 18, 1938

Rivke Litso (7 Volinska Street) ran into her man "arm in arm" with Khane Vaysfish. She didn't think long before she jumped on her competitor, starting a fistfight between the two women.

In the meantime, her man disappeared while Rivka snatched Khane's hat off her head and tore the fur collar from her coat. On top of that, she slapped her around pretty good and scratched up her face too.

Rivke came out of the fight with a gash on her left hand.

After getting help from emergency medical services, Rivke was taken to the Jewish Hospital.

87-YEAR-OLD MAN ARRESTED FOR FORCING WOMEN INTO PROSTITUTION
(He terrorized both the wanton women and other pimps.)

Moment, November 17, 1938

Yesterday, 87-year-old Khayem Tshiernetski (3 Porisovski Place) was arrested and put in prison.

Tshiernetski was accused of forcing women into prostitution, terrorizing his victims, and also of printing money.

In spite of his advanced age, Tshiernetski showed great physical power and in Povonzker neighborhood, where he was active, even the pimps, many of whom Tshiernetski attacked with knives, feared him.

⌒

You may be wondering who all these people are. Basically, they are the two-bit nobodies of Jewish history. Essentially unknown, the derelicts who populate the Yiddish crime blotter are the unsung heroes of the Jewish underclass, a group that tends to resist documentation.

Responsible for the heavy lifting in poor Jewish neighborhoods, they often are not the best and the brightest. They are tough Jews with rotten teeth and bad breath who have putrid odors steaming off their hunched, sweaty bodies. They are day laborers, hairdressers, wagon drivers, butchers, seamstresses, pimps, prostitutes, and street vendors, all of whom have been dealt a losing hand.

They do not often have steady jobs. They owe money to bookies, loan sharks, their friends, and their parents, if they know who they are. They are scarred human tragedies lumbering through life with angry snarls burled into their leathery faces. They are lifeless, slack-jawed, knuckle-dragging sluts hanging off mouth-breathing illiterates with lumpy bodies who force hoarse blasts of laughter through grimy lungs.

Theirs are dirty, barefoot children, with thick blobs of green mucus slug-trailing over their lips as they play in gutters coursing with horse and human urine. They are one-eyed, pockmarked, gap-toothed chiselers waiting to screw some dumb sucker out of his last penny. Or old women whose knotted faces sport thick misshapen moles bursting with tufts of bristly hair that wriggle about as they scream curses in the marketplace. They are grimy, soot-covered working men with pus-filled scabs crawling up their necks.

The Jews of the Yiddish crime blotter occupy the lowest rungs of the social ladder. You can find them in line at soup kitchens and free clinics. Or maybe in manacles at the police station.

In short, they are probably not the Jews you expected.

ACKNOWLEDGMENTS

This book was a lot of work, and even though I did most of it, there are people without whom it would have never happened. So blame them too.

Giant gelatinous chunks of unvarnished gratitude are to be heaped upon Sarah Abrevaya Stein, not only for threatening violence if I did not submit this manuscript but for being a most outstanding friend and colleague for what is apparently a really, really long time. Massive thanks to Margo Irvin at Stanford University Press for taking the manuscript on and doing an absolutely marvelous job. Much thanks to Nora Spiegel and Anne Fuzellier Jain, who suffered the slings and arrows of outrageous last-minute changes with great aplomb. I don't even know what to say about Mimi Braverman—she's an amazing editor. Her bosses should shower money upon her. Nancy Ball is an indexer par excellence and deserves a heaping portion of thanks. Thanks also goes to Stephanie Adams and Ryan Furtkamp. In short, I'd like to thank all the nameless scriveners at Stanford University Press. Oh—and also to Eric Brandt, upon whose desk this manuscript first landed.

Crushing blows of appreciation shall be rained on Ari Kelman and Tony Michels for their brilliant commentary and general awesomeness as friends and colleagues. David Biale's sage guidance and commentary was instrumental, and the tag team of Matthew Howard and Shelley Salamensky generously suffered through versions of the Introduction and offered brilliant suggestions. Thank you all, really and truly.

I owe a monstrous debt of thanks to Alana Newhouse, who let me publish early versions of some of these stories in *Tablet Magazine*. More of the same goes to Mireille Silcoff of the erstwhile but fabulous *Guilt and Pleasure*. Many thanks also to Sara Ivry and Sarmishta Subramanian for editorial greatness on those early outings. A huge debt of thanks also goes to Sam Norich and Jane Eisner at the *Forward*, but especially to Dan Friedman, and also to Teri Zucker for editing *Forward Looking Back* for so many years. Great pulsating blobs of gratitude also go to Roger Bennett, the soccer journo, not the gospel singer, who has long supported this project, or one that vaguely resembled it. And kind thanks to various hooligans like A. J. Jacobs and Jody Rosen, who also tried to move this thing along.

It always helps to have had brilliant professors and advisers. Thanks to Dovid Fishman, Arye Goren, Miriam Hoffman, Jenna Joselit-Weissman, Sam Kassow, Barbara Kirshenblatt-Gimblett, Alan Mintz, Dan Miron, Edna Nahshon, Avrom Novershtern, Rakhmiel Peltz, Debra Reed-Blank, David Roskies, Mordkhe Schaecter, and Jeffrey Shandler.

I love archivists and librarians, many of whom have helped me immeasurably in my quest for Yiddish ephemera: Zachary Baker, Gunnar Berg, Rena Borow, Sarah Diamond, Ettie Goldwasser, Leo Greenbaum, Brad Sabin Hill, David Kraemer, Sharon Mintz, Fruma Mohrer, George Rugg, Miriam Khaye Siegel, Loren Sklamberg, Jerry Schwarzbard, Lyudmila Sholokhova, and Vital Zajka. Thanks to all the librarians and archivists at the Center for Jewish History, the Jewish Theological Seminary, the National Library of Israel and its Historical Jewish Press project, the New York Public Library, and the YIVO Institute for Jewish Research. Next time you see an archivist or a librarian, give them a big, wet, sloppy kiss. They deserve at least one.

Much thanks to Jonathan Brent, and all my co-workers, past and present, at the YIVO Institute for Jewish Research. The most incredible archive of Eastern European Jewish life in the world, insanely great doesn't even begin to explain the wonders of YIVO and the amazing people who work there.

Special thanks to Herbert Lazarus, whose knowledge of the YIVO stacks will eternally remain unparalleled.

I've had the great good fortune to have a brilliant cohort of colleagues, friends, and nemeses, many of whom had nothing to do with this book, but they're mostly decent folk whose presence in my life means something or other. I thank them for their mere existence: Natalia Aleksiun, Andy Bachman, Elissa Bemporad, Maya Benton, Joel Berkowitz, Josh Berman, Kolya Borodulin, Jonathan Boyarin, Alisa Braun, Dan Bronstein, Paul Buhle, Alec Burko, Menachem Butler, Justin Cammy, Henry Caplan, Marc Caplan, the Cohens, Emmanuel Darmon, Jeremy Dauber, Nathaniel Deutsch, Ofer Dynes, Glenn Dynner, Gennady Estraikh, Ken Faig Jr., Edna Friedberg, Drew Friedman, Olga Gershenson, Hershl Glasser, Ezra Glinter, Itzik Gottesman, Karen Green, Stef Halpern, Phil Hollander, the Israelis, Eve Jochnowitz, Dmitri Jones, Faith Jones, Naomi Kadar, Rokhl Kafrissen, Jon Kalish, the Kaminers, Josh Karlip, Ben Katchor, Emily Katz, Alan Kaufman, Ellie Kellman, Ari Kinsberg, Rebecca Kobrin, Shira Kohn, Mikhail Krutikov, Cecile Kuznitz, Josh Lambert, Brukhe Lang, Amichai Lau-Lavie, Liz Levy, Rachel Jagoda Lithgow, Sue Lott, Rebecca Margolis, Marc Miller, Michael Miller, Allan Nadler, Roby Newman, Clayton Patterson, Roger

Paz, Shachar Pinsker, Chana Pollack, Annie Polland, Alyssa Quint, Lara Rabinovitch, Simon Rabinovitch, Reboot, Eliana Renner, Billy Rivkin, Jenny Romaine, Jeff Salant, David Schneer, Anya Shternshis, Eve Sicular, the Silvers, Nancy Sinkoff, David Sklar, the Sonins, Danny Soyer, Michael Steinlauf, Lauren Strauss, Hilit Surowitz, Vera Szabo, Barry Trachtenberg, Scott Ury, Eli Valley, David Wachtel, Nina Warnke, Kalman Weiser, Michael Wex, Azzan Yadin, Saul Zaritt, and the irrepressible Steve Zipperstein.

Apologies to anyone I may have left out.

Finally, mountains of love and thanks to my family, Mira, Ben, and Luli. I don't know where I'd be without your love and occasional aggravation. Much gratitude to my sister Rachel and her evil brood of hairy-legged men, Adam, Kobi, and Jonah. Thanks and love also to the Blushtein/Bluszstejn/Blustain families. Extra special thanks and love to my mom, Maida, who has always supported me no matter what kinds of shenanigans I was involved in. Couldn't have done it without you. I should also thank my dad, even though he's been dead for twenty years. A great lover of history, he would have enjoyed this book. And even though they're dead too, I shouldn't forget my grandparents, who instilled in me a love for Yiddish and a heightened sense of crankiness.

Now go away.

ORIGINS AND SOURCES

This collection of stories happened by accident. I fell into it while I was writing my doctoral dissertation, the topic of which was cartoons of the Yiddish press, a project that required me to sit for hours on end looking at microfilms of old Yiddish newspapers. Anyone who has ever done research using a microfilm reader can tell you that it's not that fun. Basically, you sit in front of a screen and scroll through thousands of pages of documents looking for those that will be useful for your work. It's not like working on a computer; you can't search for anything specific. You just have to wind through miles of 35 mm silver halide film, watching thousands of pages pass by and, in my case, looking for cartoons. There's also the matter of Yiddish being a language that's read right to left on microfilm that scrolls left to right. It's kind of like reading upstream.

Staring at a flickering screen as pages and pages of Yiddish text rolled by was a major part of my life for quite a few years. To put it mildly, there isn't anything anyone wouldn't do to expedite microfilm research. One of the things I quickly discovered was that the cartoons I was looking for appeared only in the Friday editions of Warsaw's Yiddish papers. As a result, I would flip the dial and hold it down in order to skip a whole week's worth of newspapers to get to Friday. One day I was looking at reels of *Moment*, one of the major Warsaw dailies. I had the first half of 1929 on the bobbin, and I was rolling from week to week at a steady clip, photocopying the cartoon images I needed for my research. On one particular roll I let go of the dial a bit early and wound up on a page from a Thursday instead of a Friday.

This wasn't unusual, and whenever it happened, I'd just keep scrolling until I arrived at the Friday cartoon page. But, for some reason, I happened to glance at the headline of a Thursday article that was in front of me and I stopped. It read, "Two Wives, Blazing Punches, and—the Cops."

"Hmm," I thought, "that's not your typical thing." I started reading the article (you can find it in Chapter 14). It turned out to be about a Warsaw Hasid who fell in love with his wife's best friend and married her on the sly. He set the second wife up in an apartment out of town and shuttled between the two of them, spending a few nights with one and a few with the other and telling the first wife that he was away on business. His older brother found out about it and was furious. He dragged his brother to the rabbinic court, where both women were waiting, as were nearly three dozen family members. After the rabbis pronounced judgment, the courtroom erupted into a massive brawl.

I sat there in front of the microfilm reader wearing a dumb smile. I was amazed. I had listened to hundreds of lectures and read thousands of pages on Jewish history during my years in graduate school, and I had never come across anything like this. "I wonder if there are more stories like this?" I asked myself. Sure enough, tucked into the back pages of Warsaw's Yiddish dailies, I found lots of them. So now, instead of skipping the entire week to get to the Friday cartoons, I began scrolling slowly, methodically scanning the headlines for little Yiddish scandal bombs. I continued to find them—thousands of them, more than I ever imagined. I even went back to the years I had already searched through for cartoons and searched again for scandalous stories. In Yiddish you'd say that I had fallen into a *shmaltz grub*, a vat of delicious chicken fat. I had found a mother lode of Jewish deviance.

During this same period, I wrote a column at a weekly newspaper called *The Forward*, the English edition of what was once the largest and most successful Yiddish newspaper in the world (*Forverts*, by the way, is still publishing). This job, which also required me to sit in front of microfilm readers for hours on end, was to provide synopses of stories that ran in the Yiddish version of the *Forverts* from 100, 75, and 50 years ago. The column, titled "Forward Looking Back," offered brief glimpses into a wide variety of news and opinion that was published in the paper from various points during the twentieth century. This required me to read the *Forverts*, New York City's biggest and best-selling Yiddish daily, in a fairly comprehensive manner. By doing so, I learned an enormous amount about Jewish immigrants in New York City, their interests, proclivities, problems, politics, and more, but I also learned about how this community was fed international and local politics and left-wing ideologies, among many other relevant matters, and how readers digested it all.

So not only was I finding incredible stories in the Yiddish press of Warsaw, but I was also finding similar material in the Yiddish press of New York. I had collected thousands of stories, but for no apparent reason. I had no idea what I was going to do with them. I managed to publish a few in a great but short-lived magazine called *Guilt and Pleasure*. Others made their way into *Tablet Magazine*, an online venue that was created after the *Forward*'s arts and culture editor quit in the wake of an editorial shake-up, part of a long-standing tradition in the Jewish press (see Chapter 7 for an example of this phenomenon). In the *Forward*, I was permitted limited space, but in *Guilt and Pleasure* and in *Tablet*, I went further, contextualizing and extrapolating on the strange historical matter I had stumbled upon. Essentially, I would take unusual episodes I found in the Yiddish press and recreate them, almost exclusively without the use of secondary sources, which usually had little information about these topics anyway.

Some of the other stories I found thanks to cartoons. When I was researching cartoons of the Warsaw Yiddish press, I found a number of images from the mid-1920s that used wrestling as a metaphor. They would show, for example, two cantors who were vying for a post at an important synagogue or two heads of different Yiddish school systems in the wrestling ring. A simple metaphor to be sure, I thought to myself, but what do Warsaw Jews know about wrestling? Distracted again, I rummaged around in the Yiddish papers and, sure enough, I found all kinds of information about Jewish professional wrestlers, some of whom led me across the ocean to find the same phenomenon in the United States and to figures like Blimp Levy.

Something similar happened during the course of my dissertation research when I first came across cartoons of the Radimner Rebbetzin, Zlate Rubin, and the winner of the Miss Judea Pageant, Zofia Oldak—except that in these cases I didn't know who the characters were, nor did I understand what the cartoons meant to convey. These cartoons were commenting on events about which I knew nothing. Here I had to do research to figure out who the central figures were and what they meant. To my good fortune, their stories not only turned out to have legs but were also compelling historically and just a little bit wild, both evoking some unruly aspects of Jewish life in the interwar period.

Although I was supposed to have been researching and writing a dissertation, I became more and more interested in these stories and what they meant to the study of Jewish history. After having taken years of classes and having read thousands of pages of often brilliant scholarship, I had never come across Jews like these. These Jews were the real *amkho*, the crass, uneducated rabble who populated impoverished Jewish ghettos in both the Old World and the New. I needed to figure out how to contextualize such a compelling element of society historically, socially, religiously, and in manifold other ways. Politics, such a prevalent theme in Jewish historiography, didn't seem terribly relevant to many of them. These Jews didn't seem to fit very well into existing categories, and because of that, they became an abiding interest.

As I mentioned in my somewhat reductive Introduction, the history of the common man has become an important trope in recent historiography. This novelty is the product of a new generation of scholarly attempts to strike new ground, often at the expense of the work of their predecessors, who focused on the great figures and great works, not average folks. The detractors of these new approaches complain that they fail to engage the primary historical realities, those that drive the machine of human history. That may indeed be true; however, the history of the common man is nonetheless worth investigating. In this case it permits us to peek into a world that no longer exists, a cultural universe that Europe expunged from its physical landscape and that has mostly disappeared in America. And that alone makes it worth knowing about. It is also worthwhile to look at the masses that were shaped, sometimes successfully and often not at all, by those who were alleged to have served as their cultural and political vanguards. If one must consider choosing either the masses or their leaders, it seems that a better decision might be not to choose but to look at all sides—the elites, the rabble, and everything in between.

When it comes to knowledge of Eastern European Jewry, most people only know how it ends. It's a bit sad that people seem more interested in the way the culture was destroyed rather than in how it lived. But considering people's interests, it does make sense. The death porn of World War II fetishizes the ways in which Eastern European Jews were killed and almost completely eclipses what the lives of these communities were like. Understanding a rich and diverse culture and the ways in which its denizens lived requires a more complex perspective than looking at Jews only as victims and survivors of genocide.

The key to understanding this world is to learn Yiddish, the rich confabulation of linguistic detritus that reached deep into Jewish history and literature as it helmed the frequently bizarre and complicated cultural lives of motley urban Jews whose culture was irretrievably Jewish. Yiddish unlocks a universe of culture and is the only vehicle you can take to travel the twisted road to Yiddishland. If you want to understand the Jewish masses, you have to speak their language and seek them out where they live and breathe. To find them in their most raw and unvarnished form, you must enter the Yiddish press. Daily chronicles created by and for the Jewish people, the Yiddish newspapers once used to wrap fish contain more history than you may know.

BIBLIOGRAPHIC SOURCES

What should be obvious here is that this is not a traditional academic monograph but a work of popular history. What this means to you is that the citations one usually finds in an academic text are not around, a fact that will doubtlessly irk some people. If I weren't the author, I'd probably be annoyed. But in lieu of citing works in the text, I have supplied a bibliography of works that I used in the writing of this book.

Obviously, the works of the journalists themselves serve as the main primary sources. By reporting on the day-to-day matters, the journalists unwittingly created a broad web of data. These stories are potentially useful to historians, allowing us to explore not only the issues presented to the journalists' readers but also a unique Yiddish perspective.

Introduction

Anderson, B. *Imagined Communities: Reflections on the Origin and Spread of Nationalism.* New York: Verso, 1991.

Aronson, Michael I. "The Attitudes of Russian Officials in the 1880s Toward Jewish Assimilation and Emigration." *Slavic Review* 34.1 (1975): 1–18.

Bal Haturim (A. Tsfanes). "Kuriozn fun der zibeter melukhe." In *Haynt yovl-bukh, 1908–1938.* Warsaw: Haynt, 1938.

Baron, S. *The Jews Under Tsars and Soviets.* New York: Macmillan, 1964.

Barth, G. "Metropolitan Press." In Gunther Barth, *City People: The Rise of Modern City Culture in 19th Century America,* 84. Oxford, UK: Oxford University Press, 1980.

Brooks, J. *When Russia Learned to Read: Literacy and Popular Literature, 1861–1917.* Princeton, NJ: Princeton University Press, 1985.

Chaikin, Y. *Yidishe bleter in amerike*. New York: M. Sh. Shklarski, 1946.

Cohen, N. "Shund and the Tabloids: Jewish Popular Reading in Interwar Poland." *Polin* 16 (2004): 189–211.

Corrsin, S. *Warsaw Before the First World War: Poles and Jews in the Third City of the Russian Empire, 1880–1914*. East European Monographs 274. New York: Columbia University Press, 1989.

Druk, D. *Tsu der geshikhte fun der yidisher prese in rusland un poyln*. Warsaw: Hatsfira, 1920.

Dubnow, Sh. *History of the Jews in Russia and Poland from the Earliest Times to the Present Day*, v. 2, *From the Death of Alexander I Until the Death of Alexander III*, trans. I Friedlaender. Philadelphia: Jewish Publication Society of America, 1918.

Feldshuh, R., ed. *Yidisher gezelshaftlekher leksikon*. Warsaw: Yidisher leksikografisher farlag, 1939.

Finklshteyn, Kh. *Haynt, a tsaytung bay yidn*. Tel Aviv: Y. L. Peretz Farlag, 1978.

Fishman, D. "Di dray penimer fun Y. M. Lifshits." *Di yidishe shprakh* 38.1–3 (1984–1986).

———. *The Rise of Modern Yiddish Culture*. Pittsburgh: University of Pittsburgh Press, 2010.

Flinker, Dovid, Mordekhai Tsanin, and Sholem Rozenfeld, eds. *Di yidishe prese vos iz geven*. Tel Aviv: Veltfarband far di yidishe zhurnalistn, 1975.

Frankel, J. *Prophecy and Politics*. Cambridge, UK: Cambridge University Press, 1981.

Fun noentn over, band 2, *Yidishe prese in varshe*. New York: Tsiko, 1956.

Gilman, S. *Jewish Self-Hatred*. Baltimore: Johns Hopkins University Press, 1986.

Gitelman, Z. *A Century of Ambivalence: The Jews of Russia and the Soviet Union, 1881 to the Present*. Bloomington: Indiana University Press, 2001.

Hertz, A. *The Jews in Polish Culture*. Evanston, IL: Northwestern University Press, 1988.

Hoerder, Dirk, and Christiane Harzig, eds. *The Immigrant Labor Press in North America, 1840s–1970s: An Annotated Bibliography*. New York: Greenwood Press, 1987.

Howe, Irving. *World of Our Fathers*. New York: Harcourt, Brace, Jovanovich, 1976.

Iks (pseud.). "Tsu der geshikhte fun der zhargonisher prese in varshe." *Der tog*, August 1, 1905.

Joselit, Jenna Weissman. "Telling Tales: Or, How a Slum Became a Shrine." *Jewish Social Studies*, n.s., 2.2 (1996): 54–63.

Kellman, E. *The Newspaper Novel in the Jewish Daily Forward, 1900–1940: Fiction as Entertainment and Serious Literature*. New York: Columbia University Press, 2000.

Kirzhnits, A. *Di yidishe prese in der gevezener rusisher imperiye*. Moscow: Tsentral felker-farlag, 1930.

Kuczer, B. *Geven amol varshe: Zikhroynes.* Paris: Editions Polyglottes, 1955.

Lewin, I. *A History of Polish Jewry During the Revival of Poland.* New York: Shengold, 1990.

Malakhi, A. R. "Der baginen fun der yidisher prese." In Shloyme Bickel and Chaim Bez, eds., *Pinkes far der forshung fun der yidisher prese un literature un prese,* 2: 253–59. New York: Alveltlekhn yidishn kultur-kongres, 1972.

———. "Der *Kol mevaser* un zayn redaktor." In Shlomo Bickel, ed., *Pinkes fun der forshung fun der yidisher literatur un prese,* 40–121. New York: Alveltlekhn yidishn kultur-kongres, 1965.

Mayzel, N. *Geven amol a lebn.* Buenos Aires: Tsentral-farband fun Poylishe Yidn in Argentine, 1951.

McReynolds, L. *The News Under Russia's Old Regime: The Development of a Mass-Circulating Press.* Princeton, NJ: Princeton University Press, 1991.

Mintz, Alan, and David Roskies, eds. "The Role of Periodicals in the Formation of Modern Jewish Identity." Special issue of *Prooftexts* 15.1 (1995).

Miron, D. *A Traveler Disguised.* Syracuse, NY: Syracuse University Press, 1996.

Mozes, M. "Der moment." In *Fun noentn over.* New York: Alveltlekhn yidishn kultur-kongres, 1956.

Mukdoyni, Aleksander (Alexander Kapel). In varshe un in lodzh: mayne bagegenishn, vol. 1. Buenos Aires: Tsentral-Farband fun poylishe yidn in argentine, 1955.

Polland, Anne. *The Sacredness of the Family: New York's Immigrant Jews and Their Religion, 1890–1930.* New York: Columbia University Press, 2004.

Quint, A. "'Yiddish Literature for the Masses?' A Reconsideration of Who Read What in Jewish Eastern Europe." *AJS Review* 29.1 (2005): 61–89.

Rischin, M. *The Promised City.* Cambridge, MA: Harvard University Press, 1962.

Roskies, David. *The Jewish Search for a Usable Past.* Bloomington: Indiana University Press, 1999.

Ruud, C. "The Printing Press as an Agent of Political Change in Early Twentieth Century Russia." *Russian Review* 40.4 (1981): 378–95.

Shmeruk, Kh. "Letoldot hasifrut hashund bayidish." *Tarbits* 52 (1983): 325–54.

———. "A Pioneering Study of the Warsaw Jewish Press." *Soviet Jewish Affairs* 11.3 (1981): 35–53.

———. *Prokim fun der yidisher literatur geshikhte.* Jerusalem: Farlag Y. L. Perets, 1988.

Soltes, M. *The Yiddish Press: An Americanizing Agency.* New York: Arno Press, 1969.

Stampfer, Shaul. "What Did 'Knowing Hebrew' Mean in Eastern Europe?" In Lewis Glinert, ed., *Hebrew in Ashkenaz: A Language in Exile.* Oxford, UK: Oxford University Press, 1993.

Stanislawski, Michael. *Tsar Nicholas I and the Jews: The Transformation of Jewish Society in Russia, 1825–1855.* New York: Columbia University Press, 1983.

Stein, Sarah Abrevaya. *Making Jews Modern: The Yiddish and Ladino Press in the Russian and Ottoman Empires.* Bloomington: Indiana University Press, 2004.

Steinlauf, M. "The Polish Jewish Daily Press." *Polin* 2 (1987): 219–45.

Stites, R. *Russian Popular Culture: Entertainment and Society Since 1900.* Cambridge, UK: Cambridge University Press, 1992.

Szeintuch, Y. *Preliminary Inventory of Yiddish Dailies and Periodicals Published in Poland Between the Two World Wars.* Jerusalem: Center for Research on the History and Culture of Polish Jews, Hebrew University, 1986.

Tsitron, Samuel Leib. *Di geshikhte fun der yidisher prese.* Vilna: Fareyn fun yidishe literatur un zhurnalistn in vilne eygener farlag, 1923.

Ury, Scott. *Barricades and Banners: The Revolution of 1905 and the Transformation of Warsaw Jewry.* Jerusalem: Stanford University Press, 2012.

Weiser, Kalman. *Jewish People, Yiddish Nation: Noah Prylucki and the Folkists in Poland.* Toronto: University of Toronto Press, 2011.

Wisse, R. *I. L. Peretz and the Making of Modern Jewish Culture.* Seattle: University of Washington Press, 1991.

Wrobel, P. "Jewish Warsaw Before the First World War." In W. Bartoszewski and A. Polonsky, eds., *The Jews in Warsaw.* Oxford, UK: Basil Blackwell, 1991.

Zipperstein, Steve. *The Jews of Odessa: A Cultural History, 1794–1881.* Stanford, CA: Stanford University Press, 1985.

Chapter 1

"The Abortion Business." *Medical and Surgical Reporter,* October 14, 1871.

"The Case of Rosenzweig Viewed by a Lawyer." *New York Times,* October 29, 1871.

"The Door of Escape." *New York Times,* November 29, 1872.

"Dutch Heinrich and Rosenzweig Granted New Trials." *New York Times,* November 19, 1872.

"The Evil of the Age." *New York Times,* August 29, 1871.

"The Evil of the Age." *New York Times,* September 1, 1871.

Frank Leslie's Illustrated Newspaper, September 16, 1871.

The Great "Trunk Mystery" Murder of New York City. Murder of the Beautiful Miss Alice A. Bowlsby, of Paterson, N.J. Her Body Placed in a Trunk and Labelled for Chicago. Many Strange Incidents Made Public. Pamphlet. Philadelphia: Barclay, 1871.

"More Developments About Rosenzweig's Operations: Identification of Another Victim." *New York Times,* September 2, 1871.

"The New York Trunk Mystery." *Daily Evening Bulletin* (Philadelphia), September 7, 1871.

"A Plea for Rosenzweig." *New York Tribune,* October 6, 1871.

"Rosenzweig." *New York Times,* October 29, 1871.

"The Rosenzweig Case." *New York Times*, November 13, 1873.

"The Rosenzweig Case." *New York Times*, November 14, 1873.

"The Rosenzweig Case." *New York Times*, December 12, 1873.

"Rosensweig's Medical Diploma." *New York Times*, September 5, 1871.

"Rosenzweig's Trial." *New York Times*, October 26, 1871.

"Rosenzweig the Abortionist: His Fruitless Attempt to Get Out on Bail." *New York Times*, September 8, 1871.

"Sins of Society." *New York Tribune*, September 13, 1871.

"Sketch of the Prisoner Rosenzweig, Alias Ascher." *New York Times*, August 29, 1871.

"A Social Reform." *New York Times*, January 12, 1872.

"The Trunk Mystery." *New York Times*, August 30, 1871.

"The Trunk Mystery." *New York Times*, October 28, 1871.

"The Trunk Tragedy." *Brooklyn Daily Eagle*, September 4, 1871.

The Trunk Tragedy; Or, The Late Murder in New York. Pamphlet. Philadelphia: C. W. Alexander, 1871.

Chapter 2

American Israelite (Cincinnati), February 18, 1976, p. 5; February 25, 1876, p. 6.

Brooklyn Daily Eagle, December 1875–May 1876.

"Dos 40te yor in dem idishn kvartal." *Forverts*, January 1, 1910, p. 4.

Idaho Avalanche (Boise), February 14, 1876, p. 2.

The Murdered Jewess: Being the Life, Trial and Conviction of Rubenstein, the Polish Jew, for the Murder of the Beautiful Sara Alexander, His Own Cousin! Pamphlet. Philadelphia: Barclay, 1876.

New York Herald, December 1875–May 1876.

New York Sun, December 1875–May 1876.

New York Times, December 1875–May 1876.

New York World, December 1875–May 1876.

Pomeroy's Democrat, December 1875–May 1876.

Rubenstein, or the Murdered Jewess: The Trial in Full. Pamphlet. Philadelphia: Old Franklin Publishing House, 1876.

Stern, Samuel. *Thrilling Mysteries of the Rubenstein Murder Never Before Brought to Light*. Pamphlet. New York: Stern & Cohn, 1876.

Sunday Dispatch (Philadelphia), April 21, 1867.

Trial of Pasach N. Rubenstein for the Murder of Sarah Alexander. New York: Baker, Voorhis, 1876.

Weitenkampf, Frank. *Manhattan Kaleidoscope*. New York: C. Scribners Sons, 1947.

Yidishe gazetn, June 1876.

Di yidishe tsaytung, c. March 1876.

Chapter 3

Forverts, October 9, 10, 1909.

Der fraynd, May 16, 1912.

Imber, Sh. Y. "Galitsien: legende un virkhlikhkayt." *Haynt*, August 18, 1933.

Lithman, Ethel. *The Man Who Wrote Hatikvah: A Biography of Naphtali Herz Imber*. London: Cazenove, 1979.

Los Angeles Times, October 4, 1897; February 4, 10, 1898.

Morgn zhurnal, October 4, 10, 1909.

New York Times, October 21, 1902; June 26, 1904.

Parry, Albert. *Garretts and Pretenders: A History of Bohemianism in America*. New York: Covici, Friede, 1933.

San Francisco Call, April 7, 12; May 3, 1896.

Di varhayt, August 25, 1908; October 9, 10, 1909.

Yidishes tageblat, October 9, 10, 1909.

Chapter 4

Evening Post, June 27, 28, 1906.

Forverts, June 27, 28, 29, 1906.

Morgn zhurnal, June 28, 29, 1906.

New York Sun, June 27, 28, 1906.

New York Times, June 28, 1906.

New York Tribune, June 27, 28, 1906; August 5, 1906.

New York World, June 27, 28, 1906.

Ribak, Gil. "'They Are Slitting the Throats of Jewish Children': The 1906 New York School Riots and Contending Images of Gentiles." *American Jewish History* 94.3 (2008): 175–96.

Di varhayt, June 28, 29, 1906.

Yidishes tageblat, June 28, 29, 1906.

Chapter 5

"Agunes freyen zikh!" *Der teglekher herold* (New York), August 27, 1903.

Forverts, 1904–1909.

"Getrofn!" *Yidishes tageblat*, May 21, 1901.

Hochman, Abraham. *Fortune Teller*. New York, c. 1895.

———. *Di geheyme kraft oder di shlisl tsu der nevue* [The Secret Power, or, the Key to Prophesy]. New York: Friedman Print, 1909.

———. *Hagode shel peysekh in reyn yidish*. New York, c. 1910.

Leshtshinski, Yankev. "Yidn zaynen ale mol geven di talantfulste un barimste spetsi-alistn af 'shvartse kuntsn.'" *Forverts*, February 18, 1934.

Morgn zhurnal, January 17, 1910.

New York Sun, August 31, 1904; October 6, 1904; May 15, 1905; March 23, 1906; September 9, 1906.

New York Times, October 6, 1904.

New York Tribune, June 24, 1907.

Di varhayt, September 24, 25, 1906; March 24, 1908; December 12, 1909; June 29, 1912; January 12, 1913.

"Vunder mentsh." *Der teglekher herold* (New York), May 12, 1904.

Dos yidishe vokhnblat, April 7, 1905.

Chapter 6

Forverts, October 3, 1913.

Der fraydenker (Lodz), 1926–1928.

Fraye Arbeter Shtime, October 16, 1891; September 19, 1902.

Hartford Courant, September 27, 1898.

Margolis, Rebecca. "A Tempest in Three Teapots: Yom Kippur Balls in London, New York, and Montreal." *Canadian Jewish Studies* 9 (2001): 38–84.

Moment (Warsaw), September 21, 1923; October 9, 1924; September 29, 1925.

New York Sun, September 22, 1893; October 1, 1903; September 20, 1915.

New York Times, September 21, 1893; October 8, 1894; September 27, 1898.

Tfilo zako (New York), September 1889.

Di varhayt, September 17, 1907.

"Yom Kiper in varshe," *Haynt*, October 9, 1927.

Chapter 7

Der fraynd (Warsaw), August–September 1913.

Haynt, August–September 1913.

Kapores (Warsaw), September 1913.

Moment, August–September 1913.

Chapter 8

Haynt, September 16, 1927; February 1931; August 17, 1931.

Kaganovski, Efroyem. "Sibes fun zelbstmord." *Unzer ekspres*, September 2, 1929.

Moment, March 25, 1927; April 11, 1927; May 5, 26, 1927; August 17, 1931; March 17, 1933; January 31, 1934.

Reb Yoyne, "Kleyner felyeton." *Unzer ekspres*, January 26, 1926.

"A spetsiele tsaytung far zelbstmerder." *Moment*, August 19, 1926.

Chapter 9

Haynt, January 19, 1928.

Moment, January 18, 1928.

Chapter 10

Fayngold, Leyb. "Ikh bin geblibn lebn." *Morgn zhurnal* (New York), January 2 and 6, 1946.

Kassow, Sam, ed. *In Those Nightmarish Days: The Ghetto Reportage of Peretz Opoczynski and Josef Zelkowicz*. New Haven, CT: Yale University Press, 2015, 72–83.

Mayzl, Nakhmen. "Tsu gast bay Urke Nakhalnik in vilne." *Literarishe bleter* (Warsaw), January 5, 1934.

———. "Urke Nakhalnik." *Yidishe kultur* 2 (1946): 17–26.

Nachalnik, Urke. "Der lebnsveg fun Urke Nakhalnik: fun der yeshive biz tsu der far-brekher-velt in tfise." Serialized in *Haynt* (Warsaw) from February 8, 1933 (no. 34), to August 23, 1933 (no. 195).

Shnitzer, Sh. *Der pogrom af der untervelt in 1905, Groshn-bibliotek*. Warsaw: Groshn-bibliotek, 1935.

Unzer ekspres, December 27, 1933.

"Yidish teater vert geshendet!" *Vokhnshrift far literatur, kunst un kultur*, no. 3, January 10, 1934.

Zlatkes, Gwido. "Urke Nachalnik: A Voice from the Underworld." *Polin* 16 (2003): 381–88.

Chapter 11

Forverts, December 21, 1927; March 23, 1928.

Morgn Freiheit, March 28, 1928.

Chapter 12

Bloch, A. and Bloch, C. *The Song of Songs: A New Translation with an Introduction and Commentary*. University of California Press, 1995, p. 128.

"Der afikoymen." *Humor Magazine* (Warsaw), April 1929.

Haynt, April 16, 17, 1929.

"Di kneydlekh fun mis yudeye." *Humor Magazine* (Warsaw), April 1929.

"Mis malke." *Humor Magazine* (Warsaw), April 1929.

Moment, March 15, 24, 26, 1929; April 1, 2, 4, 1929.

Nasz Przegląd, February–March 1929.

Nasz Przegląd Ilustrowany, February–March 1929.

"Der seder fun mis yudeye." *Humor Magazine* (Warsaw), April 1929.

Chapter 13

Haynt, July 7, 1927.

Moment, July 5, 11, 1927.

Chapter 14

Haynt, March 30, 1937.

"Interesante get-statistik fun rabinat." *Moment*, October 2, 1933, p. 5.

"A 'kheyrem' af yidishe zhurnalistn." *Moment*, February 2, 1927, p. 6.

"Kol koyre fun Varsh. Rabinat." *Moment*, March 25, 1927.

Moment, November 29, 1926; November 16, 1928.

Seidman, H. *Togbukh fun der varshever geto.* Buenos Aires: Tsentral-Farband fun poylishe yidn in argentine; and New York: Federatsye fun poylishe yidn in amerike,
1947.

Chapter 15

Haynt, January 18, 1929; August 22, 25, 28, 29, 1930.

Moment, March 1, 1916; August 24, 1923; October 6, 1924; August 7, 1927; August 13,
1928; January 1, 1929; May 9, 1933.

Chapter 16

Boesch, Paul. *Hey Boy, Where'd You Get Them Ears.* Houston: Minuteman Press, 2001.

Faig, Kenneth, Jr. *Leviathan: Some Notes On Martin "Blimp" Levy, 1905–1961.* Moshassuck Monograph Series 13. Glenview, IL: Moshassuck Press, 2009.

Farrar, Harry. "Dr. Pfefer's Groaner Ward." *Denver Post*, August 2, 1961. Reprinted in
The WAWLI Papers, 2.37, www.oocities.org/wawli/jmk06.htm.

Haight, Walter. "Pieces of Haight: All Meat and Plenty Potatoes." *Washington Post*,
January 11, 1946.

"Marital Suit Dismissed in Weighty Decision." *Los Angeles Times*, October 20, 1945.

Miley, Jack. "Jake's Juggernauts." *Collier's Magazine*, October 22, 1938.

Mitchell, Joseph. *My Ears Are Bent.* New York: Vintage Books, 2008. 109.

Povich, Shirley. "Pfefer Is the Talent Scout." *Washington Post*, December 15, 1941.

Chapter 17

Haynt, February 28–March 14, 1927.

Lemberger morgn, March 7, 1927.

Moment, February 28–March 14, 1927.

INDEX

STANFORD STUDIES IN JEWISH HISTORY AND CULTURE
Edited by David Biale and Sarah Abrevaya Stein

This series features novel approaches to examining the Jewish past in the form of innovative work that brings the field into productive dialogue with the newest scholarly concepts and methods. Open to a range of disiplinary and interdisciplinary approaches from history to cultural studies, this series publishes exceptional scholarship balanced by an accessible tone that illustrates histories of difference and addresses issues of current urgency. Books in this list push the boundaries of Jewish Studies and speak compellingly to a wide audience of scholars and students.

Jeffrey Shandler, *Holocaust Memory in the Digital Age: Survivors' Stories and New Media Practices*
2017

Alan Mintz, *Ancestral Tales: Reading the Buczacz Stories of S.Y. Agnon*
2017

Joshua Schreier, *The Merchants of Oran: A Jewish Port at the Dawn of Empire*
2017

Ellie R. Schainker, *Confessions of the Shtetl: Converts from Judaism in Imperial Russia, 1817–1906*
2016

Devin E. Naar, *Jewish Salonica: Between the Ottoman Empire and Modern Greece*
2016

Naomi Seidman, *The Marriage Plot: Or, How Jews Fell in Love with Love, and with Literature*
2016

Ivan Jablonka, *A History of the Grandparents I Never Had*
2016

For a complete listing of titles in this series, visit the Stanford University Press website, www.sup.org.